"A WELCOME ADDITION TO THE LITERATURE OF HEALTH EDUCATION. IT WILL BE A SOURCE OF COMFORT AND ADVICE TO THOSE WHO CARE FOR YOUNG CHILDREN."

From the foreword by Richard I. Feinbloom, M.D.

Other titles in the PARENTS™ Baby and Childcare Series
Published by Ballantine Books:

PARENTS™ BOOK OF TOILET TRAINING

PARENTS™ BOOK FOR NEW FATHERS

PARENTS™ BOOK FOR THE TODDLER YEARS

PARENTS™ BOOK OF BABY NAMES

PARENTS™ BOOK OF BREASTFEEDING

PARENTS™ BOOK OF CHILDHOOD ALLERGIES

PARENTS™ BOOK OF PREGNANCY AND BIRTH

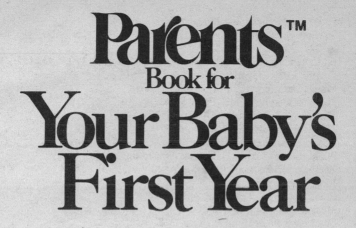

Parents™ Book for Your Baby's First Year

BY MAJA BERNATH

BALLANTINE BOOKS • NEW YORK

PHOTO CREDITS

Photo Researchers, Inc./Suzanne Szasz, p. 141

Suzanne Szasz, pp. 1, 56, 57, 74, 130, 132, 135, 150, 180, 213, 226, 236, 239, 264, 272

Ed Lettau, pp. 6, 32, 39, 83, 105, 124, 136, 138, 152, 182, 187, 190, 192, 203, 216, 223, 237, 249, 261

Mimi Cotter, pp. 10, 111, 220, 230, 290

Photo Researchers, Inc./Erika Stone, pp. 13, 206, 218

The Image Bank/Barbara Kreye, p. 17

The Image Bank/Mieke Maas, p. 22

Photo Researchers, Inc./Mary Thatcher, p. 45

Photo Researchers, Inc./Christa Armstrong, pp. 78, 86

The Image Bank/Nancy Brown, p. 92

Jorge Carva, p. 97

Erika Stone, pp. 128, 178, 242

Marina Raith, pp. 144, 165, 195

The Image Bank/Else Lewin, p. 228

The Image Bank/Bob Witt, p. 174

Photo Researchers, Inc./Ed Lettau, p. 254

Photo Researchers, Inc./Catherine Noren, p. 267

Photo Researchers, Inc./Suzanne Szasz, p. 141

Library of Congress Catalog Card Number: 82-90939

ISBN 0-345-30442-X

Manufactured in the United States of America

First Edition: August 1983
Eleventh Printing: March 1989

Contents

Expanded Contents

Foreword

Maja Bernath's *Parents™ Book for Your Baby's First Year* has all of the features of a well-written authoritative tourist guide to a great city: It tells you what to expect; what's going on behind the scenes; the effects of time, season, and mood; what to bring along; and how to pace yourself.

Here we have an entire book dedicated to the first twelve months. And it is clear from this book that the first year is deserving of such attention: It is during this period that the great human themes are first sounded. The stage is set for leitmotifs such as trust, willingness to take chances, sexuality, coping with failure, and assertiveness. While the author calls our attention to such weighty matters, she does so in a light manner that emphasizes the rich opportunities available to us rather than the heaviness of our responsibilities.

The author skillfully weaves recent research findings in infant psychology with her own keen observations (all of the little "in's and out's"), which in this case reflect her personal experience in caring for babies and observing babies and their parents in action. It all rings true. This one book provides a clear sense of what to expect without prescribing iron-clad rules for what to do. While discussing a range of options, Ms. Bernath urges parents to express their own unique solutions, to find their own way, and, above all, to trust in themselves.

This is a book for our day, rooted in contemporary American life. There are timely references to topics such as child care and working parents, traveling with infants, and parenting as opposed to mothering. Many eminently practical pointers are given for which parents will be forever grateful. As a physician, I particularly appreciate the discussion of physical safety and health as they relate to child development.

Parents™ Book for Your Baby's First Year is a welcome addition to the literature of health education. It will be a source of comfort and advice to those who care for young children.

RICHARD I. FEINBLOOM, M.D.

Parents™
Book for
Your Baby's
First Year

Introduction: Parenting in Today's World

There is a strange but inevitable effect that a newborn baby has on parents. Their home revolves in an orbit of its own, while all the changing currents of the outside world seem a bit unreal for a time. During these early baby-centered days and nights, parents may wonder at the power of a tiny infant to hold such sway over their interests. But this is a law of nature; babies must draw in their caregivers for protection to launch themselves safely into the world. Whether the baby is your first or one in a series, each baby is a new experience for the parents, but each has this same power of attraction.

And with babies, as they arrive from year to year, comes more advice to parents. In spite of the perennial platitude that "there's no one right way to raise a child," parents are flooded with expert opinions from all sides. Often such advice offers valuable food for thought. The problem is digesting it all without upsetting your own judgment. Starting out with happy expectations, it's easy to lose confidence along the way and feel you simply can't measure up. Nonsense. Any parent who is interested enough to seek advice and to listen is a caring parent, quite capable of sifting through and measuring conflicting opinions against her or his own instinctive feelings and common sense.

Much literature, for example, urges mothers to stay home and care for their babies during at least the first two years of life. But such advice is more often idealistic than practical or possible. Its overall effect may be to add feelings of guilt to the two-way pulls that working mothers have to handle. There is no evidence that a working mother who gives her baby real interest and loving attention is contributing less to his or her happiness and development than a mother who must sandwich care of the baby between hours of house-keeping chores.

There's no question that unprecedented social changes have affected family life. In earlier periods most babies lived in an extended family, which generally included three gen-erations under one roof. The baby seldom lacked for atten-tion or the mother for help. In more recent times the family has splintered into smaller units, in some cases to a one-parent–one-child family. Even the traditional nuclear family of two parents and their children is seldom what it used to be. The separation of father as *the* provider and mother as *the* housekeeper and childtender is increasingly rare. In many families these responsibilities are being shared. Parental roles are merging as economic necessity or personal choice pulls mothers out of the home and into the job world.

Out of these changes a new figure has stepped into the limelight; he is called "the new father." Certainly there have always been devoted fathers who contributed immensely to their children's happiness. The difference is that today's fathers are getting an earlier start. Many men are caught up in the new father role before their baby is born, through all the prevalent information on pregnancy and childbirth, and through participation in prepared childbirth classes. In hos-pitals across the country, fathers are acting as labor coaches and sharing in the birth of their child. A baby's birth is a sensitive and exciting time for mother-father togetherness, and this can help initiate a warm attachment to the baby.

Early bonding of mother and baby became a topic of great interest a few years ago—and also one of concern to some new parents. From a small study it was reported that women who had immediate and extended contact with their babies after delivery showed them more affection and sen-sitivity in follow-up observations. This information was re-ceived in some quarters as a dramatic breakthrough—a means of ensuring a strong mother-baby bond. Other studies, however, reported that the benefits lasted no more than the first few months. Meanwhile, some mothers—and fathers too—who for one reason or another could not be with their babies right after birth worried that they had missed the golden opportunity to have a close, loving relationship with their child.

Doctors were quick to reassure parents that, unlike bonding in other species, there is no specific time when human bonding occurs—a point that was made in the original study. Parent-child love endures much greater handicaps than separation in the early hours of a baby's life. Moreover, becoming a parent is not an event; it's a process in which the baby plays as large a part as the parents.

Attachment is the special meaning that develops from the messages that parents and child send to each other; and while it can begin to form even during the prenatal period, it continues to grow and become more "real" during the weeks and months after birth. There is no issue over the importance of bonding—just a bit of confusion. Call it bonding, call it attachment, it simply means the growth of love.

Early contact *is* important to mother and baby in easing the harsh experience of birth. Togetherness after delivery has always been, and still is, the common practice among many people of the world. A father, too, who is there to share the drama of his baby's birth has a head start in attachment over the father who first sees his baby hours later neatly combed and swaddled.

Realistic parent advisers suggest caution on becoming overly concerned with every highly publicized theory or trend that comes along. For one thing, research is open to different interpretations—the reason one expert may not agree with another; why conclusions may change from one year to another; and why it's important to give your own judgment a voice in weighing advice against your personal experience, feelings, values, and goals. Some theories are here today and gone tomorrow; some deserve only minor emphasis in the whole scheme of parenting; and some, presented as "new" findings, were second nature to mothers of previous generations—as well as common practice in many parts of the world today.

Concepts and customs, of course, can't be imported and exported like commodities. Many "natural" ways and means simply don't work in a complex society like ours. By the same token, what is suitable and advantageous for us may not be possible in a simpler society. But where the marvels of modern medicine are available, this is the safest era in history for babies to enter the world. Early in life, our babies are immunized against many diseases; antibiotics can cure illnesses that once were fatal; some congenital defects are being detected and treated before birth; and surgery has been performed on babies in the womb.

The world your baby has entered is different from the world you entered, and when your baby is grown, the world will be something else again. And here is your baby, opening his or her eyes upon a new era, and perceiving no more than his or her infant ancestors did when they peered out into their world. Your baby's behavior will take the same course that all babies have followed for centuries. But your parenting can be far more interesting than the baby tending it involves.

In these high technology times, one branch of science is focused on the ever-fascinating subject of human development. From these elaborate studies we are learning that the once-popular belief that babies perceive the world as a "great buzzing confusion" is as wrong as the old conception of the world as flat. Research has proved that babies are born with remarkable capabilities for studying the world and interacting with their caregivers in the first days of life.

When baby care is combined with insights into baby behavior, a fascinating dimension is added to all the phases of development a baby goes through. There's no stronger incentive for discovering the pleasures in parenthood than setting out to know your baby. The reality of this baby includes the quantities of energy, time, money, and patience that he or she will exact from you. But in the process of learning what parenthood is all about, you find new strengths in yourself and broaden your personal outlook on life.

A book talks to all kinds of parents about all kinds of babies. It can't individualize its suggestions; it can only express a set of views, some of which are bound to differ from other opinions. But if it spurs interest, it adds to the serious thought that today's parents are putting into parenting. Babies educate themselves, but their caregivers can do a lot to advance—or hinder—their self-education.

This book is speaking to fathers as well as mothers, recognizing that both can make unique contributions to their children's lives. The basic premise you'll find here is respect for the child. Love is a process that grows strong from this starting point. To respect an infant is to know that all infants are individuals striving to make their way in the world at one day of age, or six months or a year. The important thing to remember is that how well a baby succeeds in this early period will influence his or her entire life.

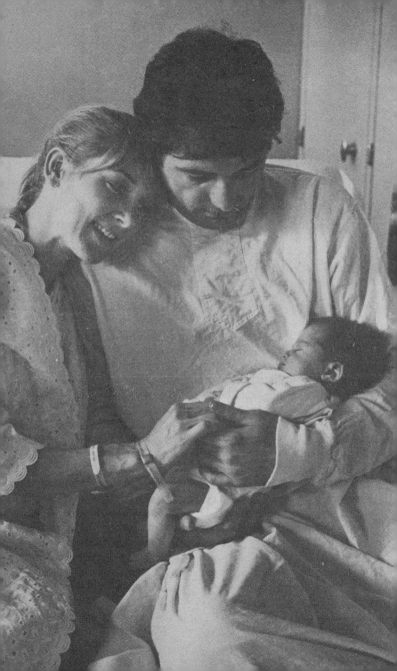

Prologue: What Is Development?

How does a baby start life? Helpless? Completely wrapped up in himself? Indifferent to his surroundings? Not at all. A baby is a competent, hard-working individual from the day he is born. He could not survive without the inner strength to demand his rights; he couldn't learn without the capacity to study his environment; he wouldn't even care to be where he is without the urge to reach out and interact with the persons who welcome him into the world.

A baby wastes no time in pulling his parents into his own life plan. He captivates them with his natural charms more than he holds them by his demands; he treats them to delightful surprises as rewards for their devoted attention. And all the while he's intent on establishing himself as the important person he is.

This first year is the liveliest and fastest learning period a child will ever have. With an enviable mixture of determination, energy, perseverance and courage, the baby develops into a sturdy little person with an upright posture and a mind of his own, who can feed himself tolerably, understand words, play simple games, and even take time out to reciprocate his parents' hugs and kisses.

From month to month we see the baby change. We say how fast he is growing and how much he is learning. But we are scarcely aware of the complex patterns making all his new behavior possible. The outward changes taking place are obvious. We can record weight and height, watch the baby's physical progress, and capture his changing appearance on film. But this only tells us he is growing bigger and stronger and older. Development is more than growth, more than the stages that a child passes through, and more than the sequence of abilities he achieves. Development is a process that combines physical, mental, emotional, and social factors in intricate patterns that keep branching out into new behavior. Each phase is infinitely more complex than the last—a blend of what the child was, and is, and is becoming.

In recording a baby's progress we tend to label the landmarks. Today Alice clearly said "mama." But Alice was communicating with her parents way back in her newborn days; and with her first coos she was training her voice apparatus for the months-later ability to formulate words. Today Kevin learned to walk. But Kevin was strengthening his legs and practicing body balance many months before he could stand. Now Alice's "first" word and Kevin's upright posture make them seem less babyish, more childlike, although there is no other discernible difference in the babies they were yesterday. Each stage of development evolves from preceding stages; one ability leads to the next, which in turn is a necessary element of another in the making.

What a baby learns to do is much more important than *when* she does it. Babies develop abilities through a series of predictable steps, which rarely vary. But all babies follow their individual timetables for arriving at various points of progress. The orderly sequence of bodily controls depends on the growth of the nervous system, connecting various muscle groups with the brain. At birth the baby's body is somewhat like a new house, complete except for the wiring. As each connection is made, rooms in the house, from top to bottom, come alive.

To learn a new ability, the baby must be physiologically ready. Her muscles must have developed strength and her neurological system must be sufficiently mature. Maturation might be called a kind of ripening. When the baby is ready for a certain skill, she is "ripe" for learning it. At each of these learning peaks the baby has a passionate urge to practice and perfect that skill. But within the range of normal development there are wide age differences in readiness for perfecting new skills.

As a baby's abilities develop, he must be protected from his lack of experience. He sees no reason not to grab a flame for a plaything or practice rollovers on the edge of a precipice. A bar of soap looks as good for biting as a cookie. He has no way of knowing whether a thing will stay put when he clutches it, as the knobs do on his chest of drawers, or separate from where it was, as the cup does from the table.

But a baby whose life is filled with stimulation, and who is allowed to investigate and take an active part in most of the things that interest him, will have better developed abilities than a child whose experiences are limited. A baby cannot begin to make sense of a world that he does not have ample chance to listen to, see, touch, examine, enter into, and enjoy. Experience will not have a stimulating effect on his learning if most of it happens to him—he must have a large part in making experience happen. He needs enough control for safety with enough freedom to pursue his goals.

All the pleasure you create for your baby and all the delights she brings you are important factors in her learning. Smooth interaction is the stimulus that keeps her alert to her own potential. It may be impossible for parents to fully realize how important they are to their baby. The interaction that takes place between a baby and the persons deeply interested in her feeds into every phase of development and remains the strongest support in her unfolding future.

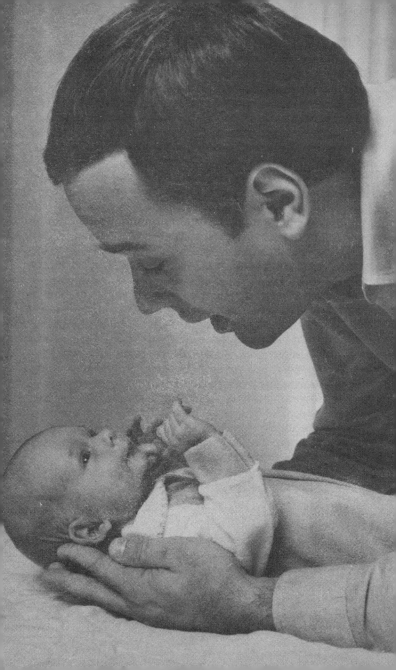

Chapter I

Day One to Six Weeks

What to Expect

Will you love your baby at first sight? You've known this child as a reality for many months, but your images have ranged far beyond the moment of birth. Suddenly, here she is. You can't expect her to look pretty as a picture after what she's just been through; or to respond with pleasure to the glare and noisy bustling that surrounds her as she's thrust into a strange new world. Of course, you'll have warm, tender feelings mingled with the tremors of excitement and discovery. And you may truly love this little individual you've never seen before. But to know and love her as a person? Give it time.

Appearance

For all their delicate appeal, just-born babies can hardly be called beauties. There's a rather gnomish look to them, with the "oversized" head (one-fourth of their entire length), narrow chest, large round abdomen, and short bowed legs. Arriving wet and slippery, coated with vernix caseosa— the white creamy substance that protects the skin before birth—the baby is cleaned up a bit in the delivery room and warmly wrapped. Later, you'll notice a downy fuzz of

11

fine hair on the body, called lanugo, which will gradually
wear off. Whether born with a thick mop of head hair or
only a fuzz, this will also be shed while being replaced by
the permanent hair. The baby's head is likely to be elongated
and rather pointed at the back, due to being "molded" during
passage through the birth canal.

Aside from plump or skinny variations, new babies are
remarkably uniform in body build. But each little face is
somehow distinctive, even though similar in a "mashed,"
pudgy way. Whoever the baby "looks like," she will be
more like her own self in a week or two. The molded head
re-forms to its normal shape, ears that may have been folded
askew take their proper place, eyelids lose their puffiness
and let the eyes look interested in looking.

The Baby's Dilemma

It's no wonder that parents need a little time to get used to
their baby. But what must the baby get used to? Try to
imagine the impact of birth—the amazing, immediate shifts
in physiological functioning that enable the baby to maintain
an independent life, the drastic change of environment with
its barrage of new sensations. The baby's senses are as-
saulted by bright light and noise (including his own shrill
voice); the feel of air on his skin, in his nostrils and lungs;
the clasp of hands on his body; contact of instruments used
to examine and ensure his welfare; the strange feel of clothing on his skin; even the sensation of his own weight on a
solid surface; for his body has known only yielding surroundings.

The baby can't be expected to adjust suddenly to this
new life. It takes time for the new functions now required
of his body to become stabilized. Meanwhile, all these new
activities—sucking for food, digesting it, emptying his
bowels and bladder—tax his energy, and he'll spend a lot
of time in sleep. Even when he's awake he'll periodically
"shut out" what's happening to and around him, as self-
protection against stress and overstimulation.

Your Baby Is Unique

Newborns differ in their adjustment to life outside the womb. Some are better equipped than others to handle the demands of their new environment, partly because of better developed bodily systems at birth. Actually, babies are not all the same age when they're born. A mother's "due date" for delivery is only an approximation; the majority of babies arrive anywhere from a few days to two weeks earlier or later than this date, which is based on the *estimated* time of conception. One baby's rate of development before birth can be faster or slower than another's, and even a few days can make a difference in some of the "finishing touches" to a baby's body before birth.

Another factor in the infant's adjustment is his inborn temperament. Babies show decided individual differences, even in their first days of life, ranging from the placid, easy-

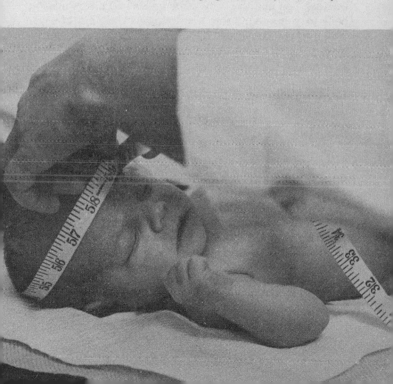

to-please ones to the wound-up-spring characters who are trigger-quick in their negative reactions, and equally alert and responsive to the pleasures of their new world.

But whatever your baby's "type"—and it will probably be somewhere between these opposites—starting out hasn't been easy. Yet you'll be surprised at how fast he becomes acclimated to this new life, and how fast you become familiar and knowledgeable with your baby. In only a few weeks "the baby" has blossomed into a personality whom everyone calls by name. By now he's "forgiven" you for the unpleasantries he's encountered. And even if this small person is still consuming great quantities of your time and energy, and has thoroughly upset your former life-style, a truce has taken place. This is inevitable. The natural process of attachment is binding baby and parents together. It's a kind of "knowing"—the nuances of understanding that pass between you and the baby as he quiets and molds his soft body to yours—and this has nourished the roots of love. Yes, now you know what it is to love this baby as a person—even when you wish he'd go away for a while.

Understanding Your Baby

Behavior

In the first days of living with your new baby, your impressions of her behavior are likely to be quite simplistic. She seems to divide her time between sleeping, crying, nursing, and noncomplaining awakeness. The latter may be deceiving until you discover what important things this very new baby may be doing. Just watching her, her behavior appears to be a kind of meaningless mixture of fragmented movements. Arms wave at random, a fisted hand opens momentarily, the tiny fingers spread daintily. Legs folded close to the body in the prenatal position thrust out in quick kicks. Fleeting expressions move across her face—a frown, a pucker, a smile, a lift of the eyebrows. In sleep, too, the fluttering eyelids, lip movements, twinges, and jerks of her body make you wonder. Why does she act so disorganized? Is she all right? Or is it simply that she has no control at all over her movements?

The Baby Brain

Until recently, newborn behavior was described, in simple terms, as a bundle of reflexes, stemming only from the lower brain and spinal nerves; not until weeks later would the "higher" cerebral cortex begin to function, making voluntary behavior possible—and at the same time inhibiting many early reflexes. This served to explain some of the surprising abilities that are present at birth, only to fade away for a period before they return in "true" form as self-directed actions.

Many scientific researchers are now refuting the belief that the newborn uses only part of his brain. Studies indicate that the entire brain is involved to some degree in newborn behavior, and that some actions that appear to be reflexive are actually voluntary. In this view, one section of the brain will not take control away from other parts as the baby matures, even though there will be remarkable changes in the integration between parts of the nervous system. Many of the baby's future abilities have their counterparts in early behavior patterns. These rudiments of skills go underground for a time, but the baby's brain has stored the experience of many repeated, though limited, actions. Whether reflexive or voluntary, these serve as the link to future skills, which the baby will be prepared to tackle when his muscles and nervous system have sufficiently matured.

Supporting the evidence of integrated brain functioning are many observations indicating that reflex action alone cannot explain how newborn babies are able to produce and modulate much of their behavior. The newborn can make choices: he can pause in an activity such as sucking and switch his attention to something he hears; he can scan his surroundings, then select an object for "study." He tries vigorously to defend himself against pain or annoyance:

He'll push or grab at a doctor's hand, or deliver a well-aimed kick with his free foot to rescue the other when it's held down for a blood sample.

In one test a cloth is lightly held over the newborn's eyes when he is interested in looking around. He tries to dislodge it by twisting his head, arching his back, then waving his arms. Repeatedly, his hands come close to the cloth. Some babies succeed in moving the cloth with their swipes; a few even grab hold of it. If the cloth is removed before the baby gets really upset, he instantly calms down and resumes his relaxed looking. Babies as young as two days of age have performed in this test.

Researchers have all sorts of ingenious ways to study babies, and they go through endless hours of recording minute details. Running filmed sequences in slow motion, for instance, they detect nuances of behavior that previously escaped the notice of even trained observers; and each bit of information adds to their knowledge of human development. Parents are often puzzled by many odd aspects of newborn behavior that are perfectly normal behavior patterns performed by all normal newborns. Yet how unexpected, even amazing, are some of these performances.

In between feeding and diapering and hoping your baby will sleep peacefully for a while, you may want to do some home testing. But wait for the right time. Your newborn won't want to show off if he's in a hazy state; his responses are best when he's calm but alert.

Behavior Patterns

How about taking your baby for a walk? With support, she can step along by herself. Hold her upright under her arms with her feet touching a firm surface. Gently bounce her a bit and she'll straighten her legs to help support her weight. Now tilt her slightly forward. She'll begin to step, lifting one foot after the other in rhythm. Some newborns perform this dramatically, lifting their legs high and prancing along like little marionettes.

Now let her play follow-the-leader. Holding her under

her arms and facing you, slowly turn with her from side to side. She'll follow your lead, turning her head and eyes in the same direction you're moving.

Here's an A-for-effort test. When your baby is lying on her back, pull her up very gently by her arms to a sitting position. Notice how her eyes snap wide open (the china-doll reflex) and how her shoulders tense as she tries to hold up her head (a righting reflex). She won't be able to steady her head for about four months, but she's doing what she can with those weak newborn muscles. A little wobbling will do no harm if you make this test slowly and steadily.

Did you know that newborn babies can actually swim? This is an ability you certainly won't home-test, but one that's been demonstrated in carefully controlled research on infant development. The newborn can glide along gracefully underwater, holding her breath to keep from swallowing water. Arms and legs move in a crawllike pattern, and the trunk swings from side to side like a little amphibian. This ability persists for about four months, then disappears until the end of the first year or early in the second year when babies can again swim rhythmically.

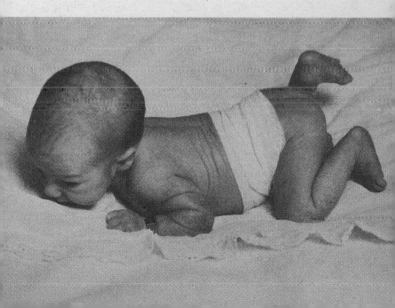

A kind of crawling, or squiggling, is another ability that may surprise you. You've made your baby all comfortable for sleep in the middle of her crib, and come back to find her curled up in one corner. She has nested herself cozily against the crib bumpers. Not intentionally—she doesn't know where she's going—but a newborn does like to find something to snuggle against before settling down, perhaps as a carry-over from womb security. In a few months, before purposeful creeping begins, she won't be able to propel herself; she'll just flail her legs and get nowhere.

The strength of a newborn's hand grip is remarkable, but it will begin to fade quickly so try it out soon. Let your baby get a good grip on your finger; you may have difficulty pulling it away. The baby can be pulled up to a sitting position while clutching your finger. He can even support his own body weight, hanging on by his hands to a thin rod in midair. (This trick should *not* be tried by a novice; the experts know just how to swing up so the baby will tighten, not lose his grip.) To a lesser degree, the newborn can also grasp with his toes. Press the sole of his foot just behind the toes and they'll attempt to curl in and take hold of the object. He may be able to briefly hold a pencil with his toes. The grasping response, which certainly seems of no practical use to our newborn babies, was crucial to prehistoric babies for clinging to their mother's body or keeping themselves safe in trees. Such reflexive acts are remnants of ancient mechanisms that have outlasted their need.

Another vestige of the dim past is a startle reflex, called the Moro. It's set off by a sudden loud sound or abrupt loss of equilibrium. A very reactive baby will perform the Moro when he's simply rolled over from stomach to back in his crib. Although the startle reflex persists into adult life, the newborn's reaction pattern is quite different. His body stiffens and arches, his arms and legs thrust outward, then quickly inward to a rigid embrace position, with arms and hands fixed as though to clutch onto something. The Moro is often called the "fear of falling" reflex.

The oddities of newborn behavior are not so strange when we consider the amazing evolution of a baby from conception to birth. All the inherent abilities that protect the baby and ensure his survival do not suddenly materialize when he enters the outside world. Many are practiced extensively during prenatal life. Systems that spring into action at birth are his heritage, his preparation for independent life. Although human infants are much less capable than the young of many animals who can fend quite well for themselves at birth, our babies have no need of many capabilities and defenses important to less-developed species. The human baby's helplessness is offset by his parents' protection and care over a long period of time. He is also safeguarded by his many automatic responses to the help he is given.

Reflexes

Put to the mother's breast immediately after birth, the baby will suck. She can even locate the source of food by rooting— a searching, reaching movement that helps her find the nipple when her cheek touches the breast. The sucking reflex is so sensitive that the newborn will try to suck on anything that touches her lips.

Sucking on a nipple is quite different from sucking on a straw, and not so easy. It involves chomping down the lips and gums to seal the mouth around the areola, then using the tongue to press the nipple to the roof of the mouth, and drawing the tongue backward to express milk. Swallowing automatically follows, but if more fluid goes into the baby's mouth than she can handle, the gagging reflex comes to her rescue to prevent choking. Gagging is also triggered if the baby breathes as she swallows. But there is a finely integrated system at work in the "simple" act of nursing; it combines the reflexes of sucking, swallowing, and breathing. Newborns somehow pace themselves, averaging about two sucks for each breath, though it takes some practice to become skillful—considering the fact that before birth, the baby didn't have to suck for her food or even breathe!

The vital reflex of breathing also needs time to become stabilized. Watching your baby asleep you'll notice how faintly she breathes for a time, then changes to deep or noisy or jerky breathing. Don't worry, it's normal for a newborn's respiration to be irregular in depth and rhythm. Sneezes and coughs help to clear her air passages of lint or dust or mucus. And that big yawn which looks so charming on a tiny baby is a means of pulling in an extra gulp of oxygen when the body needs it.

Obviously the baby, like all living things, arrives programmed with survival abilities; and many of his transient behaviors point the way to his future development. One behavior pattern that makes the latter connection very apparent is an odd passive posture you'll often see when the baby is lying on his back. It's termed the tonic neck reflex, but is aptly referred to as the fencing pose. The baby's head is turned to one side; the arm on the same side is stretched out at almost a right angle to his body; his other arm is flexed, with his fisted hand resting near the back of his head. Babies assume both right and left direction, but the rightward orientation predominates, indicating that the tonic-neck-reflex posture is the first manifestation of hand preference. This posture usually begins around four weeks of age.

If you haven't met many young babies you may wonder why you often find yours in this strange position. If it worries you a bit, and you try to "straighten him out," most likely he'll move right back the way he wants to be. And for good reason! Watch him awhile if you have the time and patience. You may catch him in the act of catching a glimpse of that outstretched hand. At first this occurs very occasionally and very briefly, only when his hand happens to move across his line of vision. But in the weeks ahead the baby's eyes will "get hold" of that outstretched hand and stare at it for long periods. This is a highly significant development—it's the forerunner of coordinated use of the eyes and the hands. Your baby is preparing himself for a few months hence, when he can direct his hand to go after those fascinating toys that only his eyes can reach out to now. Can the tonic neck posture be called a pure reflex? How many threads of intention are tied in with the newborn baby's behavior patterns?

Learning

There is no question that learning is taking place from the very beginning. "Competent" is a word you hear often now to describe the researchers' admiration of all the ways in which newborns show their capabilities. Long gone is the idea that babies are interested in nothing but creature comforts for many weeks after birth. Even in the delivery room, where a whole new world is flooding in upon the baby, she is taking in separate impressions, briefly holding on to some and rejecting others. She shuts her eyes tightly against bright light, but as she lets her eyes roam, a patch of soft light will attract and hold her attention. She'll alert to the human voice, selecting it from among other sounds.

The infant's five senses are her equipment for finding her way in this new world. However strange and sudden are many of the sensations of sight, hearing, touch, taste and smell, the newborn's entire sensory system is ready to tune in and learn from her new environment. But at this young age she needs protection from too much stimulation. Learning takes place most easily and smoothly in situations of one thing at a time. No newborn will thank you for a party atmosphere of voices, lights, music, and activity. Swamping her senses makes it impossible for her to direct her attention, and she may "go to pieces" in a long crying jag.

As parents learn all too soon, the newborn has plenty of personal problems to contend with. Hunger keeps repeating itself, air bubbles want out of her stomach, strange miseries overcome her. Often she's exhausted with the whole business and grabs every possible chance for a peaceful sleep. But wrapped up in herself as she often seems, there are many breaks in this cocoon of self, fragments of time when the baby peers into the world outside herself, gathering impressions that lure her on to explore it.

Vision

How well does a newborn see? Far better than previously

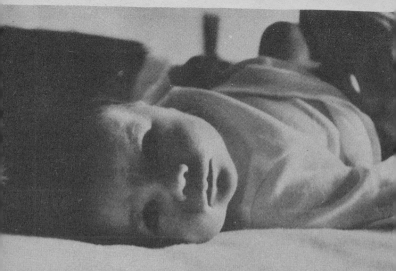

believed. When his vision was described simply as blurs of light and dark, testing techniques had not yet been devised. Hundreds of studies have since revealed a great deal about infants' perceptions. Although the newborn's visual range is limited to between eight and twelve inches, he works hard to focus on an object within his line of vision. Once he "gets hold" of it, seeing is clearly a pleasure for the baby; his eyes brighten, he becomes very quiet, staring intently. Move the object slowly from side to side and he moves his head jerkily, trying to keep it in sight. Soon he'll try to follow if it's moved very slowly up and down.

Moreover, your present-day baby can show you his preferences in modern art. If you don't want to tote him around a museum, try him on a series of prints or posters. He'll select boldly abstract designs with strongly delineated stripes and angles. The newborn concentrates longer on these than on solid shapes or patterns of diffused colors. Works of the French impressionists won't impress him. His taste runs to pure colors, with a preference for red or yellow, rather than blends or pastels. And his overall favorite for study may prove to be a black-and-white graph of anything at all, perhaps of changes in the birth rate or the value of the dollar.

A mobile may be the first "educational toy" you'll buy or make for your baby. During this period, it should be positioned to his far right or left, since a newborn generally lies with his head turned to the side. Later, when he begins to keep his head in a mid-position, you can reposition the mobile for better viewing. Music adds another dimension to a mobile, making it extra interesting as a look-and-listen toy, as it slowly circles, tinkling a nursery tune. Until the baby spends more time looking up, you can also position interesting things in his line of vision—a stuffed toy perhaps or a bold patterned piece of fabric tied to the bars of the crib.

Sometimes you'll find your baby enjoying "toys" that she's discovered for herself. She seems to be listening intently; the room is quiet; then you too hear the light, rhythmic plumping of your percolating coffee. You notice her gazing steadily in one direction; what has she found? Perhaps this time it's the interesting contrast of light and dark lines on a venetian blind, or the moving patterns playing on a curtain where sunlight is filtering through the leaves of a tree outside.

If you want to prove to yourself how much seeing means to your baby, and can bring yourself to tease her just a bit, try this experiment when she's alert and contentedly surveying her world. Place your hand an inch or two in front of her eyes to block her vision. She'll quickly look off to the side to unblock her view; if you continue to cut it off she'll continue her escape tactics. Very young infants are fairly good at this. But six-week-olds are skilled players, shifting head and eyes rapidly till you—of course!—terminate the game.

The most heartwarming test is the newborn's interest in gazing at your face. It must be admitted that she doesn't know "who" you are, but beginning in the first days of life, babies show more interest in the human face than in anything else. A picture of a face won't do for long; babies want the real thing. Perhaps movement plays a part in this preference. Who can look at a baby without "making faces"—lifting the eyebrows, smiling, moving the mouth in coos and chirps. Shiny objects attract the newborn too, making a person's eyes of great interest. Hold your baby in a semisitting position—this increases her alertness—and cup her head in your hands. Face to face she'll make eye-to-eye contact with you, often for a remarkably long period.

Authorities agree that there is much more than visual attraction involved here. This paramount interest in the human face indicates the newborn's inborn tendency to sense how important a human being is to her. In turn, parents are drawn closer to the baby by her interest in gazing at them.

Hearing

Unlike the infant's eyes, which need a few months for full development, her hearing apparatus is fully developed at birth. In fact, there is ample evidence that before birth the baby is using her hearing and reacting to outside sounds; she may move actively during a concert, or "jump" in response to the bang of a door. What she hears after birth is more amplified, of course, but the womb is not an altogether silent place; sounds from the mother's organs reach the baby.

A constant sound for the unborn baby is the mother's heartbeat. This may explain why the newborn baby is often soothed by soft rhythmic sounds. Do they re-create the tranquility of her uterine home? She will often become very calm listening to the tick of a clock, the singsong thrumming of a music box, or the age-old soother, a lullaby combined with rocking. And the hum of a car in motion is well known to experienced parents for its almost miraculous calming effect on a nervous, complaining baby. It's interesting, too, that almost all parents, whether right- or left-handed, hold their baby on the left side of the body where she can hear the adult's heartbeat. Either instinct or a few hours of experience seems to clue in the parent to the baby's preference for this holding position.

Even when the baby is nursing or sucking on a pacifier she'll inhibit her sucking to listen to a new sound, then after "taking it in" will resume her sucking. Babies become accustomed to most of the normal sounds in their household and so cease to react to them. It's seldom necessary to shush brothers and sisters ("Don't wake the baby!") unless they're overly rambunctious.

The Shut-out Mechanism

Newborns also have a remarkably efficient mechanism for defending themselves against over-stimulation. Something that causes a startle reaction, such as a bright flash of light in the eyes or a sudden bang, speeds up the baby's breathing and heart rate. If the shocks are repeated he continues to startle, putting a strain on his physiological systems. But very shortly he protects himself; he closes his eyes, curls his body into a snug bundle, and "pretends" to be asleep. What he has actually done is to control his reactions to the too-intense stimulus by shutting himself off from it. Psychologically, this is termed "habituation." It may remind you of the protective defense system of certain insects that "play dead" when gently poked. More poking, however, won't reactivate the insect; it remains comatose until you are long out of range. It's a giant leap from insects to human babies, but the contrast, rather than the comparison, is interesting. The baby *can* be reactivated by introducing a new, pleasing stimulus, such as a crooning voice or a rattle. He'll "come awake" and respond calmly to the new interest. This capacity to control his responses is a valuable and necessary ability that the newborn uses to organize his world. He needs to shut out disturbing stimuli in order to make choices and focus his attention on important infant matters.

The Human Voice

Voices, like faces, hold special interest for the newborn.

He's particularly responsive to high-pitched voices, such as women's or children's. But you'll notice that almost everyone, including men, will pitch their chatter and noises high for a newborn—perhaps because he seems too little and delicate for deeper sounds, or because they soon learn how best to bring out his bright-eyed responses. It may be that babies show this preference for higher and lighter voices because from their first days they generally hear more from their mothers than from other persons. And even in the womb, where sounds are muffled, they hear the tonal pitch of their mothers' voices.

Even though the baby can often sleep peacefully in a noisy room, he can sometimes be wakened by a whisper close to his ear. As he begins to stir and open his eyes he'll also start searching for the source of the voice, moving his head and eyes, then becoming quiet and interested when he discovers the source. Relating sounds and sights—coordinating the senses of hearing and seeing—is an important basis for learning.

Tracking a sound, like tracking a moving object, is excellent practice. When your baby is awake and in the mood for little games, shake a rattle or a bell behind her. Notice how she perks up and looks around; move the soundmaker slowly and see how she brightens when her eyes catch hold of it. Try placing yourself near her but out of sight, and talk to her, first on one side then the other; she'll turn her eyes and head toward the side your voice is coming from. A very young baby doesn't care who a voice or a face belongs to; her responses can be tested by anyone. If a man is on one side, talking to her in his normal adult voice, and a woman or child takes turns talking on the other side, the baby will almost always turn her attention to the higher voice.

Taste and Smell

A breastfed baby often stirs up a real fuss when mother occasionally tries to give him a bottle. He may flatly refuse to take it even though he's obviously hungry. But let father settle down with the baby and he'll usually take the whole feeding as smoothly as though it's his regular fare at every meal. An older breastfed baby may really be resisting the switch to bottle feeding. But with a newborn there's a different reason—connected with his sense of smell.

Newborns are sensitive to both odors and tastes; they have strong reactions to intense odors and resist sour and bitter fluids. But they do accept any sweet fluid. The breastfed baby who resists taking formula from his mother is not turned off by the taste. He smells her milk as she holds him, and that familiar odor "means" food. By five days of age, experiments have shown, babies have learned this. When a milk-soaked nursing pad and a clean unused one were held on alternate sides near a baby's cheeks, he turned his head to the milky pad. By ten days of age, babies differentiated between two milk-soaked pads—one of the mother's, the other of another nursing mother—and rapidly turned to select their own mother's. What a sensitive distinction this is!

The Sense of Touch

Of all the newborn's sensory perceptions, touch is the most highly developed. It's so natural to cuddle and fondle a baby that the paramount importance of the sense of touch may not occur to you. But the damaging effects of touch deprivation have been thoroughly documented in behavioral and clinical research. In institutions where babies received good hygiene and adequate nutrition, but lacked holding and fondling by their caretakers, the babies became retarded in all phases of development. They were subject to emotional, behavioral, and physical problems, and were more susceptible to illnesses—in some cases fatal—than family-tended infants.

The self-concept of being wanted and valued is largely rooted in the feelings of human warmth and security that a baby receives from others early in life. Lacking this, the effects carry over into child and adult life, limiting a person's ability to feel and express empathy, affection, and the confidence that comes from a good self-image. Clearly, all the manifestations of love that a baby receives from his parents are vital to his well-being.

Extensive animal research has shown that mother animals "know" how vital touch stimulation is to their young. Without all the close body contact, nuzzling, suckling, and licking they receive, baby animals cannot survive. When a mother cat tirelessly licks each of her babies she is doing much more than cleaning them. The licking activates sensory fibers in the skin, which in turn keeps all the kittens' bodily systems well stimulated.

When parents hold and caress their baby they are likewise giving him physical benefits. But much more is happening. They are communicating with their baby. Touch is the first language a baby can both understand and respond to. As by osmosis, parent and baby are absorbing their feelings about each other. What better start can the baby have for learning about love and life and his own personal worth?

Parent-Child Interaction

Crying, rather than the sense of touch, has often been called a baby's first language. More accurately, crying is his first "spoken" language, marvelously effective for summoning his caregivers. Baby yells out a demand, parent complies; peace descends; baby and parent settle down to togetherness. Now, quietly, they communicate in that other language of sensuous understanding—the language of mutual touch. The demanding cry has served its purpose.

The Spoiling Bugaboo

The newborn's cry, being self-protective, is far from subtle. Perhaps by design, nature has given the baby a strong, harsh, unpleasant cry; otherwise it might not get results so readily. And it *should* be answered promptly when it crescendos to full volume. This crude means of expressing himself is built into the baby's instinctive drive for survival. At this age, he can't grade his needs in degrees of importance; he often feels just as desperate with a minor discomfort as with the sensation of starving. When he cries he's calling for help, even though what happens and why or how it happens are far beyond his understanding. The newborn's cry for help is a defensive mechanism set off by whatever disturbs his security, and it's up to his caregivers to restore his "peace of mind."

But won't too much attention spoil a baby? Old beliefs die hard, even though a wealth of evidence refutes this one. It is, in fact, lack of attention that can "spoil" a baby. All child-study specialists emphasize that a lot of loving attention is essential for a baby's healthy development. And numerous studies have shown that infants who receive consistent care and comforting cry less as they grow older than those deprived of attention. Yet there are still people, new parents included, who think that by letting a baby "cry it out" he can be taught to conform to adults' convenience, to learn "who's boss" right from the start, and thus never become "spoiled."

A young baby cannot be *taught*, for the simple reason that he has no memory ability. But he can learn through the process of conditioning—in two very different ways. What can a baby learn in this first year of life through his relationships with others? He can learn what makes him happy and what makes him miserable; whether to trust or distrust people; to feel self-confident or timid and insecure; to approach life with zest or with anger; to love or to feel unloved and alone. And depending on what he learns he will develop a pleasing personality or one that is hard to live with.

The Ups and Downs

Right now, in these early weeks of life, many babies are not easy to live with. Even those who have few problems in adjustment use up a large portion of your days and nights. Sometimes you think, What's become of *me*? I'm with myself only in snatches. Husband-and-wife time is fractioned, if not with infant interruptions, then with expecting

them. You're tired, sometimes you're bored, sometimes
resentful. But suddenly parenthood sweeps over you again—
it's a warm, exciting feeling you get to know well—and
you think how short the time is when a child is a baby,
what a sliver out of your own life span. You want to take
up that little person and apologize for thinking even a moment of yourself. But no need. There's that demanding cry
again. You're snapped out of your reverie. And your next
round of catering begins.

What makes a good parent? Not trying to do everything
exactly right. Not blaming yourself for the gloomy times.
The formula you'll probably ease into is fairly simple. The
more you know about your baby, the more you respect her
right to be the only way she's able to be just now. By the
same token, you respect your own right to have ups and
downs in this new relationship. This way you're open to
seeing and feeling and delighting in the rewards as they
come along. Your baby will see to that!

Babies are endowed with natural abilities to pull their
parents into an orbit of loving care. They have as many
ways of charming as of demanding. Your newborn takes
hold of your finger, clasps it tightly for a moment, and
you're caught; she can almost twist you around her little
finger. You go through all kinds of antics to catch her
attention; she yawns in your face—and you're delighted.
You read about all the capabilities a newborn has, her remarkable faculties for reaching out and exploring her world.
And you think, Isn't it enough that she just *feels* like this?
Curled close to my body when I hold her, like she knows
I'll always be here when she wants me.

It's good to feel sentimental about a baby, and it's a
baby's good fortune to soak in these wonderful waves of
tenderness. What's difficult to realize in these early weeks
is how hard the baby is working to "grow up," to grow out
of being a helpless little thing. But she insists on showing
you how fast she's learning. Just a few weeks after she's
struggled out into the world, here she is, patiently waiting
for attention. She's told you she needs you, in no uncertain
terms. You've answered her soothingly. And simply by the

sound of your voice she knows that relief is coming. She lies quietly waiting for you to pick her up. How did she learn this so fast? How did she learn to wait for the comfort she needs, to "cooperate" with you in caring for her?

Certainly the newborn doesn't know he's cooperating; nor has he "learned from experience" in any adult sense of the meaning. When hunger strikes, for instance, it's an all-consuming sensation of the moment; his mind cannot tell him that relief will come, as it did a few hours before. But your presence *can* tell him. You've become part of the comfort feelings that have repeatedly replaced his discomfort.

The newborn's feelings come and go, one sensation immediately erasing another. But he is gathering impressions through all his senses, and all that he takes in is having an effect on him, helping to shape his responses and form his habits. In this way he gradually acquires a habit of contentment or a habit of anxiety. When his needs are answered consistently he has a minimum of anxiety. If he receives attention based only on arbitrary rules of "training"—out of rhythm with his needs—or haphazard attention, he suffers a great deal of anxiety. No one—especially a baby—can learn or make good use of his faculties in a state of anxiety.

Naturally, a baby can't be kept in a state of blissful contentment, for how can we possibly "read" all the meanings behind his complaints? We have to expect many blind spots in our understanding of infants. But the one blind spot that can be devastating to a baby is to say, "He just wants attention," and to deny him that. Attention is nourishment for an infant's mental and emotional development, just as food is for his physical growth.

What Does Baby Want?

By your baby's responses you can tell what kind of attention she wants, and in time you'll learn what different kinds of crying mean. For a while you'll probably answer all shades of crying, from restless fussing to outright wailing, by trying

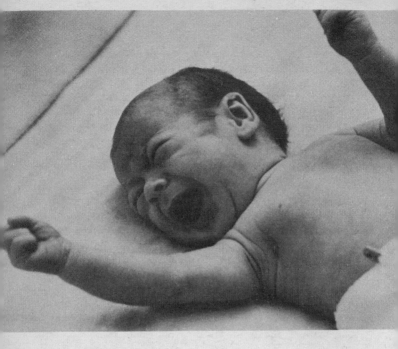

the old standbys—feeding or burping or changing. If your administrations have only a temporary effect, what next? Maybe all she wants is to be held awhile; she's lonely for the feel of you. Maybe she's bored; she's not sleepy, and she can't find anything "to do," closed off from sights and sounds in her room. Or she may be in a state of "indecision" between drifting off to sleep or stimulating herself into alertness. Depending on the hour, you'll try soothing methods or bring her into the family circle for some light entertainment.

One way that helps to ward off fretfulness and crying is every now and then to give your baby attention *before* she asks for it. Naturally you won't wake her from a peaceful sleep. But when you find her awake and uncomplaining, she'll enjoy the special treat of being held and rocked. It reinforces her good feelings and somehow instills a different meaning than the same attention when she's nervous or upset. You're in tune with her feelings—not trying to change them. Even a very young baby can appreciate this.

But your baby will be changing her own tune from week to week. Perhaps she started out scrunching herself up on her stomach for sleep after every feeding; now suddenly she resists that position, squirming and crying till you turn her over. She wants to see something more than the sheet of her crib, to look around and amuse herself for a while. Then when she's drowsy she fusses till you put her on her tummy again.

Babies are such individualists that what turns on one may turn off another. Some like to be played with; others soon signal *enough* to gentle stimulation. There are babies who even show preferences in using their perceptions, taking more interest in one kind of stimulation than another. A baby who's especially attentive to auditory stimulation will respond more to music than a baby who always seeks out the visual interests in her environment. Movement moods follow different patterns too. For some infants, gentle jouncing of the carriage is pleasing; for others, nothing but holding and walking will do.

Although rocking is a time-honored baby soother, it's amazing how particular some babies are about the way you perform it. Cadence is all-important to these connoisseurs of motion; some like it slow, some like it fast, some like a tricky little double push worked in. A smooth-riding modern rocker is just the thing for one baby. Another becomes attached to an old wooden rocker with a slight wobble and a rhythmic squeak. And as all baby and parent experts know, singing *should* be synchronized with the rocking motion.

Sometimes you find mothers and dads discussing such kernels of wisdom about their babies, and vying with one another regarding their most effective discoveries.

Is it nonsensical to think about such subtle distinctions in what a baby likes to look at or listen to or feel? Well, for one thing, it makes your baby more interesting, just as learning about a friend's opinions and activities makes him or her a more interesting person to be with. Confining conversation to remarks about the weather can get pretty boring; so can confining parent-baby communication to everyday routines. For another thing, if you've been through a few hours with a constantly complaining baby you'll be glad enough to hone up on personalized ways of pleasing her.

That Mystery Intruder: Colic

Although noncomplaining alert time gradually increases, it's still sparse with most babies. But hard crying usually diminishes during these weeks—unless colic sets in to disrupt the household. Just what is colic? It's not an illness, it's a condition—puzzling to doctors as well as parents, and miserable for the baby. Actually, colic has become a catchall term for any seizure of hard crying that seems to have neither cause nor cure. Many babies never have colic, some have it only occasionally, others are plagued with attacks of daily regularity. It usually appears first around three weeks of age, reaches its peak by six weeks, then begins to taper off, rarely continuing beyond three months.

Most commonly, the intense crying comes on in the evening. This suggests that nervous tension has built up during the day, and the baby has no other means of discharging this emotional pressure except in prolonged bursts of crying. At day's end, plenty of adults are keyed up and need to "unwind" before they can relax. A lot of factors feed into the family atmosphere at this time—fatigue and consequent impatience, dinner preparations, voices raised above the TV volume. At times it all gets to the baby. Babies are ready receptors of tension, picking up the feelings of others and the ambiance of their home like a radar screen reflecting signals. But this is a two-way situation; a baby's crying is hard on the parents' nerves; the catalyst is anyone's guess. You might say it's a case of parent-child interaction operating for worse instead of better.

But why are some babies subject to hard crying spells and not others? Some doctors have noted that colicky babies appear to have an overactive nervous system; they are especially bright and receptive to all kinds of stimuli, and so are likely to get "overdoses." When too much floods in on this type of baby it overwhelms his ability to cope with it. His control disintegrates, the same as a person who "blows up" with a surfeit of irritations or stress. In general, adults have acquired their own personal ways of coping with stress, but there's little a baby of this age can do about it except cry. As yet he has no other way to let off steam. He can't kick at a dangling toy, or pick one up and bang it, or work off tension by scooting around on the floor. He's confined to his newborn packet of meager abilities; they serve him well in a calm but are useless when he's caught in a storm.

Soothers

One ability that the newborn can be helped to use for self-comfort is sucking—sucking when he's not hungry. Although hand to mouth is an early behavior pattern, and newborns often suck on their fist or fingers when hungry, it remains a hit-or-miss action for many babies during these early weeks. For those who aren't born thumbsuckers, and don't get enough sucking satisfaction at feedings, a pacifier is an excellent prop. There was a time when the pacifier was in general disfavor with doctors, and for good reason: It was too often used as a substitute for parental attention, or for a stimulating environment or freedom to exercise and explore. But used properly, well-designed pacifiers are now often recommended by doctors for high-strung babies who need a sleep-inducer, and especially for newborns who are prone to colic.

Sucking is much more than a means of obtaining food. Unborn babies never experience hunger, yet it has long been known that some suck their thumbs. This was first evidenced by calluses on some babies' thumbs at birth, and now can be witnessed long before birth by researchers using the technique of ultrasound visualization. Touch is the earliest sense to develop before birth, and the lips are the first area to respond to touch prenatally. Thus the newborn baby is well conditioned to make use of his lips and mouth, and sucking serves as a natural, satisfying way to occupy himself.

Some pacifiers, however, are not well constructed in shape, and some are too flimsy to be safe. Your pediatrician can recommend a good brand—one that is shaped for proper development of the baby's jaws and teeth, and one that conforms to safety standards. The U. S. Consumer Product Safety Commission regulations state that all pacifiers must have a wide mouthguard with an inseparable nipple to prevent choking or swallowing, at least two ventilation holes in the mouthguard, a large handle, and no cord or ribbon attached to the handle. (A pacifier must never be hung around the baby's neck!)

If your baby needs a little encouragement to start using a pacifier, *do not* follow someone's suggestion to dip the pacifier in honey. Honey should *not* be given to a baby younger than six months old. In fact, many doctors warn against giving honey to a baby during the entire first year of life. It has been found that some honey contains a bacterium—apparently not harmful to older children and adults—that can cause infant botulism, a serious poisoning disorder.

There are a number of soothing techniques to try with a wrought-up infant. Swaddling is one. The baby is laid diagonally on a lightweight blanket, first folded up over his legs, then one side folded over the other. Snugly packaged like this, he can't flail his legs and arms and repeatedly startle himself into crying. If he dozes off while being rocked or walked he's less likely to wake himself when gently laid down. Swaddling and a cradle are a good combination. In a cradle, a rolled blanket on either side of the baby will keep him from rolling as you rock him.

Babies gulp down a lot of air with their crying and may need to get rid of that discomfort before they can relax. Often it helps to lay the baby across your knees with a well-wrapped warm (not hot) water bottle under her tummy. The warmth feels good, and gently rubbing her back or slightly bouncing your knees helps to bring up the swallowed air. The warm water bottle under her stomach and a ride in her carriage around the room is another combination that may work.

As depicted in cartoons from time immemorial, pacing the floor with the baby is the most commonly tried remedy, and it does seem to be the most effective. It's also the most exhausting during late-hours tending. With whatever method is keeping the baby quiet, taking parental turns on duty ensures a fair share of rest for everyone.

If motion isn't essential to quiet the baby, you can settle down in an easy chair, with the baby ensconced on your shoulder, and watch TV or read or listen to music. Low-keyed music with a rhythmic beat is soothing to most babies.

There's one sound instrument that may really work like a charm—a metronome. Maybe you've seen or used one of these devices. It's for help in following a regular tempo—when learning to play the piano, for instance. It works like a clock; an inverted pendulum on a metal rod swings back and forth, beating time in incessant tock-tocks. Since it can be speeded up or slowed down, you can regulate it to the beat that has the most soothing effect on your baby. There's one trick to "playing" a metronome: You have to keep yourself from being mesmerized by its monotony before the baby is as limp as you are for sleep.

The calming effect of heartbeatlike sounds is well known in infant research. When a tape recording of the human heartbeat has been piped into newborn hospital nurseries, the infants' crying was considerably reduced. Apparently this sound more than any other helps to re-create the tranquility of the baby's life before birth, when he constantly heard his mother's heartbeat.

If the baby is in a period of evening crying binges it's only sensible to forget the regular household schedule, let a lot of things go, and grab sleep throughout the day. Sometimes a better relief than rest is to get away from it all, out of the house, leaving the baby with a grandparent, friend, or experienced sitter. A substitute who's had personal experience with new-parent fatigue won't fault you for a now-and-then request for aid; nor should you fault yourself for "deserting" your post.

Baby Carriers

It's a sad fact that most babies in most industrialized countries do a great deal more crying than babies in traditional societies. Far back in time, women had to devise a way to tend their babies and keep them contented with the least possible trouble while the mothers were occupied with food gathering, homemaking, and the needs of other children. Thus the baby carrier was invented, a handiwork that allowed infants to live in the bliss of close body contact with their mothers, the lulling pleasure of motion, and an ever handy supply of food. In many parts of the world, slings and shawls and back carriers are still used extensively for infant care, and today's babies in those cultures rarely cry. If infants could make a progress report on human achievements, they'd probably classify the first baby carrier on a par with the invention of the wheel.

In our modern world, both carriers and wheels are put to good use. Manufacturers have designed a variety of equipment for toting or wheeling the baby. On wheels, choices range from compact, lightweight strollers to deluxe limousine-quality carriages. For the early months, more and more popular for both outdoor and indoor use is the front carrier worn by the parent.

Front carriers come in a variety of fabrics and provide head and neck support for the young baby as he rides chest to chest with his parent. This type of carrier, which gives you full arm and hand freedom, serves as an excellent parent's helper, keeping the baby contented while some chores get done. When selecting a front carrier, look for sturdy construction and good support for the baby's head and neck. Consider yourself, too, when choosing a carrier. Some are easier than others to put on and adjust, and some have wide, well-padded shoulder straps for comfort. Front carriers are designed for a baby up to about six months old, although some can be converted into back carriers. These are more suitable once a baby can sit without support and are discussed on pages 215 and 217.

Baby's First Smile

For most of this period, a baby's parents are kept busy trying to keep her satisfied. That may be fairly easy or really difficult. Babies differ in how they make this biggest adjustment in life—the transition from womb to world.

For all your devoted catering, you do get passive appreciation. But wouldn't it be nice if your baby could *tell* you something. And finally she does! She's gazing at your face. You see the little mouth working; the lips round, and a soft coo comes out; the mouth moves some more, the corners lift, and a tentative smile works its way up till it crinkles her eyes. This is not the meaningless newborn smile that comes and goes at random in sleep or vague awakeness. Nor is it yet a full-blown social smile. It will take a while before the baby will turn on a smile every time you ask her; and some babies are just naturally more smiley than others. Sometimes too much enthusiasm startles a baby out of a quiet contented mood when she's smiling and cooing and making soft gurgling "comfort sounds" to herself.

But these first expressions of your baby's good feelings have a remarkable effect on you; they bring out wonderful feelings of closeness, pull you and the baby together in a new kind of interaction. Now she can express more than her needs; she can keep you attentive, even busy, trying to bring out those smiles.

As soon as a baby lets her parents know that she appreciates the good life they're giving her, they want all the more to keep it that way. Thus a baby's first smiles serve a definite purpose; they create a strong reinforcement of the baby-parent bond.

Family Togetherness

Family mores continue to change, and like everything else today, the jump from one custom to another is often an about-face. It used to be routine—and still is in many families—that babies were supposed to be tucked away out of the way at an early hour every evening, with home privileges reserved for mom and dad and adult friends. It didn't always work—a decided understatement in the case of newborns. Now a lot of parents never give a thought to separating the baby from their after-dinner hours. They believe that both parents should have the privilege of sharing the new family member, that the home is for family and friends, and that the baby is as important as anyone else in this group. Granted, a new baby doesn't always feel sociable. But the fact of being accepted without reservations seems to have a remarkably beneficial effect on his behavior. Families where babies are welcome during hours when all children "ought to be in bed" may be considered too casually "modern" by some. Actually, however, they're following an old-fashioned, even ancient, pattern of family life-style. It's not that they believe the baby should be a constant in their lives, or that they don't enjoy some baby-free time. The thing is, if natural patterns of home life are more pleasant, doesn't it follow that they're commonsensible?

All in all, togetherness seems to be the cure for a vast majority of infant complaints, and the key to the best kind of infant care. When it's both practical and pleasurable for you, your baby will do his part. He'll make you the best of all possible parents for the best of all possible babies— part of the time. For the rest, you'll be good enough parents and child. And that's okay.

Routines and Care

Feeding

You'll spend hundreds of hours this year giving your baby liquid food. You deserve at least one comfortable chair in the house that everyone knows as the feeding chair. It needs two cushioned arms to support your arm that's supporting the baby. If the arms aren't cushioned, use a pillow under your arm. Without an armrest, in a half hour or so you'll think your newborn has doubled his birth weight. A footrest adds comfort. A rocker offers tranquility. And feeding, a practical necessity, brings baby and parent many islands of rest and pleasure.

What Feeding Means to the Baby

The intensity of the hunger cry gives an idea of how urgent

the newborn's stomach pangs are. Wavelike contractions are churning that small empty stomach that so recently received nourishment evenly and constantly in the womb. The unborn baby never experienced hunger. But neither did he experience the blessed relief of warm milk in his stomach. Now, with the first swallow, his cry is stilled, his body loses its tenseness, and he sets to work to save his life— instinctively. His immediate, composed response to relief tells us what feeding must mean to the newborn baby: self-preservation, self-satisfaction, comfort, human bond, all rolled into one wonderful package of pleasure.

Adult feelings, of course, can't be ascribed to the primitive responses of an infant. But however rudimentary the newborn's emotions, all are having an effect on his behavior. The more he is protected from the experience of hunger, the sooner he has a milder reaction to it.

The newborn first has a day or two of sleepy recovery from birth. Then he goes through a disorganized period when he tends to be jittery, with strong reactions to most disturbances. But if frustration is kept to a minimum he rapidly gains a more balanced state in which some inner controls begin to help him out. If he on and off sucks on his fist, for instance, this briefly alleviates his frantic reaction to hunger. Soon he's able to make some associations with feeding—such as being held or talked to—which also work as self-calming cues.

Irregularities

Perhaps the most worrisome problem for parents is whether crying *does* mean hunger. There's not much of a time-pattern in most babies' need of food during these early weeks. Until the newborn's digestive system is working more smoothly, hunger comes at irregular intervals. Sometimes, too, she gets so tired and sleepy, she can't take all she needs at one time; or she's bothered by a bowel movement coming on and needs to get that over with before finishing the feeding. If she has swallowed air while crying or during a feeding, an air bubble in her stomach makes her feel full; she goes off to sleep only to wake again soon, crying. How could she be hungry when she seemed satisfied a short while ago? Maybe the air came up while she was sleeping, or maybe the bubble is hurting her now. When she gets rid of that, she needs to fill up the empty space in her stomach before she can feel satisfied.

A baby can't seem to distinguish between hunger pain and gas pain. With gas, she'll chew on her fist, grab hold of the nipple as though she's starving, suck in a few swallows, and stop—crying. When food isn't the answer, you go on from there—to burping, comforting, perhaps diversion, and finally to whatever will lull the baby back to sleep.

Some lucky babies bring their parents good luck by being born with a well-developed digestive system that can handle food on a regular three- to four-hour schedule. If they're placid by nature, this in itself helps to keep their bodily systems in good working order—unlike babies who are easily agitated and therefore more prone to physical upsets. The "good" baby who eats and sleeps and makes few complaints keeps her parents nicely pacified, which in turn keeps the baby calm and amenable to scheduled routines.

For most parents, though, there's a several weeks' period of irregular, frequent feedings of variable amounts before the baby settles into a fairly predictable feeding routine. She'll get there as soon as she can. Meanwhile, the less stress she has over hunger—by getting service without making a tremendous fuss—the sooner she'll discover it's not a life-or-death matter.

Burping Techniques

Many young babies need to be burped once or more during the feeding as well as after, and sometimes before if they've swallowed air in crying. It's not always necessary to lift the baby to the traditional over-the-shoulder position. Try sitting him upright, leaning against you, and support his wobbly head by cupping his chin between your thumb and forefinger. The air bubble may pop right out if your baby is an easy burper; if not, it will take some coaxing. Another good position is across your lap, tummy down, his head turned sideways and supported by your hand. Back-patting shouldn't turn into thumping; gentle rubbing is just as effective and certainly less disturbing. When the baby is nice and drowsy after a meal it's best not to prolong the burping effort. Lying on his stomach in bed there's no danger of choking if a little milk comes up with the air.

Breastfed babies swallow less air while nursing than bottle-feeders. With hard sucking, the nursing baby's mouth forms an airtight seal. But if there's a copious flow of milk from a very full breast, the baby's swallowing may not be able to keep up, and he needs time-outs to catch his breath to keep from choking.

A small amount of milk often comes up with the air— the reason for a cloth over your shoulder or under the baby's chin when you're burping him. This so-called spitting up is common. And occasional real vomiting is not uncommon; it's often caused by too fast feeding or overfeeding, but *could* be a symptom of illness. Naturally you'll consult the doctor if vomiting continues. Projectile vomiting, a large amount that shoots out with great force, should be reported to the doctor promptly, as it sometimes—but not always— indicates a blockage in the gastrointestinal tract.

Hiccups are common with newborns, especially after feeding. A few swallows of water may stop them, but you don't need to bother; they don't bother the baby and usually disappear in a few minutes.

Round-the-Clock

Night feedings continue for several months at least. The one you'll want your baby to give up first is the so-called 2 A.M. feeding, the one that rouses you out of bed. A bottle-fed infant *may* be ready to do this during her second month, but a breastfed baby usually needs the middle-of-the-night feeding longer. When a baby is able to lengthen the time she can go without food, she won't be consistent about it at first; she may stretch out her sleep by three extra hours one night and only one hour the next. Go along with her, even though other feeding times get out of kilter for a few days. Self-regulation, her own natural rhythms, will get her back on track.

Breastfeeding

It's the easiest, the most economical, the most natural way to feed a baby. And breast milk is the best nutrition you can give your baby—just as the mother's milk of each species is best for the young of that species. Human breast milk has never been duplicated precisely, although today's commercial formulas come close. Breast milk has the best balance of nutrients; is the most easily digested; helps protect the baby from constipation and bacterial infections; eliminates the chance of allergy to cow's milk; and also, according to studies, helps guard against other allergies in later childhood and adult years.

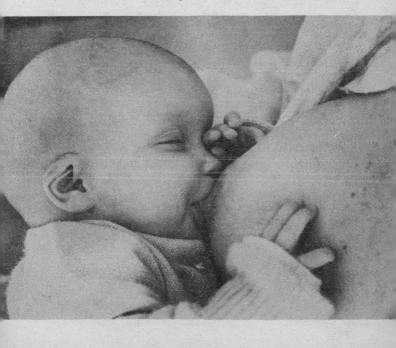

Colostrum, the yellowish fluid that the breasts secrete first, also contains immunizing substances, as well as enough proteins and fats to tide the baby over for two or three days till the true milk comes in. Clearly, nothing surpasses what a mother can offer in infant nutrition.

Along with the health advantages there's an emotional plus in breastfeeding. Mother and baby are assured of a certain intimacy, a private set of feelings that passes from one to the other. It's not that nursing makes a woman more a mother, or a better mother, but it does fulfill the whole maternity cycle. A mother nurtures her baby inside her body for nine months, and nursing is a way of extending that care to the closest comfort she can offer her baby.

Newborns would poll a unanimous yea for breastfeeding. Mothers have a lot of considerations to take into account, for practical as well as personal reasons. There are also influences—pro and con—perhaps from a woman's husband, her circle of friends, even nurses and doctors, who can be discouraging as well as supportive in their attitudes. One woman feels natural, comfortable and confident about breastfeeding; another feels nervous and strange. It's a puzzling quirk of modern society that explicit sex is widespread in literature, film, and theater, yet some people feel embarrassed when the breasts are used as nature intended.

In recent years, however, breastfeeding has been on the increase. This seems to reflect the spread of new research on infant nutrition, and a popular interest in all-around fitness and health. One group that strongly encourages breastfeeding, and offers help to nursing mothers, is La Leche League International, which has many local chapters. To find out if there is a chapter near you, look in the telephone directory or write to the national headquarters at 9616 Minneapolis Avenue, Franklin Park, Illinois 60131.

Getting Started

Your baby knows what to do if you don't confuse her. Simply hold her so that one cheek touches your breast; she'll "root" (search) for the nipple and take hold. Keep her close enough so she can take the whole areola, the dark area around the nipple, into her mouth. She has to press on that area with her gums and jaws to make the milk flow; and if she just mouthes the nipple she'll make it sore. You mustn't try to guide her mouth toward the nipple by pressing on the cheek that is not next to your breast. A newborn turns toward anything that touches her cheek, and so will turn her face away from the breast. And if you gently squeeze both cheeks, trying to open her mouth, she'll be doubly confused. Just be sure she can breathe easily while sucking; you may need to press in your breast to keep it clear of her nose.

Be careful how you take the baby off the breast. If you pull, it can hurt the nipple; there's strong suction when she has a firm hold. To break it, slip your finger into the corner of her mouth.

For a few days you'll feel cramplike twinges in your abdomen when the baby starts to nurse. This is because sucking on the breasts stimulates contractions of the uterus, which help it return to its prepregnant size.

Until the nipples become tougher from daily use, you may find it best to limit the baby's sucking time. Begin with five minutes on each breast, then day by day increase the time by a few minutes.

Extensive sucking is what stimulates milk production. Some mothers are never bothered by sore nipples when they let the baby have twenty or even thirty minutes at a feeding right from the beginning. If you start out with lengthier nursing periods it's important to feed the baby promptly whenever he seems to be hungry; he'll be much easier on the nipples when he doesn't go for his food frantically. You'll be feeding him every two or three hours during the early nursing period. Frequent feedings help establish your milk supply. And because breast milk is easily and quickly digested, an infant needs these frequent nursings. Gradually, he'll be able to go longer between feedings.

Don't be fooled into thinking your milk isn't rich enough; breast milk is naturally thin, watery looking, and slightly bluish. Comparing it, by appearance, to infant formula, you might be tempted to give your baby a little "dessert" by bottle after his nursing. This is the quickest way to diminish your breast milk. Until the milk supply is well established, which usually takes four to six weeks, "relief bottles" shouldn't be started.

Another don't-worry concern is small breasts. They'll produce as much milk as big breasts. Breast size is determined by fatty tissue, which encases the milk-producing glands. But small breasts need the support of a properly fitted bra, the same as large ones; the breasts are heavier now and this puts a strain on the supporting tissues. Sagging breasts are not caused by nursing, only by unsupported breasts during pregnancy as well as the nursing period. It's best to wear a bra during the night, too, both for support and comfort. Nursing pads inside the bra cups will take care of leakage.

Flat nipples can be prepared for nursing with a little light massage between the fingers; then it helps to press down on the areola to flatten it so the baby can more easily get hold of the nipple. Otherwise there's nothing you need do for nipple care except keep them clean with pure water— no soap—and let them air-dry after a feeding. Airing also helps relieve sorness, so go topless as much as possible for a while if you're having trouble.

Mother's Needs

Rest and relaxation are always stressed as important for establishing breastfeeding; but this is equally important for every new mother. The advantages that nursing mothers cite are no preparation, no warming, no washing of bottles. When the baby is ready to eat, her food is ready to serve— sterile and at the right temperature throughout the feeding.

Your diet? The same as it should always be—balanced: protein foods (meats, eggs, beans, nuts, cheese); fruits and vegetables (some raw); whole-grain or enriched breads and cereals; calcium-rich foods (milk, cheese, yogurt). You do need a little extra food while nursing, but your own hunger will amply take care of that. If you're worried about gaining weight, this is no time for reducing diets. Handle it the sensible, healthy way: Cut down on pastries, candies, creamy-rich foods but don't omit the daily essentials. The traditional quart of milk isn't considered necessary by many doctors if you get enough calcium via other foods or a calcium supplement prescribed by the doctor. What's important is plenty of fluids.

Are there particular foods that make a mother's milk disagree with the baby? Not in general; there's no need to give up any food unless it consistently seems to upset your baby. Some of the said-to-be offenders are chocolate, cabbage, onions, garlic, beans. Try them in small amounts at first, and if there's no problem, enjoy them, if you do. If you like beer, enjoy that too, though its much touted benefit as a stimulant to milk production is highly questionable. It may, though, help you relax at day's end, as a glass of wine will. But go very easy on alcoholic beverages; just about everything passes into your milk. Smoking, too, is suspect in reducing both the quality and quantity of mother's milk.

Baby's Needs

While emphasizing that human milk is an ideal food, the Committee on Nutrition of the American Academy of Pediatrics has established guidelines for the use of supplementary vitamins and minerals for breastfed babies.

Babies are born with a store of *iron* that lasts four to six months and helps prevent iron-deficiency anemia. Although breast milk has less iron than an iron-fortified formula, the composition of breast milk allows the iron to be easily absorbed and well utilized by the baby. As the prenatal store of iron begins to be depleted, an additional source of iron is recommended. According to the committee, the introduction of iron-fortified cereal in mid-infancy should supply adequate amounts of iron for the breastfed baby.

All babies need *vitamin D* for the prevention of rickets. While breast milk contains only small amounts of this vitamin, rickets is uncommon in breastfed infants. One explanation for this is that, like iron, the vitamin D in breast milk is easily absorbed and utilized by the baby. This, however, hasn't been confirmed, and the committee suggests that supplementary vitamin D may be indicated if the mother doesn't get enough of this vitamin in her own diet and if the infant doesn't get enough exposure to sunlight. It's the sun's rays that produce this vitamin in our bodies, and indeed vitamin D is often called the sunshine vitamin.

Fluoride for the breastfed baby is controversial, but the committee recently decided in favor of starting this supplement shortly after birth—even when the mother's water supply contains a sufficient level of fluoride. This is because human milk contains only trace amounts of fluoride. The crowns of a baby's *permanent* teeth start to calcify right after birth; so even though these teeth won't begin to erupt for about six years, fluoride can start doing its protective job in reducing future tooth decay.

Any vitamin or mineral supplements must, of course, be prescribed by the baby's doctor.

Bottle Feeding

Modern science could have done nothing more helpful for a multitude of mothers than providing the great improvements made in infant formulas. When a mother chooses not to breast feed, or stops nursing, she can supply nutrition that closely approximates human milk, which is the reference standard for commercial infant formulas. Essential vitamins and minerals are included in these modern formulas, and many are iron-fortified, which is especially important after the baby's fourth month, when her prenatal store of iron begins to be depleted. Many authorities recommend iron-fortified formula from birth on.

Whole cow's milk is not appropriate for infants. For one thing, nature has designed cow's milk for calves, whose rate of growth is three times that of human babies. It contains more proteins and harder-to-digest proteins than human milk or commercial formula; has an excess of some minerals, yet is deficient in others; and forms a larger curd that often causes a colicky reaction or constipation.

The Love Factor

There's one component of good infant care that bottle feeding *could* lack. That's the emotional element. But who hasn't heard the basic tenet: Hold your baby for his bottle. It makes no difference to the baby where his food is coming from so long as he feels security and affection while satisfying his hunger.

One nice thing about bottle feeding is that fathers can share it. And there aren't many modern fathers who don't enjoy the privilege. Grandfathers too. It's especially good in these early weeks for a mother to get a full night's sleep. But determining who gives the night feedings is up to you and your partner. Taking turns works well for some couples, unless one is more in need of rest than the other. In any case, most new mothers appreciate being relieved now and then during this "always hungry" period.

Close contact is important in early feeding for safety as well as for emotional reasons. It's not only a lonely experience to suck on a propped bottle, but it could be hazardous. The very new baby who hasn't yet got his feeding mechanism under good control needs occasional help. If he sucks in too much before swallowing, he needs to be given pauses to keep from choking. If the nipple is flowing too fast, it needs to be changed to a slower-feeding one. He'll suck in air instead of formula if the bottle slips from a proper tilt, or it's not taken away promptly when empty. And he'll be frantic with frustration if he loses the nipple. Propping a bottle might seem more necessary than it is, especially with other children around. But feeding-the-baby-time can be their time too, for special attention from you—with picture books, talking, or a bottle of juice for a toddler.

Making It Easy

Ready-to-use formula comes in 32-ounce cans, 8-ounce "six packs" and also in individual disposable bottles, a great convenience for away-from-home use. Concentrated formula to be mixed with water comes in liquid or powdered form. A day's supply can be prepared and refrigerated, or it can be mixed bottle by bottle as needed. Follow the proportion of water to formula as stated on the container unless your doctor specifies differently. He or she will advise you how many ounces to put in each bottle. You'll probably need at least six bottles in a twenty-four-hour period.

If you mix a day's supply, the easiest method is to sterilize bottles and formula together—called terminal sterilization. You dilute the concentrated formula with the prescribed amount of water, mixing it well in a large pitcher. Divide this into the individual bottles; put on the nipples and caps, loosening the screw-on caps one-half turn; place in sterilizer with two or three inches of water; put lid on sterilizer and boil gently for twenty-five minutes. Let the bottles cool in the sterilizer, then tighten the nipple collars, and store the formula in the refrigerator.

You can eliminate bottle sterilizing if you fill each one just before use. A day's supply of mixed formula can be stored in a sterilized jar in the refrigerator; then you pour the specified amount into a clean bottle, feeding by feeding. Many doctors also okay using tap water if you want to prepare each feeding as needed. Just add the correct proportion of concentrated formula to the correct amount of water in the bottle, and shake it till well mixed. In almost all municipal systems, water directly from the tap is pure. But if you or your doctor think best, boil the water for five minutes and keep it in a sterilized container until ready to use. Prepare a fresh supply each day.

If glass or plastic bottles are washed shortly after use they're easy to clean with a soapy bottle brush; rinse with running tap water or in your electric dishwasher. Another choice is disposable "bottles." These are thin plastic containers that fit into a holder. They're packaged in a roll, sterilized; you tear off one as needed and throw it away after use. But you do have to boil the nipples and caps.

Nipples and caps for all bottles should be boiled for five minutes, drained, and stored in a sterilized jar. When washing nipples, use a nipple brush to clean the inside, then test the flow: Fill the nipple with water, holding the stem between two fingers, and press your thumb over the open end of the nipple. If water doesn't squirt out it's clogged; use a toothpick or pin to clean out the hole. For feeding, be sure to snap the nipple properly into the collar of the bottle. (It *does* pay to read the carton instructions if you're a real novice.) It's best to test the formula flow each time before feeding: Turn the bottle upside down; formula may spurt out for a moment, but then should change to a steady dripping, not a stream. If it's too fast, discard that nipple. If it's too slow, loosen the screw-on top slightly for a better flow. If your baby is a consistently weak sucker you can buy a special type of nipple made for preemies. And if all regular nipples feed too fast for an especially strong sucker, you can buy blind nipples and puncture them with a fine, red-hot needle. But don't try to hold the needle in your fingers while heating it! Stick the eye end into a cork to use as a handle.

Must the formula always be warmed? It's not a must; according to some studies, even refrigerated formula can be given to the baby without apparent harm. But this is just too unnatural for most parents'—and doctors'—tastes, not to mention the baby's. It seems too much like a cup of cold coffee when you've just gotten out of bed. The baby won't mind waiting for that extra comfort if you hold him for the few minutes it takes to warm his bottle. An electric bottle warmer shuts off automatically at the right temperature. But take the precaution to test it, the same as you do when the bottle is heated in a pan of water. Shake it first, then dribble a little formula on the inside of your wrist; if you can scarcely feel it, it's body temperature—just right. If you do decide to go the cold formula way, be consistent; it's not good to change back and forth.

How Much Should Baby Eat?

The one thing you don't want your baby to get from a bottle is a stomachache from swallowed air. So the bottle must be tilted up to keep the nipple and neck filled with formula.

And he must never be allowed to go on sucking when the bottle is empty. Hold him close, leaning against you, in a semisitting position for easier swallowing.

The newborn will need about twenty minutes of active sucking to finish his quota of formula. If it goes down much faster it cuts down on his sucking pleasure and also may upset his digestion. If the nipple hole is too small he'll be taking in air and soon feel a false fullness. But even with a properly flowing nipple, these early feedings usually stretch out. It's tiring for a little baby to keep up the sucking-swallowing effort; let him have rest breaks without trying to rouse him by jostling, or jiggling the nipple in his mouth.

Remember that a breastfeeding mother has no way to tell how much milk her baby is taking at each feeding. She has to trust her baby to take as much as he needs. So should you. At first the amount may vary from feeding to feeding. If he takes only half what's in the bottle it may satisfy him this time as much as a full portion the next time. All you need to watch is whether he seems hungry after consistently finishing each feeding. Then you add a half ounce or so to each bottle. It's really best if there's always a little left; then you know he's taking all he needs.

Chubby babies are cute. And the fatter the better was long considered a sign of infant good health. But medical opinion has changed. Recently, scientists presented data indicating that fatness in infancy could create problems of obesity in adulthood. It was suggested that overeating during infancy produces an excess of fat cells that remain with a person for life. Other studies, however, have not substantiated this theory, and have indicated that there is only a slight tendency for fat babies to become fat adults. But medical opinion in general is opposed to excess fat in babies as well as adults. At any age, excess weight tends to handicap a person in getting sufficient exercise for fitness, and may predispose to health hazards. Good appetite is one thing, but overeating is a hard-to-stop habit, and a baby shouldn't be coaxed to take "just a little more." It's also well to keep in mind that there are many reasons for crying besides hunger.

Feeding is the most important event in a newborn's day, and it's charged with emotion—first with the anxiety brought on by hunger, then with the eager anticipation of food as he's picked up and held, and finally with a warm flood of relief, the instinctive sense that all's well in his world. This is the nourishing emotion that can be given to a baby whether he's fed by bottle or by breast.

Sleep

How much sleep does a newborn need? As much as she takes. She'll get along fine even when she seems—to her parents—"never" to sleep. A sleep chart based on research studies may show that newborns *average* sixteen hours of sleep out of twenty-four. But don't let that average mislead or worry you; it includes normal newborns who sleep less than ten hours, and others who sleep more than twenty hours in a day. You'd be hard put to find your own baby in any set of statistics. On a sleep chart she could be at either end or somewhere between. Moreover, most newborns' sleeping time varies considerably from day to day and week to week.

The link between food and sleep is so strong in the early weeks that *some* babies sleep from feeding to feeding, scarcely taking time for any outside interests. Very little disturbs them besides the discomfort of hunger. They seem to be convalescing from the upheaval of birth, resting and gathering strength for a busier life ahead. But few babies are this well organized. Until their bodily systems mature and function more smoothly, their sleep is disturbed by uneven digestion and stomach or intestinal discomfort.

The Nature of Newborn Sleep

The sleep pattern of all newborns is much more fragmented than it will be in later periods. It's broken into brief cycles of deep and light sleep. As the baby grows, sleeping periods and waking periods both lengthen, although for some time there is little change in the total amount of sleep in twenty-four hours.

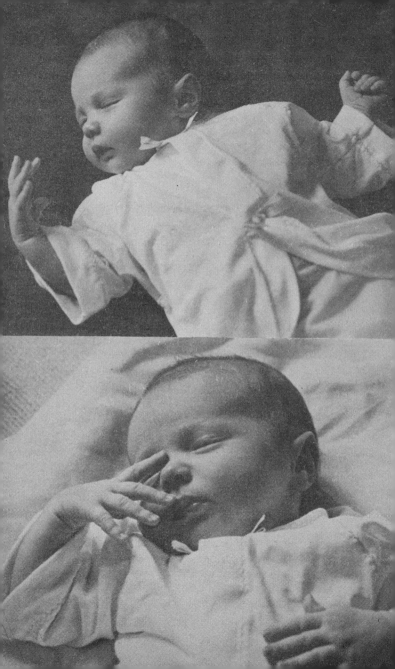

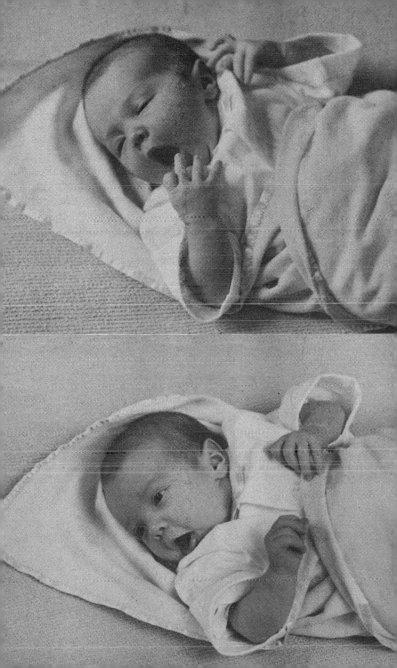

Changes in sleep patterns follow the development of the central nervous system. The ability to *sustain* sleep is acquired in the same way as other abilities. The baby can't learn to see better, or develop hand skills, or crawl or walk—or sleep for long periods—until the necessary hookups have been made as his neurological system matures.

During these early weeks, the baby's asleep and awake states are not always well defined. Because his central nervous system is very immature, he's often in an intermediate state, a kind of twilight zone, in which he's not well enough organized to "decide" which way to go—that is, to come out of sleep or go back into it. At other times a hard-crying awake state changes abruptly; crying stops and the baby falls asleep the next instant.

In persons of all ages, there are two basic levels of sleep cycles—deep and light. During deep sleep practically nothing can wake the baby. Sudden noise or bright light won't disturb him. If he's moved abruptly his body may briefly twitch, but then quickly quiet again. After such a disturbance he seems to try harder to keep himself "inside" sleep, tightening his eyes and his body against outside interference, and continuing his rhythmic, deep breathing.

REM Sleep

Light sleep is scientifically referred to as the REM state, which stands for rapid eye movement. Underneath closed lids the eyes can be seen to continually dart here and there. When adults are in REM sleep they are dreaming. Do newborns dream? If they do, no one knows what their dreaming consists of. Certainly it is very different from the subjective and complex dreaming of an adult. In infants, REM sleep is considered to represent the workings of instinctive drive centers of the brain. In fact, the newborn's brain appears to be very busy during REM sleep. The electrical energy being discharged by the brain can be recorded on an EEG (electroencephalogram) and these brain-wave patterns are very similar to those of an awake baby in an alert state.

When you first notice your baby in the REM state of

sleep you may be concerned. His eyes may be slightly open; his eyelids flutter; twitches, grimaces, and fleeting smiles play across his face. The smiles are little more than a slight curve at the corners of his mouth, quite different from the "social smile" he'll soon acquire. These newborn smiles used to be called "gas smiles," but are now considered to be part of the discharge of nervous energy that occurs during REM sleep.

Newborns spend 50 percent of their sleep in the REM state (premature babies even more). This diminishes in the months ahead until, by toddler age, the dream state occupies only about 20 percent of sleep time, which approximates the quota in adult sleep.

The Workings of Sleep

At any age, sleep cannot remotely be considered a "blank-out." It is an active function, tied in with all fundamental processes of the body, and related to all phases of living and growing—development, behavior, memory, health, and illness. During the early period of life, the brain grows at a rapid rate, and the baby's neurological system is under tremendous pressure as it tackles the extensive learning that's taking place—from bodily controls to complex skills such as talking. Much energy is expended in this rapid learning, and part of this energy is being discharged while the baby sleeps.

With all the extensive research in recent years on the mysterious state called sleep, there are still many unanswered questions. Sleep is as individual as people; there are wide differences in sleep behavior at all ages, among children in the same family, and in any one person at various times. Why some people, of any age, need more or less sleep than others is still a moot question. But the fact that there are great individual differences in the actual need of sleep is important for parents to know. The appetite for sleep cannot be increased by trying to force it, any more than forcing food will have a beneficial effect on appetite for food. Starting in infancy, an individual needs only to be given the opportunity to take as much sleep as he or she needs.

Organizing Baby's Sleep

Although the newborn baby can't be "trained" into changing her natural sleep rhythms, she can be helped to organize her sleep behavior. In the same way that you begin to recognize what different types of crying mean (hunger, a soiled diaper, loneliness, overstimulation) you can begin to read the signs of sleep needs. Then you can help the baby to help herself.

In that hazy state, for instance, just on the edge of sleep, she'll like the feeling of drifting off in a soothing atmosphere of soft singing and rocking in a dimly lighted room. In bed, the normal stirrings and whimpering that sometimes occur in REM sleep may indicate that she doesn't "know" whether she wants to wake up or sleep some more. She may be capable of shifting herself into deep sleep. But REM is a fragile state that can easily be altered. If it's interfered with, if you hurry to pick her up or talk to her, she'll be roused awake. If left alone to work it out for herself she may shortly be sleeping peacefully again. When she seems to be working herself up into alertness, perhaps some quiet soothing in bed—gentle stroking, soft crooning—may help to nudge her back to sleep. At such times of infant indecision, the arms of Morpheus may be more welcome than your own.

Crib-time Particulars

A sleepy baby should be allowed to stay sleepy. He won't appreciate being fussed over "to make him more comfortable." He couldn't care less about a slightly wet diaper; if it's changed he'll wet the new one in a few minutes anyway. There's no point in arranging his covers "just so"; he'll probably disarrange them before he settles down. When he's quiet and still you can check.

Babies are often made warmer than necessary. This is because their feet and hands are normally cool when they're perfectly comfortable—and also when they're too warm.

You can tell by feeling the back of the baby's neck; if it's hot and moist there are too many covers. But the baby does need to be checked a few times during sleep. His body's heat-regulating system is immature, and he can become chilled more rapidly than an adult.

Never use a pillow under the baby's head. On a firm flat mattress he can turn his head easily from one cheek to the other for clear breathing space. Tummy down is the position many newborns favor, and it's the safest for after a feeding. On the back a baby might aspirate milk that comes up with a burp.

Even though the crib mattress is moistureproof, constant wettings will do it no good. The mattress should be topped with a waterproof sheet, preferably the kind that's flannelized on both sides, which keeps it from slipping and allows some air to circulate. This should then be topped with a regular fitted crib sheet. You'll seldom have use for a top sheet; lightweight crib blankets are best for daily use. You'll need several to keep ahead on laundering and drying, plus a couple of warmer blankets for cool-weather use. The so-called receiving blanket is more a garment than a blanket. It's smaller than a crib blanket, and is used for swaddling and also as a wrap when the baby is out of bed.

In general, room temperature that's comfortable for you is right for the baby. In warm weather, be sure he's protected from drafts from open windows or fans, or from currents of cold air from an air conditioner. In cold weather, you can freshen the air in the baby's sleeping room—while he's in another room—by opening the window for five minutes or so.

Equipment

There are federal safety regulations for cribs. These include: crib slats no more than 2 3/8 inches apart; drop-sides with safe, secure locking devices that cannot be accidentally released or released by the baby; safe metal hardware with no rough edges; crib sides that lock at maximum height. You should be sure, too, that the mattress fits snugly; if you can fit two fingers between the mattress and the crib side, the mattress is too small and should not be used. Also be sure that there are no dangerous cutouts in the head and footboards of the crib, openings in which a baby's head could get caught. If you install a padded crib bumper, which is a good idea, be sure it goes around the entire crib and is secured with at least six straps. The crib can be as fancy or as simple as you wish. Your *main* concerns, in any price range, should be safety and sturdy craftsmanship, since this lightweight, relatively passive newborn will soon be a big active baby.

Check for all of these safety precautions if you are using a second-hand crib, and if you find that it's not up to par, don't use it. If you are considering buying or borrowing a cradle, you'll want to be sure that the slats are no more than 2 3/8 inches apart and that the mattress fits snugly.

Your baby will like a modern cradle as much as great-grandmother's babies liked theirs. But for all its charming qualities, a cradle can't be used as long as a standard-size crib. A bassinet on wheels has a short use-life too, but a nice advantage in that it fits through doorways and you can take the baby along from one room to another. With some you can also detach the basket from its wheeled stand for easy carrying. This is especially handy if you live in a two-story house. To avoid all that stair climbing, bring the baby downstairs during the day, and arrange a baby nook for keeping basic clothing and duplicates of the baby toiletries you have upstairs.

There's a wide selection of baby furniture—from co-ordinated sets of crib, chest of drawers, and chifforobe to simple dressing tables with bins or shelves for storage. Or simply arrange for storage space (baby things do take up a lot of room) and a place to dress and bathe the baby. One thing that's important is to have your baby's dressing table of proper height to avoid bending over, and within easy reach of your "place for everything and everything in its place."

An item you'll probably want right off is a baby carrier-seat with adjustable backrest. Little babies like to be propped so they can see things "straight" instead of having a side or up view of the world, as they do lying down. And it's a rest for the baby, as well as dad and mom, not to be held and toted all the time. You can take the carrier from room to room to keep the baby company when she's awake. Or you can take it with you when you go visiting; the baby can sit in the carrier and even go to sleep in it. But there are precautions to take when buying or using this kind of carrier. It is made for use only by young babies who can't yet sit up alone; many accidents have happened with bigger, active babies who toppled themselves over. The carrier should have a wide, stable base; a nonskid bottom surface; a supporting device that locks firmly in place when adjusted to different positions; and a waist and crotch safety strap. Although a little baby can't maneuver herself up to sit without support, she can shift her position by squirming, so must always be strapped in. When using the carrier on any off-the-floor place, you must always be within arm's reach of the baby, and make sure she's out of reach of any hot or dangerous object. The floor is a safe place—unless there are frisky dogs or children running around who could topple her.

Bathing

The one rule for bathing is: Never leave the baby for a moment, either in the tub or out on a flat surface. The littlest baby can wriggle out of position. Have everything you'll need close at hand, and keep a hand—not just an eye—on the baby whether she's having a once-over lightly on the dressing table or a real tub bath.

Little babies don't get dirty, except in particular spots—the diaper area, of course, and around the chin and neck folds, where dried milk dribbles could irritate the skin. Otherwise, the very new baby would rather not be bothered with an all-over bath. So for a start, simply take care of the important places.

The Diaper Area

Prompt changing and thorough cleansing are essential after a bowel movement, which is a strong irritant to the skin. The newborn's small b.m.'s can usually be well cleaned off with disposable towelettes or baby lotion and several tissues. If not, use a washcloth with bland soap, rinse the skin well and blot it dry with a soft towel. Be sure to clean the folds of skin, and wipe the baby girl's vulva from front to back.

Newborns wet so frequently that it's impossible to keep their skin free of urine, but it rarely causes irritation. There's little point in frequent changes, and no point in disturbing a sleeping baby to change a wet diaper. If there's diaper rash, however, more frequent changes and special care are needed. (See pages 70 and 71.)

If your baby boy is circumcized you'll need to keep the scab from sticking to the diaper while his penis is healing. Your doctor may recommend petroleum jelly or other ointment. This can be coated on a small square of sterile gauze and wrapped around the end of the penis. The ointment keeps the gauze in place and makes it easy to remove and replace with a fresh square as needed. The uncircumcized penis needs no special care. When the baby is about six months old, the doctor may advise you to try to gently retract the foreskin during the baby's bath, wash the end of the penis, and then return the foreskin to its original position. If the foreskin cannot be easily retracted, try again in a few months. About 96 percent of male newborns naturally have nonretractable foreskins. By about three years of age, this percentage has dropped to some 10 percent. As your child learns to bathe himself, you can show him how to clean beneath the foreskin. The important thing to remember is that the foreskin must always be returned to its original position.

Two things you should know about baby penises: Erections are common, especially just before or during urination. And this tiny appendage is capable of squirting quite some distance; don't get caught unawares when the diaper is off.

The Navel

The umbilical cord shrinks and turns black within a few days. In a week or ten days it will drop off; you'll probably find it during a diaper change. There'll be a small raw spot left on the navel that will take about another week to heal. No dressing is needed. Just try to keep it clean and dry by fitting the diaper below the navel. Once or twice a day, dab the spot with absorbent cotton moistened with alcohol, which is cleansing and helps to dry it. The only thing to watch for is redness of the navel or surrounding skin; this indicates infection, which requires prompt medical attention.

Skin Care

It will take a while for that petal-soft skin to lose the common newborn blemishes, and for dry, wrinkled areas to gain a dewy fresh look. Wrists and ankles are often dry and peeling, and can be softened by smoothing baby cream or lotion in the creases. Baby powder or lotion helps to prevent chafing and to relieve it, but you mustn't use both at the same time; the combination can cake in the creases and folds of the skin and cause more irritation. Powder shouldn't be sprinkled from the container directly onto the baby, as she could inhale flying particles; shake it into your hand and then smooth it on—just a light coating.

Those tiny newborn hands may have fairly long fingernails that can inflict real scratches if the baby paws at her face. It's easiest to clip nails when she's asleep, and safest with blunt-end baby nail scissors. Your fingernails should be short and smooth too; and bracelets, wrist watches, and rings with protruding metal or stones should be removed before handling the baby. Watch out, too for large beads or buckles that could press against her and cause a bruise, or a scratchy sweater or jacket that could irritate tender baby skin.

When to Give a Bath

One problem in the early weeks is *when* to give a bath. It

shouldn't be right after a feeding when it could upset the stomach, or the chance for a good sleep. And it can't be managed when the baby is frantic for a feeding. Wait for a good-mood time, after about a week at home, and see how it goes for both of you. At least it will probably make *you* feel better to have your baby freshly bathed, even if she's made strong objections during the process. But maybe she won't; a lot depends on how adept you are, and that may take some practice if you're inexperienced.

The Sponge Bath

Some doctors advise sponge bathing instead of tub bathing until the baby's navel and/or circumcision are healed. Sponge bathing, by the way, is really a misnomer, because what you'll use is a soft washcloth; a sponge retains too much soap for quick rinsing out. The advantage of this method is that it's easier on both you and the baby. It eliminates lifting him in and out of a tub, and it's less disturbing to him since he's bathed piecemeal.

Have his clean clothes on hand; a basin of comfortably warm water (test it by dipping your elbow); a soft washcloth and drying towel; and the baby toiletries you use. Except for the diaper area, you can omit soap if you like.

The baby can lie across your lap on a big towel or on a tabletop with a cushioned pad under the towel. A rather low chair makes you a better lap for keeping the baby from rolling. Undress him—but leave the diaper on—and cover him with a receiving blanket. He's probably still a little nervous about the surprise of air on his skin, so keep him covered as much as possible, exposing just the area you're washing and drying as you go along.

The face is first, with the washcloth wrung out of clear water. The newborn's facial skin is too delicate to tolerate the mildest soap. Babies hate face washing, so make it quick, and dry by gently blotting with a soft towel. If you're tempted to fuss over any particular, put it off till later. But never probe into the nose or ears. Ear wax is there for protection. Dried mucus is usually sneezed out. If mucus seems to be clogging the nostril opening, you can use a twist of dampened cotton to ease it out.

Chest, arms, and hands are next. Don't bother about the lint that collects between fingers of the little fisted hands; you can clean them sometime when he's relaxed. If you're using soap, lather your hands to smooth it on. The baby will like this gentle skin stimulation. After rinsing and drying (always blot, don't rub, with the towel) cover his upper body again. Then wash and dry his legs and feet, and cover them with the blanket.

Now turn him slowly onto his tummy, wash and dry his back, then roll him right side up again. Keep these movements firm but gentle so he won't be startled. The diaper area is last, and this does need soap. If he's had a bowel movement clean his skin first with tissues or towelettes, then lather and rinse well—remembering not to neglect the skin folds, and always to wipe the baby girl from front to back. Blot the whole area dry, put on the clean diaper and clothes. Now your baby will probably tell you that after all this "nonsense" he'd like a feeding followed by a good sleep.

Tub Bath Techniques

This is when expertise counts. A wet and soapy baby is slippery, but with proper hand holds you can keep her safe. You may want to eliminate soap during trial runs to simplify things. The room should be a little warmer than "room temperature" (75 to 80 degrees is good) and protected from drafts.

To lift the baby in and out of the tub, slide one hand under her neck; with her head resting on your wrist, circle your hand around her shoulder with a secure but gentle grip. With your other hand, clasp her ankles, keeping two fingers between them (this avoids pressure on her ankle bones). Hold the baby close to your body as you lift and move her— slowly. Sudden movements and air on her skin can give her a "lost in space" feeling and trigger the fear-of-falling reflex (the Moro) that throws her whole body into a startle.

When you start to use soap, wash the baby's face first

with clear water. Then lather her body on the bath table to keep tub water clear for rinsing. Use your hands for soaping; she'll like that gentle massage and may lie quietly, especially if you lean close to her face and talk to her. In these early baths, the newborn isn't ready for fun and games, as she will be later. Now, a kick of her legs or a slight roll of her body can set off a series of startles followed by crying, so keep your hands on her body to steady her.

Once in the water she'll probably feel calmer. Even if your baby bath has a hammock, it's best, at first, not to let go of the baby; she'll feel more secure if you keep your hand clasped around her shoulder. Be careful not to splash her face as you rinse. If you tie a bath towel around your neck, or wear a big terrycloth apron, you can quickly wrap it around the baby as you lift her out of the tub, saving her the upset of air on her wet skin. Remember not to rub her skin; just carefully blot it dry with the towel.

The typical baby tub is made of molded plastic, although a somewhat new slant on infant baths is an inflatable vinyl tub. This type has a shallow middle and helps free the parent's hands since the baby is supported by the tub's soft, rounded sides. Many plastic tubs come with features to help make baby bathing easier and safer, including slip-resistant and cushioned bottoms, and detachable hammocks. A hammock also gives a parent more hand freedom because it cradles and supports the baby in the tub. In addition, there are a number of helpful tub accessories. One popular item is a contoured poly-foam form; placed inside a plastic tub, it supports and cushions the baby's body and head. With a baby tub you can give the bath on any table or countertop and have clean clothes and all other items at hand, or move your towel-wrapped baby to her dressing table. The family bathtub is all but impossible for bathing a young baby because of the awkward kneeling position it puts you in.

Baths during your baby's early weeks will probably be whenever you can fit them in. The time of day doesn't matter; that will more or less establish itself as the baby's habits become more predictable. Perhaps you can plan on twice-a-week bathing for a while, and change to daily baths when the baby shows he likes the idea. Two baths a week are usually all a baby really needs—except in very hot weather—until he's big enough to be down and around where he can get dirty. Long before that, though, the daily bath becomes a highlight in a baby's routines, whether he needs it or not.

The Shampoo

For the once- or twice-a-week hair washing, there's a special holding technique. Called the football hold, it guards against soap and water running down the baby's face. Tuck him against your body, face up, with his buttocks and legs resting on your hip, his back resting on your forearm, and his head in your hand. Tilt him slightly headdown while you lather his hair and rinse it several times with a washcloth. Dip the cloth in a basin of clear water, and squeeze out excess water each time. A newborn rarely objects to this kind of shampoo; held so snugly, he can relax and enjoy all that nice warmth on his head.

Don't be hesitant about washing "the soft spot" on top of the baby's head. This is one of the fontanels, the places where the skull bones are not yet fused together. During delivery, these places allowed the bones to overlap a bit and "mold" the baby's head for passage through the birth canal. The so-called soft spot is the largest of the fontanels (the others are scarcely noticeable) and you can feel it pulsating, or possibly see it bulging a bit when the baby cries. This is normal—no cause for worry. The soft spot is covered with a thick protective membrane and should be washed as well as the whole head.

Skin Problems

Apropos of the soft spot, "cradle cap" sometimes gets a start when the baby's head is washed too timidly. This is a scaly crust on the scalp. If it doesn't come off with mild soap and a washcloth, don't try to comb or pick it off when dry. Rub petroleum jelly or baby oil into the area and leave it on a few hours or overnight. The crusts should be well softened and lift off easily with the next washing. Then you can gently comb and brush all the flakes out of the baby's hair.

A pink pimply rash called prickly heat usually means you're overdressing or overcovering the baby—winter or summer. The rash usually appears on the shoulders and neck, and sometimes on the chest, back, and around the ears. To relieve it, sponge the areas with clear water and dry well by gently blotting with a soft towel. Then use absorbent cotton to pat on a light coating of baby powder or cornstarch. Also soothing is a bicarbonate of soda solution (one teaspoon to one cup of water) dabbed on several times a day. A rash that becomes quite red or that develops blisters or a bruised look should be seen by the doctor.

Diaper rash can usually be arrested before it spreads. At each diaper change, check the baby's skin; if there is any spot of redness, cover it with a diaper rash ointment before putting on the fresh diaper. If you use disposable diapers, or cloth diapers from a commercial diaper service, you have a perfectly clean diaper at every change. Home-laundered diapers might retain some traces of soap or detergent or bacteria. Chlorine bleach should kill bacteria, and three rinses should remove the washing powder.

Diapers should be washed separately from other laundry. There are excellent laundry products for disinfecting and softening diapers, and for soaking before washing. A b.m.-soiled diaper must be rinsed out in the toilet before adding it to the urine diapers. And after discarding the soak water, give the diapers a spin in the washer before laundering. To retain their absorbency, don't overuse a liquid fabric softener; and don't leave them overlong in the dryer, as this makes them harsh.

If diaper rash does get a start, apply a protective ointment, and if you use waterproof pants, discontinue using them until the rash clears up. One of the best curing agents for diaper rash is air. A baby without a diaper can present problems, but at this young age it's not difficult to manage. Put a folded diaper under him and a light cover over him. The rash will get much more air this way than it does under a closed diaper. Have the skin free of diaper rash ointment for this treatment, and repeat the airings several times a day.

Be sure to consult your doctor about any rash on any part of the body that persists, that worsens, or that you can't easily identify.

Dressing

You have all these little garments neatly stacked in or near the baby's dressing table. Now comes getting the baby into them. She'll either be wriggling and kicking or as quietly cooperative as a rag doll. The easiest shirt to put on a newborn is the wrap style. You spread it open on the dressing pad, lay the baby on it, push her arms through the sleeves, lap one side front over the other and fasten. An over-the-head shirt should have an expandable or lap shoulder neck. This kind you bunch into a loop at the back of the baby's head, then pull it down and out, stretching it enough to clear her face. Push her arms through the sleeves, and lift her up by the feet to pull the shirt down in back. A sleeveless shirt can easily be put on "backwards"—over the feet and legs instead of the head.

It's easy to put the baby's arm through the armhole of a sleeveless or short-sleeved shirt. With long sleeves it's a little trickier. The best way is to start her hand and arm through the armhole, then slip your hand up the sleeve to meet her hand and pull it on through. If you try to push her arm through from the top, her fingers are likely to get snagged on the way. Use this system, too, for other long-sleeved garments, such as nightgowns or kimonos.

Newborns don't like all the fuss of being dressed and undressed, and shouldn't have to put up with fancy clothes, except perhaps for one high-style occasion such as a christening. Shirts and diapers are the basics. Kimonos and nightgowns help keep her cozy. Sacques give her a more "dressed" look and so do the "stretchie" coveralls that have become a mainstay of so many baby wardrobes. One additional item you'll want if your baby arrives in cold weather is an all-in-one blanket-sleeper. The important thing to keep in mind is not to overdress the baby. If you think she might need an extra wrap, feel a part of her body that's covered—but not her hands and feet, which, remember, are normally cool.

The baggy look is always in style for a well-dressed newborn. She'll soon grow into oversized shirts, and would rapidly outgrow the smallest size. In this regard, the loose-fitting gowns and kimonos usually outlast shirts. You have to keep checking your baby's clothes for comfort—non-binding armholes and necks, easily stretchable chest and stomach width, ample room for diapers, and sufficient leg room in gowns and stretchies. And if you can't resist using a pair of charming bootees now and then, be sure they're not tight around the ankles.

All infant's and children's sleepwear, sizes 0 to 14, must meet federal standards for flame resistance. To retain the flame retardancy, sleepwear must be washed with detergent, not soap, and ideally it should be rinsed twice. Always read the care labels inside your baby's garments for proper laundering instructions.

Diaper Choices

Considering the thousands of diaper changes you'll make this year, nothing could be more work-saving than disposable diapers. But whatever you decide—cloth or disposable—you'll want to have some of the others on hand. If you use cloth, a box or two of disposables will see you through those times when you don't get diapers laundered before you run out, or for use on outings or trips. By the same token, a few cloth diapers will see you through if you run out of disposables.

There are three fabric choices in cloth diapers—gauze, bird's-eye and flannel. Gauze is a little less absorbent and durable than the other two, but is lighter, cooler and faster-drying. There are also style choices—fitted, prefolded, snap-closing—as well as the traditional flat. Departures from basic white include a variety of prints, which can be coordinated with layette items. If you use cloth diapers, you will also need several pairs of waterproof pants. (Disposables have a waterproof covering.)

Outings

Unless your baby is born at home, his very first outing will be out of the hospital or birthing center. In a car, your arms are not the safest place for an infant, and could be the most dangerous in case of an accident. An infant auto restraint is one piece of equipment the baby needs right after birth, and will use for months ahead—in yours or relatives' or friends' cars.

Car Safety

All children's auto restraints manufactured after January 1, 1981 must meet rigid federal safety standards. When shopping for an auto restraint, look for a label giving the date of manufacture. Most restraints made today are the "convertible" type—that is, they can be used with infants and then be converted for use with older babies and young children. Infants weighing up to 17 or 20 pounds ride facing rearward in a semireclining position. Older babies and young children ride facing forward in an upright position.

But even the safest auto restraint must be used correctly if it is to provide protection. The baby must always be secured in the restraint and the restraint itself must always be secured to the car with an adult lap belt. When shopping for an auto restraint, ask to see the instruction booklet and be sure the restraint will fit properly in your car. If possible, try it out before buying. Keep in mind that if a restraint comes with a top anchor strap (as some do), the strap *must* be installed and installed correctly. In some model cars, installing a top anchor strap poses difficulties. If this is the case with your car, or if you think you might not install the anchor strap, you should choose a restraint that doesn't require one.

The following publications can supply useful buying information: *Don't Risk Your Child's Life!* (35¢), from Physicians for Automotive Safety, P. O. Box 208, Rye, New York 10580; *A Family Shopping Guide to Infant/Child Automobile Restraints* (single copy free), from Division of Public Education, American Academy of Pediatrics, P. O. Box 1034, Evanston, Illinois 60204. For each publication, include a stamped, self-addressed long white envelope. Either of these organizations will also answer specific questions, which is especially helpful if you are using a borrowed or secondhand restraint manufactured before January 1, 1981. Many of these may give good protection; others, however, are not safe. To be sure, write to either of these organizations.

Carriage or Stroller?

For on-foot outings, you have several choices for toting your baby—front carrier, carriage, or stroller. For a little baby, a carriage is cozy, especially in cold weather. In fact, full-size carriages tend to be more popular in colder climates and also in cities where sidewalks make the traditional carriage ride easy and convenient. Some strollers, however, are almost as comfy as a carriage, with padded interiors and windbreaker sides, adjustable backs, and snug-fitting canopies. And for the pusher and shopper, some strollers feature swivel wheels and ample carrying baskets or bins.

Whatever you decide, check for these safety features: a back that doesn't tip the balance when the back is in its lowest position; a wide base and large-diameter wheels; tightly locking brakes, preferably two- or four-wheel brakes; a canopy that locks securely in forward position and rotates to downward position in rear; no scissorlike mechanism in adjusting devices; a firmly attached safety belt; a shopping basket that's mounted in front of, or centered over, the rear axle for stability. (Safety and comfort features of front carriers are discussed on page 38.)

Now you have only to decide whether you and the baby and the weather are ready for an outing. Naturally, at this young age, you won't take the baby out in very cold, damp,

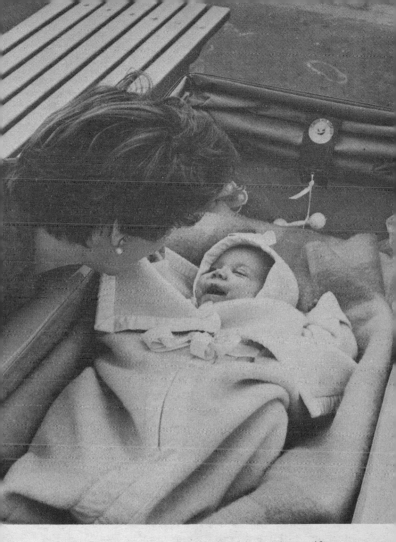

or windy weather, and you'll check with the doctor if your baby is delicate in any way.

The baby will be comfortable in about the same amount of clothing that feels right to you, but in cool weather he should wear a cap that covers his ears. Be careful to shield him from direct sun, but don't bundle him up just *because* he's outdoors, if it happens to be warmer outdoors than in. You do need to be prepared for sudden breezes, so take along an extra cover. Outdoors in cold weather you'll need to put the baby inside a bunting or pram suit. When your baby has to wear all this outdoor gear, he'll rapidly get overheated indoors, so have yourself ready to go as soon as he's zippered up.

The most sudden temperature changes usually occur in stores. If you're shopping where you can wheel the stroller indoors, you may have to add cover or take it off. Store temperatures are often many degrees different from the outdoor temperature—too highly air-conditioned in summer and too heated in winter. Even for brief trips, be prepared with the basic take-alongs—disposable diapers, tissues or towelettes, and a bottle of formula if you're not breastfeeding.

Long trips by car or plane could be upsetting to a newborn, who is having enough trouble getting himself stabilized and accustomed to home routines—not to mention the difficulties that traveling with a newborn may cause his parents. If, for any reason, a long-distance trip is necessary during these weeks, be sure to check with your baby's doctor for advice and instructions.

Other Caregivers

Parents do need a break now and then from the closed circle of new-baby care. The thing to decide is whether these early weeks are the time to take breaks together. You can always find "a" sitter. But the responsible, experienced, good-in-emergencies kind of person? You're lucky if a close friend or relative who's familiar with how you do things is available and willing to take over for a few hours.

A lot of couples feel better to forgo together-evenings-out right now, and treat each other to an occasional solo outing with friends. Today's fathers have their hand in baby care right from the start. And even if a dad is nervous the first time around, he manages. It's his little kid, and that bond can mean as much as experience in how he fares with a "sitter."

Comes an occasion when you do leave the baby with someone for the first time. For your own reassurance as well as the sitter's, leave the phone number where you can be reached, along with phone numbers of your doctor, the police and fire departments, and a neighbor who could be called for advice or assistance. Show—not just tell—the sitter where all the baby's things are kept, and any particulars about the house that might be unfamiliar, such as regulating the thermostat or air conditioner or securing door locks. A standing rule should be: Don't unlock the door for any stranger, including delivery persons.

Once you're out the door, you'll have only one problem: to shift mental gears and leave baby concerns behind. If you let worrisome thoughts brake your pleasure every few minutes you won't really get far from home, no matter where you go. Inevitably, you'll be asked: And how's the baby? Just tell them: Fine—already beginning to smile! and maybe you can keep yourself on that positive track.

Pediatric Note

You'll be taking your baby for his first regular medical checkup at about one month of age. *Well*-baby checkups are fully as important as any calls you make to the pediatrician in between, for reasons of illness, worries or instruction.

See Chapter VI for information on general health care.

Chapter II

Six Weeks to Three Months

What to Expect

If you could see your six-week-old infant side by side with himself at three months, you'd be amazed by the contrast. From a relatively passive, straight-faced little person, he changes to a charmer who can beckon you with smiles and gurgles to come and enjoy him. This period is the season of a baby's social coming-out. Day by day he works at developing the qualities that make him undeniably a member of "the human family," and these very qualitites activate you in helping to make him a social being.

Not that an infant isn't an endearing little person from the very beginning. But if the newborn period extended much longer, you might find it an unrewarding state of affairs. All those weeks while you tended him devotedly, your baby gave you glimmerings of what he was *becoming*, but not much substantial evidence of the progress he was making. Even those first smiles started out as fleeting maybe's, promises of what was to come. Now, during the weeks ahead, he'll turn on his smile in a flash, and use it to keep you with him.

Before, you were closest during quiet interludes; now,

there's action in your togetherness. You can keep each other going for a half hour or more. Your baby uses his whole body to express himself; he kicks and waves, pants with excitement, vocalizes and smiles—using all his wiles to keep you using yours. Comfort has taken on more meaning too. He knows how to cuddle. When you hold him he relaxes and sometimes looks at your face intently. Even when you're talking to someone else, you may find your baby studying your face.

All the attention and stimulation a baby gets makes him more responsive to everything around him. He likes to watch and listen to what's going on in a room—movement and voices and music. And when no one's around you'll find him enjoying his toys and smiling and cooing to them. Much as he loves attention, you are by no means exclusive in his interests. At times he may even resent an intrusion on his business of the moment, and give you a glum stare, for instance, when you change his position and cut off something he was studying.

Natural Differences

Your baby will have her own little mannerisms and quirks, and she can't be expected to fit her moods to yours all the time. But some babies can be broadly "typed" by the wide individual differences they show, even babies in the same family. The quiet ones, called "good" babies, linger on longer in the easy-going newborn kind of life, eating and sleeping and merging comfortably into their surroundings when awake, but seldom getting overenthusiastic in their responses. The high-keyed "sparklers" may become as demanding in their bids for entertainment and companionship as they first were for food and comfort; but their zest for living keeps them going in self-play too, getting every drop of interest out of every new accomplishment. In-betweeners in temperament have up days and hours and down days and hours, asking only that you respond in kind to their moods of the moment. Overall, babies are not only different from one another, but are different at different times.

What Will Be Will Be

Baby studiers have no crystal balls. They make no claims as to predicting with any accuracy a baby's future "style," based on how he performs today. They can only point out what many babies have in common as they move along from month to month. Changes in the baby and influences of his environment will both help to steer his course. This mystery of the future adds a lot of fascination to your own baby-watching. It should also make you turn a deaf ear to those all-too-common foolish remarks: "That boy's going to have a temper as bad as his Grandfather Joseph's," or "She's going to be as quiet and prim as her Aunt Martha." Too many people just don't understand what goes on in a baby's world.

Perhaps your baby can give you hints now of what to expect of him in the future, a future that is beautifully open, though unpredictable. But the real pleasure comes from tuning in on your baby all along the way. These weeks won't come again.

Understanding Your Baby

Behavior

After six weeks of living in the outside world, your baby's whole action system is better organized. Her movements are slower and smoother, though she'll still revert to quick, jerky movements when upset. She could ride a bicycle very well—lying on her back; for exercise she rhythmically cycles her legs and waves her arms to the world. Lying on her stomach she lifts her head and holds it up, at first briefly, but soon for many minutes. The head lift progresses to the chest lift, with weight resting on the forearms, giving her a good look around in the tummy-down position. Until the neck muscles are stronger, however, the baby's head will still bob forward when she's held upright.

New Patterns

With maturing of the digestive system, there's more regularity in feeding and sleeping patterns, and waking periods become longer and more contented. Being less involved with bodily comforts, the baby can forget about her stomach a good part of the time and switch her attention to outside interests—and also to her own new-found abilities. When she's alone, she'll smile and talk to herself with throaty gurgles and vowellike sounds, obviously pleased with this new way to use her voice.

Crying is still an important means of communication for a large part of this period. But around the three-months' birthday, crying diminishes dramatically, often replaced by patient whimpering to express a need. But she'll still let you know, with a cry that means business, if you impose on her good nature. If she's been a colicky baby, that phase too may disappear almost magically, as it does for *most* babies by three months of age. The mysterious reason seems to be that a baby is now finding ways other than bursts of hard crying to release her tensions. She can communicate in exciting ways with people; her vision has improved remarkably, allowing her to take in a whole room full of interests; and she's discovered those novel ways to use her voice—for amusement instead of needed relief.

Phase-outs

Now you'll notice that the baby's early behavior patterns are changing. Some of the rudimentary abilities of his newborn days are beginning to merge with voluntary controls, and this may cause some disorganization for a while until he learns the new systems for coordinating his muscles and mind. His hands, kept fisted most of the time in the newborn period, are now mostly open, and the strong hand grasp is fading; he may not be able to easily hold on to an object when you place it in his hand. The strong startle reaction, the Moro, diminishes from the rigid clutching-at-air reaction to a much milder "normal" kind of startle. And for many months to come, he won't be able to take a little walk with you as he could in his newborn days; when you hold him upright he'll just stand on his toes without planting a foot down or attempting to move. Squiggle-crawling is phasing out too; the baby stays more or less where you put him in bed. The amazing newborn performances of crawling, walking, and swimming will have to wait quite a while before the baby gets them under voluntary control. But he's already busy on preliminary practice for using his hands.

Hand Play

One sign of this forthcoming new ability is the fading of the tonic neck reflex, the "fencing" posture that seemed so

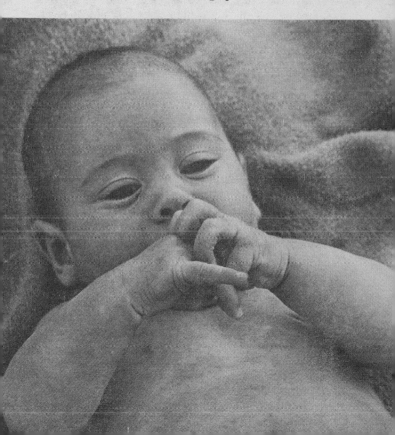

strange and meaningless when it started in the newborn period. During the second month, this habitual posture leads the baby to do a great deal of hand gazing, since her head is turned in the direction of her outstretched arm. Looking at her hand is thus the beginning of eye-hand coordination. But in the third month, as the baby loses the tonic neck reflex and begins to keep her head in the midline, another progression takes place; she can coordinate seeing and touching. Holding her hands above her face, she watches and feels, fingering her fingers in delicate little dances. Sometimes she catches one hand, holds it a few moments, then pulls her two hands apart. Thus the baby's hands are the first toys she can actually grasp and examine, and this is a fascinating pastime weeks before she'll be able to reach out an arm and latch onto a tantalizingly close-by toy. Now a crib gym is a good idea. Positioned across the crib, it encourages the baby to reach for an object and grasp it, but before this complicated skill is mastered, she'll be doing a lot of batting and swiping at those interesting objects in front of her. Look for sturdy construction when selecting a crib gym, with safe, easy-to-grasp objects, and be sure it attaches securely to the crib. As the baby begins to keep her head in the midline, you'll also want to reposition her mobile for better viewing. In the beginning, when she kept her head turned to the side, it was best positioned to her far right or left.

From Head to Foot

Muscular control does not take place evenly throughout the baby's body. It follows the spine downward in what is called, biologically, the cephalocaudal law, and, in addition, from the center of the body outward. From general large-muscle movements, the baby's control progresses to specific small-muscle actions; he grasps with his whole hand, for example, before he can use thumb and forefinger in a delicate pincer grasp.

Countless fine "tentacles" of the brain's nerve cells are constantly maturing and thrusting out from their cells to connect with particular muscles and make them perform. Because of the short distance from brain to face, hookups are first made there, with the result that the face muscles are the first to be used intentionally (smiling); then the throat (cooing and gurgling); the neck muscles (to hold the head steady); on to the arms and hands (reaching and grasping); and the legs and feet (crawling and walking).

All along, the baby's tireless hours of practice are preparation for the increasingly complex skills that will follow. He is strengthening his legs with kicking and stretching long before he'll put them to use for crawling and walking. He is working hard with face, tongue, and throat muscles, coordinating their movements to produce speech sounds long before he'll be able to master the most complex and highly developed skill of all—talking.

All this purpose in a baby's behavior is certainly not apparent as you live with him day to day. He goes on doing much the same things, and only occasionally does a new trick pop out to delight you. Actually, there's a continual merging of abilities that precludes separation; and the pre liminary preparation is usually overlooked until a resulting accomplishment *seems* to occur suddenly.

The sequence of all babies' developing skills follows a remarkably uniform order; only rarely is there a deviation from this preordained process of nature. But the speed of normal development may vary widely; one baby accomplishes an outstanding act weeks, even months, earlier or later than another—and the time for both is well within the normal range.

In this particular period of a baby's development it's difficult to know just what's going on in the way of physical progress; indeed it's probably pretty confusing to the baby. His newborn behavior patterns are still overlapping and merging with the more intentional behavior that will gain power in the months that lie ahead. Meanwhile, his new social powers are plenty of compensation and satisfaction for himself and his family.

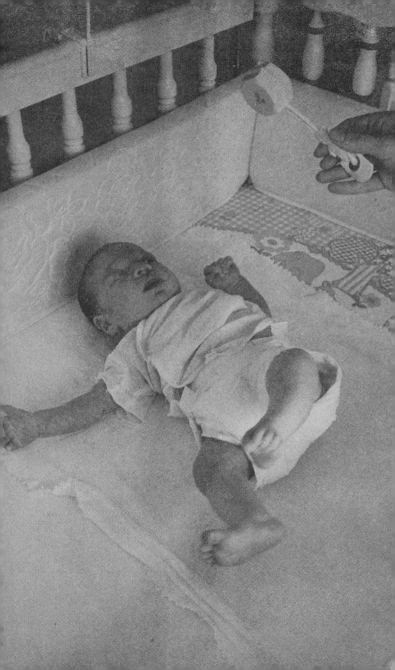

Learning

The baby is now using her tools for learning much more regularly. Things she did occasionally and briefly are now becoming frequent performances with more holding power. And things you may not have noticed—which researchers have uncovered for us by patient study—now become very apparent, part of the baby's repertoire of daily activities.

Vision

For example, your baby's looking pleasures. The newborn first got her visual treats in bits and snatches, and she was limited to close-ups for fairly clear vision. She had a hard time keeping both eyes on track; just when she was really trying, she'd suddenly be cross-eyed, or one eye would wander off to the side. It was hard work to follow a very slowly moved object, held just the right distance—about eight to twelve inches—in front of her. But during her second month, her eyes far out-distance those inches; they can reach out several feet to follow a moving object.

The newborn did, however, do some quite sophisticated maneuvering within her limited range. If her eyes slightly overshot their mark when following an object, or when shifting from one thing to another, she could adjust her aim—"retrieve" the object—by making a very slight head turn. But what a difference by three months of age—both head and eyes sweep around freely to take in a wide vista, and for minutes at a time she'll watch an activity going on clear across a room.

Making Sense

A baby often seems to be passing his time in idle curiosity. But his curiosity is never idle, it's constantly working for him. "Witness" this evidence of how a baby learns by storing information gathered through his senses. To test whether young babies could relate visual and auditory information, researchers separated babies and mothers by a glass barrier. Through a speaker system, the baby could hear his mother talking to him while watching her face at the same time. Then the sound was switched to make her voice come not from her moving lips, but out to the side of her. Each baby tested became obviously distressed by this strange occurrence that didn't "make sense." These babies, between one and two-and-a-half months old, had already learned to coordinate the sound of a voice with the sight of a moving mouth. Denying them this correct expectation was very upsetting; it violated an important piece of learning. The magic of ventriloquism can't amuse a young baby; he's too intent on the logic of putting two and two together.

Yes, researchers do occasionally play unpleasant tricks on their little testees. But this wealth of new information on the processes of development and learning is raising infants to the high esteem they deserve. It wasn't too long ago that these little bundles from heaven were thought to want little more than food and clothing and lullabies from their mothers, a little tickling from their fathers, and a helping hand when they began to walk. They received much more than that, of course, being charming creatures whom no one could resist. Even so, newborns were considered as mental "blanks" who would gradually be patterned and shaped by their elders. It was not suspected that babies arrive *as* persons, *as* individuals, *as* complex and competent human beings who start right out to make their personal mark in life.

Of course, the impudent question might be asked: So how did babies grow into reasonably adequate adults in the past, when scientists as well as parents knew next to nothing about them? Babies use their own powers to take care of that. Research has now shown that babies not only respond to their environment but actively use these responses for learning. By their interaction with their family and with what they find in their environment, they help to shape their own life as much as life helps to shape them. But note the key word—interaction. Without a satisfactory amount of that, a baby is subjected to an increasingly dull existence and a rapid diminishing of the powers he was born with. Yet it's remarkable how little help a baby requires to keep on using his capabilities. The ancient wisdom embedded in the human race gives a baby his direction for learning. And his learning is the incentive that keeps his parents on the track of helping him to learn.

Two-Track Action

About the fastest a newborn can learn is one thing at a time. But just graduating out of newbornhood, she showed—by her displeasure with the ventriloquist trick—how well she'd learned to coordinate two senses. Soon she'll show you that she can perform a two-things-at-once trick of her own—sucking and looking at the same time. This counterpoint activity takes some doing. Way back in her early days she kept her eyes tightly closed when sucking; it required a lot of effort to keep that operation working smoothly. Then she begins to nurse in bursts and pauses. After a brief steady spurt to take the edge off her hunger, she sucks a few seconds, then pauses to take a peek at you. The pauses then take on further interest; she can look away at something that attracts her attention, keep hold of the nipple—but not suck it. Sucking in bursts interspersed with looking-pauses continues as a regular pattern for a while. And finally she makes the combination work—looking and sucking at the same time.

Doing two things at once is a big step away from one-track learning, and a significant start in the ability to concentrate with more than one faculty in operation. We give no thought to all the things we do in conjunction—writing a letter, listening to music, tapping a foot, shooing a fly. But all second-nature kinds of things date back to their difficult beginnings in infant learning.

Voice Play

It's sometimes said of a garrulous person who carries on endlessly about this or that, "He's in love with the sound of his own voice." Perhaps he didn't do enough prattling in infancy, for this is the time when the remark accurately fits the case.

The early soft sounds that a baby makes give him a wonderful sense of achievement; he is voluntarily using his voice for pleasure. Before this, the main impulse was involuntary—crying to have his needs satisfied and rid himself of tensions. Now begins the delight of playing with his voice, hearing his own sounds, and *feeling* himself make them. It may seem incredible that your baby is grooming his voice for talking. But that's exactly what he is doing. Feeling the sensations in his throat, tongue, and lips as the sounds come out is not only a large part of his pleasure but an important part. He is exercising the components of what will eventually develop into speech, many long months from now. Just as all the other abilities that will come along— grasping, crawling, walking—are getting a lot of preparatory exercise now, so the ability to talk has its rudiments in these delicate sounds your baby is making.

There's another aspect of this early voice exercise—an odd kind of play that derives not from comfort feelings but as an aftermath of discomfort. It's like a winding down, a transition from a state of discontent, almost a talking over, to himself, of the complaint he's just coming out of. There's an intermingling of discomfort sounds with the repetitive patterns of pleasure sounds, finally merging into pure voice play. Think what an accomplishment this is! The baby has gained mastery over a state of discontent, and achieved a pleasure state, through the use of his own voice. He has no clear feelings, of course, about what he is doing, but it's evidence of the importance of play in learning. A baby's sounds of himself serve as playthings; in turn, as a means of emotional control; and all the while as instruments for learning the rudiments of speech.

Learning Through Feedback

It's not surprising that a baby's progress in socializing is a strong impetus in learning. All the feedback she gets from others stimulates her efforts, resulting in a continual gain in self-motivation. The repetition involved in socializing is also a basic part of the learning process; a baby retains a great deal in the form of impressions and habits that she'll put to good use later.

As social skills increase, the baby will go into her act for almost anyone, with sisters or brothers often out front in getting the most ready responses. What is it about children that captivates a baby? Surely she can't yet perceive that they're closer to her in size. It seems to be their qualities of naturalness. They're not into any acquired role, they're simply who they are, acting themselves, coming and going when they want to. Adults, by contrast, assume various roles, some of which they naturally enjoy more than others. It's not as pleasant to change a dirty diaper as it is to rock a baby to sleep, or to try to stop her crying as to play with her when she's happy. The baby picks up on these differences and even at this young age learns a modicum about human nature. An older child can be a playmate, but he can't be what the baby learns instinctively—that a parent is much more than that.

Parent-Child Interaction

However different babies may be from one another, the pair of parents they get are individuals too. At a very young age, a baby is aware of this, and soon handles their differences without a ripple of trouble. In fact, she has good control over both, whether they realize it or not. At the same time, each parent's personality is having an effect on the baby. She is influencing them and they are influencing her, in a kind of ever-changing blend. There's no need for a constant parent-child "fit"; all along it's being adjusted by accommodations on both sides.

The advent of smiling, more than anything else, stimulates baby-parent interaction. It's like the sun breaking through a subdued landscape, or the warm greeting of a friend. Smile meeting smile says all the feelings you knew were there. And this is a verity—in spite of the fact that your baby's first smiles are not motivated by all the smiles you've given your baby. This can't be so, because blind

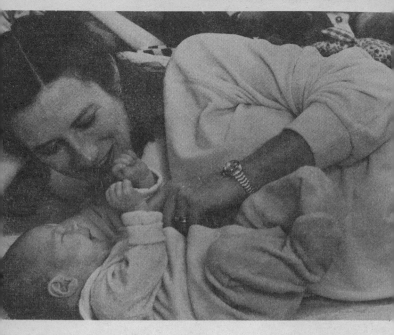

babies begin to smile right "on time," according to the developmental schedule for this ability. Normal babies of this age will not only smile at anyone's face, but at an ugly Halloween mask. Faces in general are what young babies like.

But no matter. Developmental smiles rapidly become responsive smiles for the natural reason that *you* respond. A baby who's unfortunate enough to lack this interaction soon stops smiling. Yet continued smiling is not dependent on vision alone. Parents of blind babies can discover a variety of ways to communicate their happy feelings to the baby. By responding with touches and tone of voice, they can convey their appreciation of the baby's smiles and so keep them effective; and the baby will learn to keep on using her smile to elicit responses from her parents.

For normal babies, as well, the sense of touch remains

all-important. Holding and caressing will always tell your child you love her. Now touching can also tell her she's fun to be with. You gently poke her nose or her tummy, she smiles, you poke again, another smile, and the two of you have invented a little game. Touch-and-smile, a game that takes two to play, is a new kind of companionship.

For many long weeks your baby has told you in other ways that your care has taken effect. Now that she's found a delightful new way to express her good feelings, these responses will keep on growing. Do believe, if you wish, that even that very first smile was personally meant for you. A rainbow is for the beholder, isn't it?

Consistency = Trust

You can count on your baby to reciprocate your attentiveness by fitting himself into family life more smoothly week by week—*if* he's given the chance. He has to be able to count on you for consistency. Without an organized environment of care he can't organize his own habits. This doesn't mean that you confine him to specified feeding, sleeping, and play periods—not at all. It's simply a matter of keeping intact the sequences a baby has come to expect.

He alerts you with a hunger cry. Then he hears you coming, and before he even sees you, he stops crying. While you carry him to the dressing table, change his diaper and talk to him, he looks expectant but a bit serious, not in a mood for play. Feeding is what he's waiting for. Now if that doesn't follow, if you put him down in his crib again, he can't sustain his patience; he bursts out in protest. Breaking a sequence that the baby expects is like breaking the rules of a game. And how can anyone learn to "play the game" well, or to trust the coach, if rules are constantly being changed? Once in a while it will happen, for one reason or another, and certainly without lasting harm. But it's important to keep as much continuity as possible in the baby's care. This way there's an interchange of understanding between you—the basis for getting along well with persons of any age.

Changeability

Sensitive understanding of a baby comes from accepting him in three phases at once—who he was, who he is now, and who he is becoming. This is an empathy that most parents acquire naturally. No one expects a baby to suddenly *be* two months old, or to *act like* three months old on a given day. One stage merges into another, always retaining some characteristics of the previous stage, and indicating work in progress on the coming stage.

Your baby flashes you a big smile, activates his whole body with such energy it seems he's on the verge of taking off on a fast crawl. A short while later he's nestling in your arms, tapering off his crying with one last whimper, and soaking in your soothing just like his weeks-ago newborn self. He wants to and needs to be treated appropriately in all the phases of himself. If he gets a little competition from the baby down the street, any comparisons are lost on him. Because Johnny "almost never cries any more" is no reason your baby shouldn't cry when he feels like it. Turn a deaf ear when Johnny's praises are sung, just as your baby does.

Talking to Your Baby

If you had cried every time your baby cried, in a good imitation of her wailing style, you certainly would have reinforced that noise-making. Babies respond to the cries of other babies, joining in till they have a whole chorus going. Strangely (or naturally? Who can be sure?) a baby will react most forcefully to a tape recording of her own crying. Fortunately, you needn't carry on any such experimental research; you've had a good deal of experience with crying by now.

Your natural aim with the reinforcement principle is to encourage your baby's pleasant behavior, and the more you respond to her, the more good humor she gives you. Actually, you've been doing this all along by responding to her demanding calls for attention. In crying, she's using her voice for practical purposes; now she's begun to use it for pleasure. These twin impulses—practical use of the voice, and pleasure in using it—continue throughout life, and retain a certain power over others.

When a baby begins to enjoy her own voice, she's doing what an older child or an adult does when he sings to himself or for others. A baby can't sing for her supper but she can use these expressive new sounds to summon you for companionship. You may notice her watching you, and then hear a smilelike gurgle come bubbling out. Who could resist that invitation to "come talk to me."

Try to follow your baby's rhythms when you talk to her. Her vocal responses will be slow at first, but she'll "talk" with her whole body, waving her arms and legs, then quieting for a few pensive moments. She'll look away, look back, make tentative sounds in between, or maybe just smile. When she sobers, use light touches to activate her interest. Pauses are important. If you keep up a steady stream of your own, she'll have trouble getting a word in edgewise. Ask her questions and wait for an answer. These little buds of conversation are worth your patience, for they're the rudimentary beginnings of the art of language.

Imitation of speech sounds will come later. In all the languages all over the world, babies start out by making the same basic sounds. To learn their native tongue, they must hear hours and months of the distinctive sounds that make up a particular language. Somehow, it's not easy for most persons to "talk straight" to a baby. But very soon it's important to use real words in a natural tone of voice. Your baby is watching you as you talk to her. The movements of your face and lips are interesting, and in time she'll unconsciously be imitating them. When you've watched close-ups of faces in foreign films with dubbed in speech, you've probably noticed that the actors are not speaking your language. Your baby can't get the proper feel of language, by sound or by facial movements, if you speak only gibberish to her.

Talking to your baby is good socializing. But more than fun is happening. Long before she can make the intricate sounds required in speech, she is internalizing many segments of sound units for later use. Soon you'll begin to hear some of these as her repertoire of sound-making grows.

Routines and Care

Feeding

Your baby may express his hunger just as emphatically as ever, but once started on appeasing it, he's interested in more than food. The social side of feeding—all the close attention that comes with it—means more to him, now that food doesn't seem such a vital event. It has always come, it will come again, so he can relax and better enjoy the whole procedure. This is what a "self-demand" or flexible start in feeding accomplishes. By fitting feedings to the baby's natural rhythms of hunger, he loses that early intensity about getting sustenance into himself. Hunger becomes a less urgent matter and probably a less hurting sensation as his system is able to handle food more efficiently. Gradually he can take more at one time, digest it more evenly, and hold out longer between feedings. By now a pattern has developed—perhaps not a perfect pattern, but a predictable one.

Keep It Relaxed

You may have a tendency to want to hurry the baby through her feedings more than you did before; after all, she has good control, sucking doesn't tire her, and you have plenty of other things to do. But as we've seen, the baby has started taking her time, nursing in a regular pattern of bursts and pauses. During the pauses she looks at you or takes notice of some sound or sight nearby. You may think you ought to discourage this, help her keep her mind on the business of eating. So you tap her lightly on the cheek, talk to her, jiggle the nipple in her mouth to keep her going—and you're actually defeating your own purpose!

This is yet another bit of behavior that's been tested. When mothers let the suck-pause pattern take its course, the pauses were found to be shorter and the whole feeding faster; when mothers made hurry-up attempts during the pauses, it seems they were alerting the baby to the social pleasure of the feeding time, and so stretching it out!

It's not easy to change a baby's determination to follow her own inclinations; there's purpose in the smallest matters. Because sucking has a calming effect, quieting random body movements, it induces use of a passive skill such as looking; in turn, the pauses between bursts of sucking attract the mother's attention, encouraging her to communicate with the baby. You might say it's like keeping a little conversation going during a meal, a social grace that's generally appreciated. Who likes to dine with someone who wolfs down food?

Adjusting a Schedule

Essentially, and initially, a baby sets his own schedule for feedings. By the time he's skipping the middle-of-the-night feeding (which *may* be during the second month for a bottle-fed baby and a little later for a breastfed infant) he has pretty well organized his late evening or so-called 10 P.M. feeding as well as his daytime feedings. The trouble may be that one or another comes just when you don't want it to, at your own dinner hour, for instance. It's easy enough to change this pattern without upsetting the baby. The trick is to make the change gradually so that he doesn't even know it's happening.

Assuming that the daytime feedings are fairly well set, you feed him ten or fifteen minutes earlier or later than usual at each one. If it's later, he's usually willing to play with you that short while, or at least be carried around. If it's earlier, and he's used to being fed as soon as he wakes up, gently talk him awake a few minutes early. You may have to make yourself do this; it's so nice to have a little extra time for yourself, and all through the newborn weeks it was virtually against the law to disturb your baby when he was sleeping. But by using this system of a gradual shift in the feeding times, in a week or so you'll probably be enjoying a peaceful dinner while the baby is either sleeping or lounging on the sidelines gurgling about anything except food.

Delayed Scheduling

If you haven't yet been inclined to work out any kind of schedule, you won't be doing your baby any harm by continuing with self-demand feeding; but you may be tiring yourself out. The baby will be taking care of his own nutritional needs, probably with a series of more short than long rations, depending on how often you *think* he's hungry. A baby can get in the habit of "snacking" on formula or breast milk and never be hungry enough for a full feeding. You may be putting a nipple in his mouth when he doesn't really want it, and he'll oblige by taking a small amount each time. This will keep the middle-of-the-night feeding going too, since he'll seldom have a large enough feeding to tide him over many hours. Or, he may get in the habit of taking a larger feeding in the morning or afternoon, followed by a six-hour sleep, and start up his demands for frequent feedings during the night.

The thing to realize about self-demand feeding is that it's the only sensible and considerate way to treat a baby *as long as* his system remains immature. Sometime during this period, practically every baby becomes satisfied for four hours at a stretch if he takes a full feeding at a time when he's really hungry. There's certainly no exact cut-off age for self-demand, or any reason to ever be rigid about feeding times. Like everyone else, a baby sometimes gets hungry before or after his schedule says it's time. But you can be flexible *within* a system. Babies like systems in their care because they're trying all the time to organize themselves. And how can they get an inkling of what's going on unless there are some regular key events in their days?

By keeping track of the hours when you feed your baby, you'll know in a few days how to aim for a regular schedule. When he lets you know you're on the right track, he's surely

ready to cooperate in organizing family life. And maybe
he's already done it all by himself.

Breast Is Still Best

If it's going well, you're probably sold on the idea of breastfeeding. There's no reason you shouldn't go on nursing for
a year or more if there's nothing to interfere with its convenience value for you. Many mothers in our society, as
well as in simpler societies, follow the natural system of
letting the baby decide when she wants to give up the breast,
and there's not one baby who would opt for that until several
months hence.

Nursing becomes much less time-consuming as the baby
grows older. Between two and three months, the number
of feedings begins to taper off; also, the need for extra
sucking satisfaction begins to fade after about three months.
When the newborn keeps on sucking for a half hour or
more, she's not taking in milk all that time—she'd burst if
that were the case. She's gotten most of the milk from the
breast in five to ten minutes; from then on she's sucking
for pure pleasure.

Early Weaning

If for any reason you're planning on weaning, the baby
should start sampling formula well ahead of time. If she
has a "relief bottle" a couple of times a week—to give you
a respite from nursing—she'll have an easier time when
you begin to make a gradual switchover to bottle feeding.
With these first months of nursing you've both had many
benefits from the experience, the baby's digestive system
has had time to mature and work smoothly, and she's taking
an alert interest in many things outside the lovely warmth
of mother-baby intimacy. Even so, nursing is a strong emotional attachment that you'll both be reluctant to break, so
the change should be made slowly.

It will be harder for the baby to accept a bottle from
mother than from someone else. Try it first in the middle
of the day instead of at a cozy bedtime hour. She may take

part of it because she's hungry, then want to finish with breast milk. Or she may have no part of it to start with, but be willing to try some after a short nursing and a little play time in between. If you have no luck at all, keep trying two or three times a week, not forcing, not making her mad. And if she just won't take a bottle at all from you, arrange for someone else to give it while you absent yourself from the whole scene.

Keep on omitting that one breastfeeding regularly till your milk production has had time to adjust to the lesser demand. Then substitute a bottle for another regular breastfeeding. With a waiting period of several days or a week in between each added bottle feeding, you may not have any problem with an excess of milk. If you do, you can either express some milk to relieve the pressure, or let the baby nurse just a minute—during a playtime, not a hungrytime.

Very gradual weaning from the breast helps to protect both mother and baby from emotional hurt. If some circumstance makes it necessary to hurry the whole procedure, another factor may add to a mother's doldrums in giving up this relationship with her baby. When there is a sudden decrease in milk production, hormonal change can bring on a brief period of low spirits similar to the postpartum "blues" that affect many women for a time after the baby's birth.

Bottle Plus Thumb?

The baby should still be getting at least twenty minutes of sucking time at each feeding. With use, bottle nipples get flabby and faster flowing, and as the baby's sucking strength increases, he can polish off a bottle in ten minutes or less. So old nipples should be replaced with new ones as often as necessary.

All babies have a strong need for sucking pleasure during their first three months; then this natural urge begins to taper off. But although the need slackens, some babies cling to the pleasant habit of sucking for months to come, using thumb, fingers, a pacifier, or toys as food-nipple substitutes.

All the experts put together cannot ascertain why some babies suck their thumbs and some don't. They can suggest what encourages thumbsucking, what will or won't discourage it, but they can come up with nothing that will prevent it. Also puzzling is why some parents think it's a cute habit and others can't abide it. Opinion is equally divided on pacifier in place of thumb. Only the baby who never indulges in either is left out of these discussions; no one bothers to mention him.

Most pediatricians agree that there's more thumbsucking (or fingersucking) among bottle-fed babies than breastfed. This is attributed to the tendency of most nursing mothers to let the young baby continue to suck for long periods because it's obviously a great comfort to him. Twenty minutes is about the limit for a bottle, since slower feeding would make the baby have to work too hard. And unlike sucking on an empty breast, he would take in a lot of air if he sucked on an empty bottle. Twenty minutes satisfies some babies and falls far short for others. This is why doctors often advise a pacifier for a baby who seems shortchanged on sucking—if he's not one who already knew how to get thumb to mouth when he was born. Love of thumb is so strong in these precocious suckers that they usually reject a pacifier.

What worries some parents about letting thumbsucking get started is the thought of their baby becoming a preschooler who stands around all day with his thumb in his mouth. Excessive thumbsucking of this kind is rare, and there can be many reasons for it—reasons often beyond a parent's control. Most children with a satisfying life need this comfort less as they grow older. But a comfort it is, and many happy children use it at times of stress and times of relaxation. There's no point in projecting into the future if a baby pops his thumb in his mouth when he's upset, or while staring at something of interest, or when contentedly falling asleep. Trying to prevent thumbsucking in a baby, or nagging or teasing an older child about it, are the surest ways to entrench and prolong the habit.

One worry to dispense with is the effect of thumbsucking

on the teeth. Dental authorities state that even if the first
teeth are pushed out of line, there is no effect on the permanent teeth *if* thumbsucking is given up before they come
in, which starts around six years of age. And a pedodontist,
a dentist who specializes in treating children, is usually
excellent in the art of gentle persuasion to talk a late thumb-
sucker out of the habit.

Bottle Plus Pacifier?

Parents who are reluctant to start their newborn on the pacifier also harbor distasteful thoughts of older babies who
seem to be contented only when their mouth is plugged with
a nipple. Actually, it's much easier to prevent dependency
on the pacifier than on the thumb—and not by the mean
trick of simply taking the pacifier away from the older baby.
The kind trick is to be aware of the time when the young
baby doesn't need it any more. The intense instinct for
sucking is a developmental phase that usually begins to
lessen at the end of this period.

   If your newborn often tried to get his thumb in his mouth
after a bottle feeding, or needed a soother for fretful or
colicky times, and you found that he liked a pacifier, you
did him a favor by supplying it. The pacifier served a good
purpose in satisfying a natural need. But as the need begins
to fade away, it's time to watch your baby for signs of
disinterest in that little helper.

   When the pacifier falls out of his mouth he may not even
notice, and promptly get busy on another interest; he may
even spit it out when you offer it. If you respect those cues,
and answer your baby's signs of boredom or bids for comfort
in other ways, the pacifier will become only a now-and-
then desire, soon tapering off to a lost habit. Unlike the
thumb, a pacifier can be out of sight, out of mind—if
caregivers break *their* habit of using it as an easy out for
all the baby's whimpers of discontent. After all, the handy
little gadget is supposed to be a baby's helper, not an adult's.

   As you gradually wean your baby from the pacifier,
relaxed bottle-feeding times will mean more to him. All

through the day, too, you'll find yourself enjoying his company more; he'll look and be more alert and expressive. You'll just naturally pay more attention to each other without that poky pacifier coming between you.

Sleep

Day sleep is diminishing. Instead of returning to slumberland every time her stomach is full and comfortable, the baby is spending more hours in the interesting world of wakeland. She's now taking long and short naps during the day. You can stretch out the time between naps—and hopefully add to her night sleep—by keeping her entertained. This doesn't mean you have to do all the entertaining; by this age she's learning to do pretty well on her own. Sometimes your baby doesn't bother to tell you she's waked up from a nap. When you peek in the door, there she is, lying awake and enjoying the antics of a crib toy that she can activate with a little activity of her own. Don't be tempted to hurry in and tell her how cute she looks. She's content with herself because she's busy. A baby needs time to sharpen up her faculties without being diverted by a confusion of interests that keep her darting her attention from one thing to another.

Night Sleep

During this period, six or seven hours at a stretch becomes par for the course of night sleep. This depends, of course, on whether the middle-of-the-night feeding is being skipped. Once that's established, you'll want the baby's long sleep to coincide with yours. If your baby has developed into a good sleeper, she may have obligingly arranged that pattern without help, perhaps napping after her early evening feeding and going right into her long night sleep after her late evening feeding, just before you go to bed. Most babies, however, want to enjoy some family life before settling down for the night. And the after-dinner hours are usually

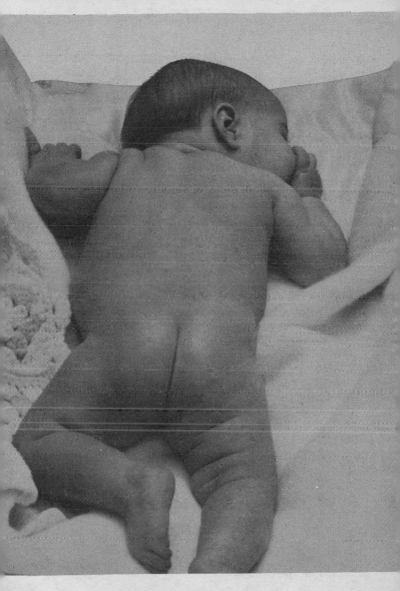

the best time for mom and dad and the baby to get together and entertain one another.

Respect for Unsleepy Times

The one thing to avoid is pushing the baby into a disenchantment with sleep by trying to force it. Sleep should be a welcome rest, not an imposed one. What can be more boring than lying in a quiet, dark room when one isn't sleepy? And what can a baby do about boredom except complain. Then if he's picked up and rocked in the same dark room, in an effort to soothe him into sleep, he has a taste of companionship that makes him want more. A baby has a right to be not sleepy the same as anyone else. The "cure" is to let him enjoy himself and work off energy until he's really ready to relax. After all, a baby can't settle down with a book and read till his eyes begin to droop.

Avoiding Night-Owlishness

Entertaining a not-sleepy baby is quite a different matter from stimulating the baby who's in the midst of a sleep period. Who would do that? Many parents—unwittingly. Without realizing that they're helping the baby out of sleep instead of into it again, they hurry to administer some attention as soon as the baby begins to stir and make a few minor complaints. Maybe she wants a diaper change, they think, or a little rocking. Being picked up, in particular, is her cue to come awake, and no matter how calmly the soothing is done, it usually has just the opposite effect of the caregiver's good intentions.

The baby is still in the process of regulating her sleep cycles—the natural patterns of deep sleep sandwiched between periods of light REM sleep. In these semiawake states the baby's energies begin to surface; she'll squirm and fuss, quiet, perhaps coo, cry briefly, then settle down with her fist or thumb to soothe herself. Maybe. It won't always work this way; at times she'll rouse herself into a state that does need help. But if given the chance to self-regulate her natural sleep rhythms she can often snuggle herself back into sleep. Interrupting these shifts from light to deep sleep can condition the baby to wider-awake intervals. This is how night owls are often made.

Cry-outs Are Not the Answer

Finding a happy medium is the challenge here. Helping a baby to help himself learn to sleep in smooth, ever-changing cycles is a patient process, far removed from a harsh crying-it-out method. You need to judge whether the baby needs your prompt response, or whether he'll get himself under control by letting off a little steam in the transition from light to deep sleep. It's well to remember that all changes take place gradually. During the early weeks, irregular sleep, the same as irregular feeding, was the norm. By now the baby's overall development is leading to more systematic sleep. During newbornhood there was a lot of hazy drowsiness and catnapping, with deep sleep rarely lasting more than twenty minutes at a time. Now the baby can sustain that sleep cycle for an hour. His awake time is also much more clearly defined. He can be entertained and entertain others with an alert responsiveness that keeps him busy. If you help him use up energy this way during the day and evening, he may make better use of his night sleep time; he'll be more inclined to help himself through those REM sleep periods without coming fully awake. This is where your help consists of waiting awhile to see if he makes it on his own.

It's not hard to train yourself to do this during the hours before you go to bed, when there are many ways to distract yourself. But in the quiet of the night, two minutes of baby-fussing puts you on edge, and two minutes of crying may seem unbearable. If quiet descends, you still feel you ought to check to make sure the baby's all right. And with too much broken sleep you end up exhausted in the morning.

Bundling

If your baby doesn't soon become an easy sleeper, and night waking continues to plague you, there's another way of helping her make smooth shifts from one cycle of sleep to another. That way is simply to be there where she can touch you, and feel comforted and secure in your presence. And how is that accomplished? By crouching over the crib all night? No, just by deciding you need a good night's rest—and bringing the baby into your bed.

If this strikes you as a doubtful idea, it's because authoritative advice to the contrary has long been prevalent. The point is made that if the baby is trained to sleep alone, preferably in a room apart from the parents, mom and dad will get more rest because they won't be alerted by every whimper and squirm of discontent, and they can even learn to ignore crying if it doesn't become frantic. In actual practice, many parents find that they can't relax at all except during absolute lulls; they're attuned to those whimpers, expecting them to intensify, straining to hear, hoping they won't have to drag themselves out of bed again. The other point made is the aforementioned practice the baby gets in teaching herself to self-regulate her sleep cycles—a valid enough objective. Parents are simply asked to sacrifice part of their night's repose—as long as necessary—to achieve this goal. Some authorities temper their advice with the kindly counsel to sit beside the crib until the child finally falls asleep—a suggestion that shows empathy for the little one, but leaves parents out in the cold.

Meanwhile, there's a grassroots movement afoot that believes in equal tranquility rights for parents, and that endorses the parents' bed as a practical pacifier for a baby. Many nursing mothers feed their babies in bed during the night and sleep with them, either because they believe in the practice or because they can't stay awake after a feeding. And both nursing and bottle-feeding mothers find that a baby passes through restless periods quite smoothly simply by lying close to them in bed.

To be inflexible about child-parent separation in sleep, they contend, benefits no one, and moreover is clearly unnatural. Warmth and protection for the young is not only the rule in the nighttime animal kingdom, but in human cultures back through the ages—and today. Indeed, there are many adults in the world who have never slept alone since they were born. They started out in their parents' bed, progressed to sleeping with their brothers or sisters, then with their spouses, and finally, full circle, to sharing a bed with their own offspring.

Anthropologists point out that child-care practices reflect the ultimate aims of particular cultures, which differ even in modern industrialized countries. The traditional American culture is aimed toward independence, and so starts out to try to establish this in infancy. Learning to sleep alone is a first lesson. Does it work? Does an infant "get the point" of nighttime separation, and thus become more self-reliant? Or does she finally begin to sleep less restlessly simply because, and as, her development dictates? At what age can a child dispense with the comfort of close body contact, the sense of touch that is the first—and an enduring—means of communication? It does seem a strange contradiction that while close physical contact is stressed as a basic infant need, parents are generally advised to disregard this need and put distance between themselves and their babies in the long dark hours of the night.

Although newborn babies show no fear of the dark, by two or three months of age, some show distress when left in a dark room; and many older children develop intense nighttime fears. But according to most child-care advisers, parents will regret ever starting the bad habit of sleeping with the baby. Never take the baby into your own bed, promptly and firmly return a straying toddler to his own bed; these are the governing rules for fostering nighttime independence in the child.

Proponents of bedding down on occasion with a baby assert that nighttime togetherness does not inhibit, but actually promotes the growth of independence, because a child's sense of trust in his parents has continuity—it's operative in twenty-four-hour cycles, not switched off during the night. Giving comfort when needed, they say, is not starting a bad habit, it's breaking the undesirable habit of periodic night crying.

There always have been doctors who smiled on the idea

of parent-child bundling, and recently there are others who no longer frown on it. Times and professional opinion do change. It wasn't so long ago that doctors who advocated self-demand or flexible feeding were viewed as radical mavericks by professionals who adhered to the rigid-schedule practice of infant feeding. In time will there be a unanimous reversal of the separate-sleeping rule?

Meanwhile you, along with many other parents, are probably playing it by ear—enjoying privacy when all's quiet on the baby front, and when it's not, visiting her crib or letting her visit your bed as you see fit. For either choice you have strong supporters.

Bathing and Dressing

The baby's almost daily bath probably has a regular time slot in the day. If it's in the evening it can be part of his family socializing, with mom and dad sharing the event. But if evening is a time that can't be counted on—because of drop-in visitors, TV programs, whatever—it's best to schedule the bath during the day so that there's less chance of its being skipped.

The baby doesn't care when it is, just so he's not too hungry and it's not a hurried time. He's gotten over his early-days nervousness. Now the feel of air on his skin is exhilarating, and in a warm room he can have a no-clothes exercise period before he goes into the tub. Free-form kicking and waving is interspersed with wide-open smiles and squeals. Stay right next to him and don't look away for a moment while he's carrying on atop his dressing table. Or put him on a pad on the floor and watch him perform in safety. Going into the tub usually sobers him; most babies this age are still a little timid about splashing in water. But the whole bath routine has a perk-up effect, and it's good to keep it a daily event. (Techniques for bathing the baby are given on pages 67 and 68.)

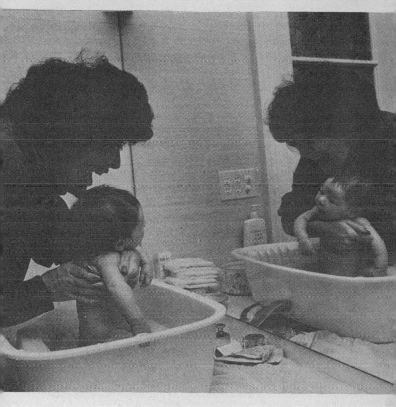

Toggery

Most mothers keep the baby in basic newborn clothes till he's sleeping less and socializing more. But by now your baby has probably grown into some of the more "stylish" clothes you first tucked away. One style that you'll continue to find indispensable is the "stretchie" coverall. It can be worn day or night, and indoors or out in moderate weather.

Many of the easy-care fabrics used in newborn garments are carried over into top-and-pants sets, overalls, and short-leg rompers. There are plenty of ruffles and bows for girls, and tailored styles for boys, and just as many with an either/or look. All your baby is interested in is how comfortable clothes feel. A dainty dress may look lovely, but if the texture is rough or if it hampers your child's movement, it may leave her feeling irritable and unhappy. Since this is a period of rapid weight gain, you'll want to keep checking your baby's clothes for proper fit.

Outings and Travel

Outdoor naps are good for the baby now, even in cold weather. She has enough fat insulation to keep her from getting chilled if she's dressed properly and it's not damp or windy. In winter, the middle of the day hours are best, and in summer, before or after those hours, and in a shaded spot. Down inside a carriage she'll be warmer than you are in cool weather, and may need less covering than you think; better to add a blanket after checking rather than take one off when she's hot.

Wintertime visiting or shopping with the baby can take you in and out of hot to cold temperatures. If you're staying more than a short time indoors, it's worth the trouble to take off the baby's outdoor clothing. Babies enjoy all the color and glitter of store strolling—if they're comfortable; whenever you see one fussing or crying she's usually miserably bundled up.

Outdoor Playtime

By now you'll be wanting a safe roomy place where your baby can spend some time outdoors, and also indoors to have a change from the crib. This piece of equipment was formerly called a playpen but is now known as a play yard. Full-size play yards are square and usually measure three feet by three feet, although some are a few inches bigger. There are also smaller rectangular play yards that are made to fit through a doorway. Some of these have legs that can be adjusted to crib or play yard height, and so double as portable cribs. Virtually all play yards made today have mesh sides rather than slats.

The U. S. Consumer Product Safety Commission advises parents to look for these safety features in play yards: mesh netting with a very tiny weave, so tiny that buttons on a baby's clothing will not get caught; a strong floor and railing; secure locking devices to prevent scissoring; no sharp edges, points, or protrusions. Look for these safety features, too, if you are using a secondhand play yard, and if it has slats be sure they are no more than 2 3/8 inches apart. Check the play yard for any rough spots or torn vinyl, particularly on the top rail, which eventually your baby, at stand-up age, will be inclined to use as a handy teether. Pay special attention also to the size of the weave in a secondhand mesh play yard; some of the earlier models had large openings, which are *very* dangerous. If you hang toys from the play yard rail, be sure the cord is less than 12 inches long or so short that it can't wrap around the baby's neck. And when your baby is older, there should be no large toys or boxes inside the play yard that the baby could stack, climb on, and possibly "use" for falling overboard.

If you don't have a yard or porch or patio, but do have a big enough car, why not transport your baby's play yard to a shady park sometimes, where you can enjoy the outdoors together. There's no better perk-up than a change of scene. If the grass isn't high, you can protect the baby from tiny crawlers and creepers by putting the play yard feet in small containers of water. Ants can paddle, but it will take them a while to get across the moat, and most won't bother to try.

When the weather is warm enough, let your baby have her nudist pleasures in a shaded, sheltered spot outdoors, lying on a big cotton blanket. She'll enjoy soft air playing on her skin while she looks around through the strange vista of open space, without walls or even the play yard mesh to haze her view. Perhaps she'll locate flowers or moving leaves to watch. Here you'll have to be on the lookout for flying creatures as well as ground ones. Make sure, too, that no patches of sunlight are filtering down on the baby. Even in full shade, where the sky is open overhead, the baby's skin will be getting some coloring from reflected rays of the sun. A baby's tender skin is so vulnerable that she can enjoy only briefly the wonderful warm sensation of sun covering her body. To protect her from sunburn, you must follow strict rules and also consider certain factors that affect the sun's burning power.

Sun Safety

Sunbaths should be out in the open where air can circulate around the baby, but never at the beach or poolside, where reflections from water or sand intensify the sun's rays. The baby should lie on a cotton towel or blanket, not a plastic surface, which doesn't absorb perspiration. To protect his eyes, place him so the top of his head is toward the sun, and if glare seems to bother him, put on a brimmed hat to shield his eyes.

A baby's time in the sun must be measured by the clock— *not* judged by the appearance of the skin. Sunburn does not become apparent until several hours after exposure. By the time a flush appears, the skin has already received an overdose that will rapidly develop the red, painful effects of a bad burn. And clock-watching includes the time of day. The ultraviolet rays that cause burning are most intense when the sun is high in the sky—that's between ten in the morning and two in the afternoon by sundial time; by daylight saving time, these hours read eleven to three on the clock. Baby's sunbaths should be either before or after these high sun hours.

A fair-complexioned baby's first exposure must be limited to four minutes, and that brief period must be divided between back and tummy-down positions—two minutes of sunning on each side. Very fair-skinned blonds or redheads should be started with even less. A dark or olive-complexioned baby may be safe with a first exposure of four minutes on each side. If the sunning is daily, the same number of minutes may be added each day—to a maximum of fifteen to twenty minutes on each side. This maximum must not be exceeded, no matter how much tan the baby has acquired.

Timing schedules are not foolproof. If your baby's skin shows a red flush at night, keep him out of the sun altogether on the following day, and subsequent days, too, if necessary. Until the pink tone is gone, his skin will be vulnerable to a burn. After this interval, cut back on his timetable; start again with a lesser amount of sunning, then adhere to the gradual daily increase.

Very gradual exposure gives the skin a chance to protect itself. Here's how it works: Cells below the outer layer of skin contain a pigment called melanin. The sun's invisible ultraviolet rays stimulate the release of melanin, and this pigment works its way up, darkening the outer layer of skin to shield it from sun damage. But the cells produce melanin only gradually; an overdose of sun results in a burn. The skin of dark-complexioned persons has a large amount of melanin to begin with, and so can tolerate more sun than a fair skin, which has very little. But the color of skin is not always an indication of its sensitivity to the sun; persons of any color and any age may have a type of skin that has a low tolerance to sun. A baby's skin, regardless of its natural color, is thin and delicate and especially vulnerable to burning.

The time of year also has to be considered. You may feel that your baby's bare legs and arms are safe from sunburn if you take him for a stroll on a warm day in April or May; in reality, the sun can be just as intense then as on a sizzling day in August. Remember that the sun reaches its annual zenith at noon on the longest day of the year— June 21 in the United States. Before and after that date, its angle to the earth is gradually changing. Since the slant of the sun's rays determines their burning power, the temperature on a given day is a guide only for the baby's outdoor comfort, not for his safe time in the sun.

Don't depend, either, on the look of the sky. On an overcast or partly cloudy day, the scattered, reflected rays are still getting through.

Your baby may be nicely tanned from being outdoors at

home. Then comes a vacation in a locality miles away. If you're northerners going south, even within the United States, beware; the nearer to the equator you go, the more intense are the sun's rays. They're stronger, too, in high altitudes than in low. Beaches and poolsides call for extra precautions; the sun's intensity is often doubled by reflections from sand or water. At these places the baby's exposure to sun must be cut back to half the quota that was safe at home; then he must be kept in the shade altogether or dressed in cover-up clothing, including a hat. A beach umbrella or open shade does not offer full protection, since reflected rays from sand or water still reach a person. And be sure to limit beach or poolside outings to the early morning or late afternoon hours—not the midday hours when the sun is high in the sky.

Now that you're duly prepared to protect your baby—and the whole family—from sunburn, there's one more note of precaution if you take your baby to a sandy beach: Don't forget the baby powder. Sand scratches; even a few grains can irritate tender skin. It's hard to remove from damp skin, particularly in the diaper area. But sprinkle on powder first and the sand will easily brush off with a dry towel.

Car Travel

This period of your baby's first year is ideal for trip-taking. She's still having long naps, which the lulling hum of a car may make even longer. She doesn't want the frequent exercise and snack breaks that an older baby needs. In fact her great satisfaction is simply having you close during all the hours she's awake.

What baby gear you take along depends, of course, on your destination plans. For city sight-seeing, a lightweight folding stroller is good. And wherever you are, you'll undoubtedly find a lot of use for the soft front carrier that baby rides in and dad or mom wears. The baby carrier-seat with an adjustable backrest is also useful on a trip. It's fine for visiting; the baby can be in the center of things; then when she's tired of it all, she can fall asleep right where she is, with the carrier adjusted to its reclining position. One place you'll especially appreciate a carrier is in restaurants. You can't very well enjoy those meals you don't have to fix while holding a wiggler in your lap. *Never* leave the baby alone in a parked car, even when she's sound asleep and the car is in view; there's no counting the things that could happen. (Information on buying and using front carriers and baby carrier-seats is given on pages 38 and 62 to 63.)

You want your baby to feel at home away from home, and traveling by car you can take along much more than by plane or train. But that's the trouble; you're likely to make your car a beast of burden that arrives back home with a lot of unused things you don't even remember packing. Meanwhile, you're often dragging out five things in the car trunk to reach one item. You can count on finding disposable diapers all along the way, even in many off-the-beaten-track villages. If you're bottle-feeding, ready-to-use formula in disposable bottles is a great convenience; but it might not be as readily available as disposable diapers, so it's best to restock when you come to a large pharmacy or supermarket (stops you can happily skip if you're nursing).

Large plastic bags are a must for used diapers and tissues, and can be disposed of in trash receptacles each evening. If you pack your diaper bag before setting out in the morning, there'll be no need to dig into suitcases while you're on the road or before leaving the car for some sight-seeing. A roomy bag will hold diapers, a clothing change, baby toiletries, two or three bottles of ready-to-feed formula, and premoistened towelettes—an indispensable item for all kinds of cleanups.

"Early to start and early to stop" is a good rule for motor trips. If you avoid peak restaurant times by an hour or so you'll have faster and better service and a more tranquil mealtime atmosphere. In populated areas, motels fill up fast in the evening. Well before sunset is the time to begin looking for your night's lodging; if you drive into the night, you may have to settle for less than desirable accommodations. Off the road early, you can get the baby bathed, fed, and settled down, organize things for a top-of-the-morning start the next day, then relax with maps or travel brochures.

Many chain motels will make reservations for your next stop and also reserve a crib—although you may not want to consider using a motel crib and mattress for your baby. The crib might be an old one, not up to the safety standards now required for cribs (explained on page 61). A multiuse take-along that your baby will use many times is a rectangular play yard that is also designed to double as a portable crib. As discussed on pages 112 and 113, this type has legs that adjust to crib or play yard height. A travel bed or bassinet is another possibility and is very suitable for these early months. It is *not*, however, to be used in the car, where the only safe place for your baby is in an approved auto restraint. The baby must be correctly secured in the restraint and the restraint must be correctly installed in the car. (Information on selecting and using an auto restraint is given on pages 73 and 74.)

Getting there ought to be as pleasant as being there. Once you've escaped a city's mad traffic, do take breaks for your own sakes, no matter how contented your baby is to keep going. Turning off a throughway to browse through a country village or have a picnic lunch in a grassy park gives you a refreshing change from seat-belt confinement in the car. Your muscles, circulation, and eyes all benefit from interruptions in long-distance car travel, and this contributes to safe driving.

Plane Travel

Basics for the baby are the same however you go—diapers, clothing changes, food, and a place to sleep. The difference in air travel is that you'll need less enroute and can have most supplies checked through to your destination. A carryon bag that fits under the seat will hold more than enough for the trip—and do pack it with somewhat more; delays are by no means uncommon. Still, you're tied to a strict schedule, which must be arranged well ahead of departure.

Make reservations at least two or three weeks in advance,

and if it's a holiday period, much earlier. Confirm your reservations and time schedule the day before takeoff, and also recheck on any baby equipment you may have requested. Some airlines supply bassinets; if not, you may want to bring your own travel bed or bassinet with you. Also ask if bulkhead or front-row seats can be reserved for you. These have more leg room than other seats and may accommodate a bassinet. Most airlines will warm bottles but you shouldn't count on any baby supplies being available. It's best to go prepared with your own diapers, baby foods, and toiletries. Although most airlines charge no fare for a child under two on domestic flights, the baby will not have a separate seat unless you reserve and pay for it. If there's an available seat, however, the flight attendant may offer it after the plane is airborne. It's good to have the extra room for diaper changing—if the baby isn't in a bassinet—and for your comfort and convenience. But before you buy a seat for your baby, inquire about any family-package price specials.

A nursing mother has considerable privacy for feeding in a window seat with her husband next to her. It's good if that doesn't concern her one way or the other. If it does, she can ask the flight attendant to accommodate her in the flight attendant area; but that can only be between takeoff, meal-serving, and landing, and so may not work out. When the seat belt sign is on, the belt must be fastened only around you, and the baby held in your arms. Ascents and descents often cause ear pain. Frequent swallowing helps to clear ear pressure during altitude changes, so it's a good idea to either nurse the baby or give him some formula or water by bottle during such times.

If you're traveling alone with your baby, ask a flight attendant to watch him if you have to leave your seat. Never take your baby with you into the lavatory, even if you have him in a soft front carrier. The space is much too confining, and sudden altitude changes can throw you dangerously off-balance. The baby can be comfortably transported in this type of carrier, which leaves your hands free, or in a small folding stroller, which can be taken aboard the plane. And however light you go with luggage, you'll appreciate a luggage carrier on wheels to pull around through airports. Many large airports have nurseries with good provisions and some supplies for travel ease with a baby. Inquire about this if you can't schedule a nonstop flight or in case of a delayed flight.

Train Travel

Few people still take the smooth, easy riding of the rails for long trips—and even fewer do with babies. The family car, taking off from your doorstep, is by far the most convenient; the plane gets you there faster; and you can combine plane with rental car to cover a lot of territory. You can combine train and car, too, but the long distance jumps consume more time by train. Your baby, who's not interested in a travel view from any angle, will be as happy with one means as another for getting from here to there. So it's left to her parents' preference and pocketbook. For the latter, you'll have to do some comparative figuring.

A plane eliminates the expense of motels and meals on distance travel by car. On overnight train trips you'll want a roomette for your own rest; this is considerably more expensive than coach but it does offer privacy. It's confining, manageable with a young baby, but a not very happy place for an older child.

As with plane travel, a baby under two usually rides free on a train but will not have a reserved seat. But again, inquire about any possible family plans or excursion rates. Purchase your train tickets in advance to avoid long waiting lines, and ask for a car as near as possible to the diner. Generally, no baby items are available so take along all that you will need, including a travel bed or bassinet if you have a roomette.

Carry-on bags should be limited to your minimal needs, and other baggage shipped on ahead. Remember to double-check your baggage stubs for correct destination, and to confirm your time schedule the day before departure. It saves a lot of worry and bother if you can be routed with the least possible train changes. When you do have to change, put your trust in station clocks on cross-country trips; you might forget to reset your watches as you pass from one time zone to another.

For any trip with a stay-put destination, it's best to have the name, address, and phone number of a pediatrician whom your home doctor recommends. Otherwise, telephone the local medical society for a recommendation. And in an emergency, the hospital is the place to go. Always take your baby's medical record book with you on an extended trip away from home.

Other Caregivers

The stay-at-home parent needs to get away from home without the baby in tow, and both parents need to be together and free of the baby now and then. Naturally you want a baby-sitter who's dependable in all respects; but it's important, too, to find someone who's dependably available. Then you don't have to "train" a new person each time, and your baby will be happier with someone who knows her. A good sitter can be male or female, in his or her sixties or teens, who's capable of taking responsibility for your baby's safety. Aside from that priority, your main consideration should be the person's rapport with your baby.

Test out a prospective sitter with a couple of paid visits while you're home. Go through the methods that your baby is accustomed to in her regular routines, and give the sitter plenty of chance to handle the baby alone. Your baby will tell you within an hour whether she's going to take to this person. Although the situation will be different when you're not there, at least you'll know that the person your baby has "chosen" is capable of handling any initial upset when you leave and has the warmth and sensitivity to bring out the baby's good feelings.

The Baby-Sitting Pool

If you know parents with babies or toddlers, they may be interested in cooperating on a weekly plan that gives each of you a morning or afternoon break—free of charge. The group should be small, preferably only three youngsters in all, so that it's not too much for one parent to handle. Each of you takes turns tending the children in your own home. On your free day you deposit your baby with one parent and take off for the hours agreed upon. It may be only a once-a-week exchange or more frequent. It's best to make it businesslike, with one parent in charge of keeping a record of the hours put in by each parent. There'll be times when the arrangement must be adjusted for one reason or another. But at least the plan lets you count on some free time for yourself without the expense of a paid sitter.

Support for Working Mothers

The number of mothers who work outside the home continues to grow. If you are planning to return to a job—either because of financial necessity or to continue a career or for personal fulfillment—you are no doubt giving a great deal of thought to what this will mean to your child. Out of all the research that has been done on children in day care, two things seem to be quite evident: A child can do very well in a good day-care arrangement, and no substitute caregiver will ever take the parents' place. Keep in mind, too, that your baby's sense of well-being is intimately linked to your own; if you feel secure and confident about working, your baby will most likely make a good adjustment to substitute care.

This is not to say that finding a good day-care arrangement is easy. Unless you can call upon a relative, it usually takes a lot of determination and work. So do allow yourself sufficient time to find a child-care arrangement you feel comfortable with and a caregiver whose approach most approximates your own.

Juggling motherhood, home, and a job isn't easy either.

One of the principal problems working mothers cite is that they have little or no time for themselves. Certainly it's essential to limit outside commitments, streamline household chores, and focus on what is most important: family and self. But just as necessary is father involvement. Mothers who are best able to manage the triad of parenting, work, and home point out that they have spouses who not only support their decision to work but who share child-care and household responsibilities. This is when good communication between mother and father is essential. The time for them to discuss their feelings and thoughts, and to come up with a realistic plan of action, is well before the mother returns to work. For a growing number of working parents, this shared involvement starts with finding a day-care arrangement for their child.

Day-Care Alternatives

There are three main types of day care: in-home care, family day-care home, and center-based care. Many professionals and parents believe that in-home care is best for a baby. In fact, it's been estimated that nearly 50 percent of preschoolers whose parents work are taken care of in their own homes. In-home care, however, can be very expensive, although the cost varies considerably depending on where one lives.

A comfortable alternative for many parents is a family day-care home. With this arrangement, a woman, usually a mother herself, takes care of two or three children in her home. A family day-care home can provide individualized attention for a young baby and a social environment for a toddler, together with a warm, homey atmosphere. Some family day-care homes are licensed but most function as informal sitting arrangements. Licensing usually means that the home has met certain health and safety standards but is not necessarily an indication of the home's emotional climate.

Center-based care is the most difficult to find for a baby. In fact, only about 5 percent of *all* preschoolers whose

parents work are in a group center. Quality day-care centers are scarce and generally expensive; many centers that charge on a sliding scale according to the parents' income have long waiting lists. In addition, most centers do no accept babies and young toddlers, only youngsters who are already toilet taught. Day-care centers are more subject to government regulation, but neither licensing nor cost guarantees quality. Any type of day-care arrangement that is being considered must be thoroughly investigated.

Of utmost importance is the caregiver's personality and ability. You want a warm, affectionate, competent, and reliable person who can tend to your baby's needs and on whom your baby can depend. You also want someone who will do things pretty much as you do them. When interviewing a prospective caregiver, have your baby there and see how they respond to one another. If you are visiting a prospective day-care home, observe the interaction between the day-care mother and the children. If you are visiting a group center, pick out one child to observe and then one caregiver.

Always ask for references and be sure to check them by telephone. You should never be hesitant about asking for references or about asking questions. A good caregiver understands and respects a parent's interest and concern. If a prospective caregiver makes you feel defensive, she is not the right person for you.

If you are considering a group center, you will want to know the ratio of children to caregiver. Look for a ratio of no more than three babies to one caregiver. Babies need individualized attention, which is a principal reason why most group centers do not accept them. Having enough staff members to meet the needs of infants would drive the cost of care beyond the reach of most parents. In a group center, too, you will want to be sure that one person has primary responsibility for your child.

A safe environment is another criterion when investigating a family day-care home or a group center. Ask, too, about meals and snacks, about where your child will sleep, and whether he'll have a place to keep toys and other possessions. Discuss what will be done in case your child gets sick during the day. At a group center, is there a sick bay and a pediatrician on call?

Whatever type of child-care arrangement you may be considering, it's always best to investigate at least several possibilities. This will give you more confidence in your final decision.

Working Mothers Co-op

If you plan to work part-time, you may want to consider starting a co-op arrangement with another mother who will also be working part-time. For example, say you work Mondays and Tuesdays, and another mother works Thursdays and Fridays. On the days each of you works, the other mother takes care of the children, thus eliminating the cost of an outside caregiver. You may already know someone who may be interested in such an arrangement and who has flexible working hours. If not, talk to friends, relatives, and neighbors, or put a notice on the bulletin boards of your church or synagogue or at the pediatrician's office.

You may have to work, or you may want to work. Carefully consider all the possibilities open to you for providing your baby with the kind of care that most approximates your own. If he's with a person who gives him comfort and attention and pleasure during the day, he'll adjust to the change with a minimum of trouble—and so will you. More about this in the next chapter.

Pediatric Note

At age two months your baby's immunization schedule starts. Don't miss this medical appointment. Diseases that the medical profession has greatly reduced by large-scale immunization programs still exist, and from time to time break out anew in epidemic proportions. This is because some parents become lax in keeping their children properly immunized. Yet what a simple matter it is to spare a child the suffering and sometimes permanent damage of many serious diseases.

A complete schedule of recommended immunizations and tests for infants and young children is listed on page 276. The immunizations given at approximately two months of age are the first DTP shot and the first TOPV. DTP stands for diphtheria, tetanus, and pertussis (whooping cough). TOPV stands for trivalent oral polio vaccine. Note the date of these immunizations in your baby's personal record book, which you'll need for reference many times in the future.

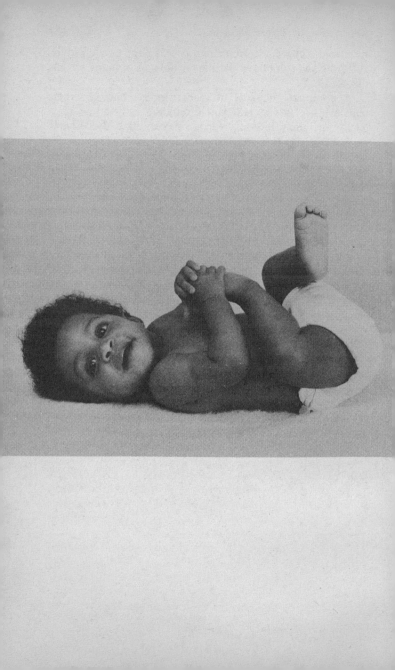

Chapter III

Three Months to Six Months

What to Expect

Fun is a new word in your baby's vocabulary. Those crinkly smiles get entangled with her developing voice, and out come real chortles. This brand-new fun sound will probably surprise you more than the baby, for you may hear it first when she's playing alone. She'll be trying to blow bubbles with her lips, or make a crib toy dance, and every time her little game succeeds she lets out a chortle. It comes spontaneously, like laughing at her own private joke, and until the "mechanism" gets under better control, she may not laugh for you. Then something you do will tickle her funny bone when you least expect it. Soon those first little chuckles develop into gleeful laughing that jiggles her stomach and quickly brings her a captive audience.

Sometimes she startles herself with a new sound that comes out; she'll hit high C with a squeal, or a good deep bass with a growl. A "talkative" baby enjoys long conversations with herself—part of the time. But all babies, like all good actors, appreciate a responsive audience.

New Skills

The baby wakes to play and plays to stay awake, in her own particular style. Her brand of play may be quietly satisfying or noisily active, but it's all fun and learning. She has fun with you, with her hands and feet, her voice and eyes and muscles and mouth—and soon, even with toys. Toys have been nice all along, but mostly for looking at, or—when she's helped to latch onto them—for holding briefly and mouthing.

What a thrill it must be, midway in this period, when the new teamwork of eyes-mind-hands enable the baby to reach out and grab hold of a toy. Her eyes tell her mind what she wants, her mind tells her hand to get it, and all of a sudden there it is, a shiny bright thing caught tight in her little fist. Her mouth wants it, and in it goes, for the nice hard slick feel against her gums.

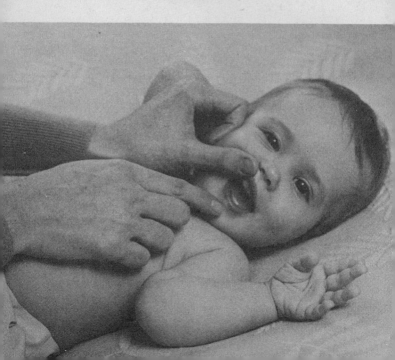

First Tooth?

Teething is one of the few things that may dilute the baby's flow of pleasure. During the day she's generally too busy to take much notice of teething discomfort, but during the night, little nagging tingles may interfere with sleep. Many babies, however, are not bothered at all by these first tiny baby teeth, the lower central incisors; they push up through the gums with the greatest of ease, and the first one may announce itself by a click on the feeding spoon.

Six months is the average age for a first tooth to appear, though much earlier or later is perfectly normal. An excess of drooling may tell you that a tooth is on the way, and if there *is* discomfort, it sometimes causes fretfulness for weeks before the tooth breaks through. Teething also may cause some loss of appetite. But don't blame any unusual symptom on teething, including a continuing poor appetite; any sign of possible illness should be reported to your doctor.

Slower Weight Gain

In any case, you can't expect your baby to continue gaining weight as fast as she did in her first three months. Growth is normally slowing down, though she'll reach twice her birth weight during this period. At the monthly pediatric checkup, the doctor will tell you whether your baby's weight gain is progressing normally. There's no point in more frequent weight checks, as the gaining may be somewhat irregular, though normal.

Other Variables

What else is new? Possibly eye color and hair color. If your baby's eyes were destined to be darker than their indefinite slate-blue color at birth, you may notice a difference now; flecks of color may be gradually changing them to brown or hazel. A dark-skinned baby may now have shiny black eyes. And a blue-eyed newborn may retain clear blue eyes or acquire flecks of color that turn them to green or gray.

Your baby has been shedding the hair she was born with, and a new crop is growing in. It may be a different color and texture than the fuzz or the mop she arrived with. What if she turns out a dramatic redhead? Dispel the myths! Red hair does *not* predispose a child to a hotheaded disposition; redheaded children are *not* prone to more illness than other children. However, they may be more susceptible to sunburn, since redheads often have very light skin. The only other "problem" you can expect is possibly choosing colors in clothing that enhance rather than clash with that handsome, distinctive hair.

Sibling Relations

Affection is growing stronger between the baby and her brothers and sisters or cousins and child friends. Her real out-loud laughing delights the kids, and they can usually bring out better performances than adults can. Now, before the baby can get around and into their things, she's no source of annoyance for them. And later on, these early ties of affection will help them handle the baby with more tolerance and understanding.

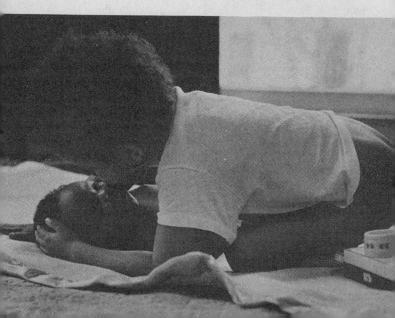

Understanding Your Baby

Behavior

These are delightful months. Baby and family are on the best of terms. He's less trouble than he used to be, and still not big enough to get *into* trouble. He can "do" enough now to be much more interesting for the children in his life. Smiley and "talkative," it's no wonder he invites so much attention.

Social Ups and Downs

How a baby reacts to visitors at home depends partly on his daily environment. If it's lively with drop-in friends and children who run in and out, he'll be more accepting of a variety of persons. But usually by this age a baby will be changing some of his easy-going attitudes. He may not smile at just anyone as he did before. Almost all babies now begin to develop reservations about who to accept as friends. This is because they're gaining the ability to discriminate differences, and so become more selective in many ways. It's also because adults differ greatly in their approach to babies. The "pouncers" don't give the baby a chance to collect himself, and he withdraws in protective silence, or sometimes in wails. Children, however, usually can do no wrong as far as a baby is concerned; he'll often reach out to pat a strange child as readily as his own brother or sister, or take a ruffling from a child, which he wouldn't tolerate in an adult.

An only-child baby, or one who doesn't see many people, may be quite antisocial with unfamiliar persons; and unfamiliar may be a "known" person who arrives at the house looking different—wearing a hat or glasses, for instance. The baby is now wise enough to seek safety—perhaps clamming up or clamoring for his parent—when that stranger tries to poke or sweet-talk him into a smile. Grandparents and friends who don't see him regularly can have their feelings hurt by this little sober-faced person who so recently welcomed them with ready smiles.

The Changing-Tunes Trick

If visitors keep their distance for a while, perhaps ignore him, a four- or five-month-old may soon get tired of that state of affairs and switch from an unsocial to an oversocial attitude. He's used to being part of, even the center of, a small group situation. He may start smiling and babbling, trying to get attention. And if the visitors are engrossed in conversation with his parents, the baby may start babbling to them, trying to divert attention to himself. He can get so loud that he practically drowns out the grownups' talk (which may also be pretty high-keyed, and interesting to imitate). If you move him out to another room he'll be understandably outraged.

This is one of those conflicts of interest that's hard to get around. You've been encouraging your baby to be an outgoing little person, and here he is, going too far. The proper amenities of social give-and-take are a fine distinction a baby can't be expected to make. Perhaps you can stop his social overreaching with a teething biscuit to chew on, or seat him in front of the TV to be diverted by cavorting characters there. Whoever may frown on "spoiling" a baby by such considerations and compromises is still living in the era when children were supposed to be seen and not heard.

Muscle Fun

Action fills hours of the baby's day now. There's a glow of pleasure all through his body as he puts it to work on new maneuvers. Watch him twist, thrust, struggle, striving to get somewhere, if only over. He may make the complete rollover by the end of this period; if not, he's strengthening every muscle it takes, readying himself for the near-future joy of flipping with ease from back to tummy and back again.

Watch him work toward reaching and grasping. All those

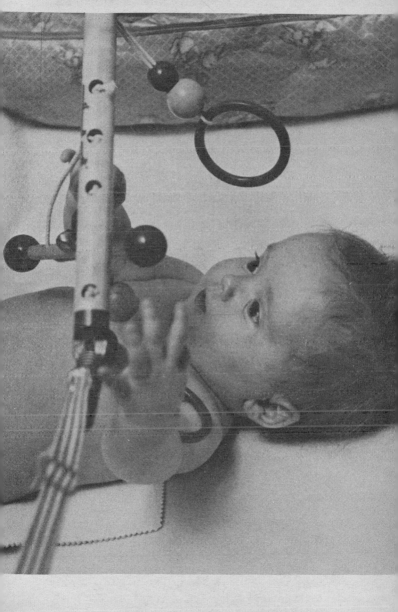

enticing toys that long satisfied his eyes are objects he now wants to get hold of. Delicate mobiles must be positioned well out of reach. For practice the baby needs sturdy toys to swipe at and bat, to pull on and kick, to squeeze, shake and rattle. Long before he achieves good control you'll see the tremendous effort and patience he puts into mastering this skill. It took months of visual development before he could focus well enough to coordinate what he sees with movements of his arm and hand. He first swipes at what he wants with closed fist. Then he reaches with his fingers spread out, his eyes wide open, concentrating, straining. He swings at a toy, misses it, tries, misses, makes contact but fails to close in. At last everything works together; he's got that thing caught in his hand; he can pull it to himself to feel, examine, and if he can get it as far as his mouth, to taste. Safety should always be a principal consideration when selecting toys for your baby. They must be sturdy and nontoxic, have no sharp points or edges or small parts that could be swallowed.

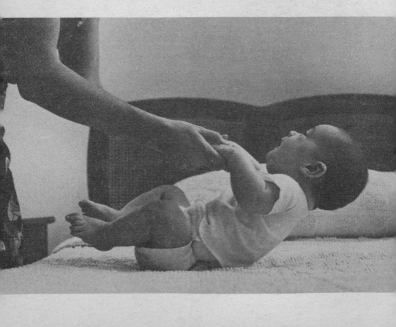

Neck and back muscles are now much stronger. Just entering this period, the baby can hold his head erect in line with his back as he's pulled by his hands to a sitting position, and his head no longer bobs forward when he's upright. He'll also begin to help when you pull him up, leaning his body forward and pulling in his knees. By five months, good head balance will be continuous. With back support he can sit propped in a slight backward slant for a good half hour without tiring, people-watching, or playing with toys. By six months he'll be putting more movement into his sitting, gaining balance as he's safely strapped into his seat or held on your lap.

But his best play position is still on his back. A flat firm surface feels more safe and secure, more natural than when he's upright. There, too, he can use his feet for amusement. A foot flies up into view, he grabs it, pulls it to his mouth and sucks on a toe. By his fifth month he has the strength to lift and hold his feet off the ground, with his legs stretched out straight. When he does this lying on his stomach, his arms, too, are lifted, his back is arched, and he rocks like a little boat. That's quite a muscular feat. Try it!

Your baby's athletic program affects his all-over behavior. With plenty of chance to exercise, and an admiring audience to appreciate his efforts, he'll feel physically fit, alert, happy, and obviously proud of his abilities.

Learning

Everything is now coming together for the baby to facilitate her first major thrust in learning. Eye-hand-body controls combine to help her do more with herself; her developing voice helps her pull people closer for all the learning that comes with social development.

Visual Fitness

In the baby's fourth month her vision is reaching normal adult standards. This means that in addition to the valuable

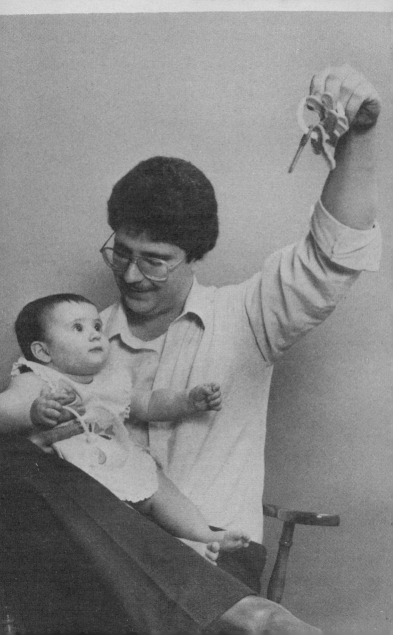

but limited vision of the newborn, the eyes can now perceive depth, adjust easily to different distances, and clearly discriminate all colors of the spectrum. The baby can also coordinate her eyes and head rotations almost as well as an adult, and she uses the same style of movements: Her head leads her eyes when she wants to look at a stationary object; her eyes, which move faster, lead the head when the object is moving. Thus, as her reach-grasp ability improves, she can take sure aim on dangling toys as well as on fixed objects.

Touch Learning

During this period, you'll notice that your baby is showing great interest in touching things, not only to get hold of them, but to examine how they feel. She scratches at a sheet or a sweater or a fuzzy stuffed animal, catches your hair in her fingers, rubs and pats a tabletop with the palm of her hand, squeezes a soft yielding toy.

From the beginning, the sense of touch has served as one of the most important avenues of learning. When the baby was younger, pleasurable touch was a passive experience; it acted upon her, with no effort on her part, creating sensations and lasting impressions. Now she is using the sense of touch to actively further her learning; touching opens up a new world of meanings. For months ahead, she'll continue to explore her surroundings by holding and looking at things, feeling them with her hands and mouth, examining differences in texture, shape, weight. Gradually she learns what to expect of certain objects by mentally combining and transferring various experiences.

A typical experiment that researchers have used with six-month-old babies demonstrates this kind of learning. A wooden star is placed in the baby's hands, but it is blocked from her view by a screen. She handles the star toy with great interest, examining it by feel alone. Then the star is brought out in view and a ball of similar size is placed beside it. The baby picks up the ball and ignores the star. She has made the connection between touch and vision; she already "knows" the star, and so selects the ball as a new thing of interest to explore. Psychologists suggest that the baby's ability to take in information with one sense and transfer it to another may form the basis for symbolic thinking.

It's easy to overlook the importance of what a baby is doing, to dismiss it as idle child's play. There is nothing idle about it, of course, even though the baby is not consciously or systematically trying to teach herself. But learning is steadily flowing through her as she experiences differences in the things she touches and holds and mouthes. Simply the sensation that there *are* differences constitutes a chunk of learning. To realize this we would have to unlearn most of what we know about our environment, perhaps imagine ourselves in an extraterrestrial place where the nature of each thing we touched was a surprise.

There is a way, though, to get some idea of what the baby is doing. If you can "isolate" the sense of touch it will seem like a pristine experience for yourself. Close your eyes, and as you touch or hold one thing at a time, try to "absorb" its feel—a smooth tabletop, the rough bristles of a brush, a pillow, a flower petal. If you can concentrate on only this one sense, you have some awareness of what your baby is finding in all that busy handling and feeling of everything around her. You may even discover that a few moments of savoring the feel of things gives a lift to your routine chores.

The sense of touch may have already given the baby a start in learning to know something about herself. For example, when she has a finger in her mouth, her mouth is feeling the finger and the finger is feeling her mouth. This two-way feeling is called self-sentience. It's a sensation that does not involve thought, but that will become an awareness of separate parts of herself.

The World and I

It's impossible to know when a baby begins to sense that he and the outside world are separate. But an inkling of this must begin to take form when the baby can see himself act—when he can select a particular object, reach for it and grasp it. Whether he can distinguish his feet from other objects is problematic. He can hold and mouth and play with a foot, then lose it the same as any other toy. When his feet are out of sight they no longer exist for him; they are as "gone" as any object he can't see or feel—not missed, not wanted, of interest only when it reappears in front of his eyes or in his hand.

Hands are more reliable than feet in the baby's life. He has long used them as toys to suck; for a period he used them as interesting things to gaze at, and then to study as he fingered his fingers. Soon after he uses them for procuring toys. But does he see his hands as part of himself? They may still be as nebulous in his realization of self as are his eyes and ears, which are also instruments for contacting the world around him.

The process of self-discovery is extremely slow and involved. But a concept of self is clearly not necessary in the learning process, for the baby has obviously been learning since the day he was born. He absorbed impressions through all his senses, retained and used these impressions to learn a great deal about his surroundings and other persons. All this was perceived as part of or an extension of himself, yet it affected and changed his behavior. A caregiver, for example, was first a feeling, then a happening, and in time a meaning. From the beginning, these phases formed a strong baby-parent attachment, and this will be even more important to the baby as he gradually learns more about himself and moves toward independence.

A Modicum of Memory

During his early months, the baby's field of interest is a series of things and events that come and go. People and objects mysteriously appear, disappear and reappear. But by four months the baby has acquired a memory span of a few seconds. Brief as this is, it's an important development, for it helps him learn how to repeat an action.

He bats a dangling toy and it jingles. Making the sound is at first accidental, for he doesn't connect it with the batting. But every time he bats, comes the sound. Soon he links the two, and keeps repeating his action for the effect. And when he has performed this many times over, a memory trace is established in his brain, so that relearning this feat from one day to the next is unnecessary.

In another month or so he has gained a little more hold on the immediate past. After much practice in reaching and activating toys, he has a sense of before and after. This alerts him to look for a toy he has dropped—but only momentarily; he'll abandon the search if he can't readily see or feel the missing object. "Out of sight, out of mind" is still his overall limitation.

The Babbler

Language learning has started in earnest. The baby is not only using her voice to chortle, squeal, growl, and belly-laugh, but she's beginning to use quite refined speech sounds.

Consonants are being inserted between the vowel sounds. Babbling is a rhythmic chain of these sounds that the baby puts together in endless repetition. Lip sounds, such as b, m, p, are easy to make, since the baby is practiced in using her lips for bubble blowing. Adding on a vowel, she can babble a string of be-be's, ma-ma's, pa-pa's or a growing number of combinations—none of which have any meaning for the baby as yet except her pleasure in making them. But pleasure is the greatest incentive to learning.

In babbling the baby begins to make an association between hearing and speech. Hearing one of her voice sounds triggers release of the next, stimulating a rapid succession of rhythmic voice activity. When someone responds to her babbling, the interplay of her own voice with another leads her to the rudimentary realization that sounds have meaning; and this leads her, in time, to attempt to imitate the speech sounds she hears.

The babbling stage of a baby's voice play is a critical period for deaf babies. Without the exciting stimulus of hearing her own voice, the deaf baby makes no association between the sensations she feels when occasionally using her voice; and she does not associate sound with the movement she sees on the lips of others. She experiences no interplay of her own and other voices—with a gradual gleaning of its meaning—to ready her for speech. This is why hearing aids are now recommended for deaf babies at a very early age. A small, lightweight but high-powered hearing aid can be worn in comfort by a baby, encased in a cloth harness and worn as part of her clothing all through the day. In this auditory training method for deaf babies, a child does not lose out on this critical period when language learning is taking form. But without the opportunity to hear, which is the faculty that normally impels language skills, a deaf baby's vocal activity subsides in the babbling stage.

In the normal baby's development, all senses and abilities are linked together, aiding and stimulating one another as she learns a little more each day about her small world, herself, and the important persons in her life.

Parent-Child Interaction

Have you decided yet whether your baby is going to be a "doctor, lawyer, merchant, or chief"? Or is he mechanically, musically, or dramatically inclined? Perhaps you can't yet be *quite* sure what his aptitudes are. But nonsense aside, some babies do show individual interests at a young age.

Encouraging Special Interests

A baby who's especially interested in listening will be fascinated by subtle sound toys. If you string a few bells across the crib and activate them separately, he'll listen intently to the differences in tone. Try him on music; perhaps you'll notice that he's much more attentive to a classical guitar piece than to a rock group.

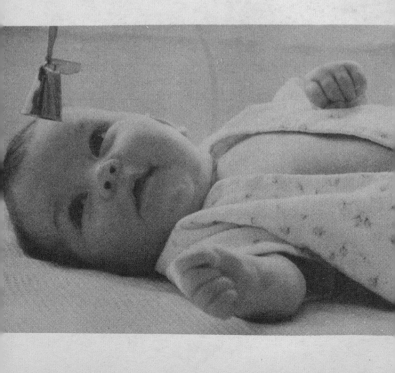

A baby who's gesture-inclined will begin early to use that language if you encourage it with meaningful gestures of your own. Before picking him up, for instance, hold out your arms to him and wait till he tries to say "yes" with jerky arm waving or definite reaching. He may be an early learner in bye-bye waving—and perhaps in shaking his head "no" as well!

A lively babbler will delight in voice play with you. He'll look surprised and pleased when you imitate his voice variations. Then you can reverse the game, making different sounds and waiting for his answer. He'll soon learn how to imitate you. This interplay gives him a head start in learning that language is communication.

A quiet, self-contained baby may study his voice ability more privately, experimenting in soft trilling and volume control. Less interested in socializing, he may be busy studying his world visually, comparing colors and shapes and the actions of people. This kind of baby appreciates enough uninterrupted time to concentrate on his own methods of learning.

Your baby can tell you a great deal about himself, his individuality, the amount and the kind of interaction he enjoys. And all the while he needs encouragement in his personal pursuits, the developmental skills he's striving to master.

Reaching a Goal

Your baby is hard at work on her new goal of reaching. Perfecting this skill isn't easy, but it will make a big change in the baby's life. Imagine looking and wanting and not being able to get things for yourself. Those interesting toys you supplied were there—shining, swaying, tinkling, within reach but out of her power to reach except when you helped. Finally all by herself she manages to latch on to toys, to study them from every angle—and she's embarked on new adventures in play and learning. Imagine, too, what this new-found ability does for a baby's self-esteem!

You have to keep a bit ahead of your baby by anticipating

what she's up to, and acting upon the right need at the right time. As soon as she's attempting to reach, toys that were only for looking and listening pleasure must be put out of reach. When you're holding the baby, or she's seated in her baby carrier or stroller, take care that she's not close enough to anything dangerous that she might reach out and touch or grab. Make sure, too, that she *does* have safe playthings within easy reach.

How You Can Help

The urge to do is a compelling force that the baby must and will get control of as the time for each new ability comes along. Some babies take these big steps in stride, calmly and patiently working away till they're over the hump; some become frustrated but want to fight it through on their own, resenting any outside interference; others do better with an occasional helping hand. Your own baby's style of confronting problems is your guide to the kind of encouragement he needs. But remember that he *wants* to tackle new problems; diverting him from his efforts will only prolong the learning period.

If you see, for instance, that a dangling toy is making him intense and agitated when his round-house swings fail to connect with their target, it won't do much good to pick him up and cuddle him like a newborn baby. He's an action baby now, who wants to get on with his work. Slowly guide that toy to his hand so he can hold onto it. Help him out, too, by putting stationary toys within reach; dangling things swing when they're batted, and moving objects are much harder to catch. The next time you find him upset, try talking to him—not sympathetically, but admiringly about the good tries he's making—before you offer any assistance. No matter that he can't understand words; your voice conveys interest in what he's trying to do, and that alone gives him comfort and support for renewing his emotional energy.

Down-to-Earth Fun

A baby can actually double the time he ordinarily spends

in play when one of the family joins him. Literally getting down to his level delights a baby. If he's one who thinks tummy down is only for sleep, you can show him it's a good position, too, for play and exercise. When he can't readily see you, he may get mad when you turn him onto his stomach or get sullen and lie like a lump. But get down on a mat yourself, face to face with him, and he'll perk up in spirit and action. Before a baby learns to roll himself over he's mostly back-oriented for play. That way he naturally has good use of his arms, but other muscles are being neglected. With short periods in the tummy-down position he'll stretch and exercise his whole body. Toys will help to keep him interested, but there's nothing like back and forth play and talk with another person, right there at close range, to keep him delighted.

The Crack-of-Dawn Baby

A lot of daytime exercise and an active evening play session (before the quiet, relaxing last feeding) *may* help the baby to sleep later in the morning. For most babies, however, the first sliver of light is the alarm clock that alerts them to the busyness of a new day. During these months, a baby can't contain herself for long with lazy finger sucking; her surge of energy for mastering new skills is too exciting. If she's a tummy sleeper she'll start right in, squirming, twisting, lifting her legs and arms off the mattress and rocking on her torso. But that kind of workout is tiring; besides, it's not what she wants; she's eager to get going on her important work in toy control. And if she's handicapped by no turnover skill, she may be yelling even sooner for attention. If the household isn't geared to early rising, and you try to ignore her, hoping she'll give in and go back to sleep, the likely result is a roused-awake, grumpy rest of the family.

One thing you can try is rollover lessons during the day. With a little help your baby may master this maneuver sooner than by figuring it out for herself. When she's lying on her stomach, hold a toy out to the side of her face. Make sure she's looking at it, then move it slowly up so she has to twist her body to keep it in sight. Watch how she moves and places her legs and arms as she twists; this will show you the leverage points that are important for taking her on over. Give a little push to those points to help her complete the stomach to back roll. Only light, subtle help will work; the baby has to get the feel of the movement mechanisms that result in a body roll. But when she does it, she can amuse herself alone for a longer time when she wakes with the birds in the morning.

Bear with your baby. Developmental urges swell and wane, affecting her habits and changing the patterns of her days and nights. A night waker or an early bird won't always be one. The driving forces that propel a baby make the first year of life the time when she learns tremendously more and faster than she'll learn in any other period of life. What she puts into this is bound to take something out of you, just as your babyhood cost your parents a few inconveniences. If you treasure an hour or so extra sleep in the morning, it's not worth a fight with your baby to get it. Anyway, you can't win—until nature decrees a change in the baby. But if you're naturally an early riser, or have adjusted to the need, you already know the charm of a baby fresh from sleep, wide-eyed and eager for the wonders of a new day. That's a mood worth preserving.

The Tie That Binds

Don't ever think that playthings can replace parents. No matter how much your baby is learning to do with his toys, *things* can never replace you in his interests or his affections. Sometimes when you've been talking and playing with him, he'll squeal with frustration when you leave him.

Why are you more important to your baby's play than his toys? He can get reactions from playthings too; some of them do lively, amusing things when he simply moves them; he can make them make noises by shaking or squeezing them. In short, both toys and persons respond to the baby's actions, and the baby responds to toys' actions by smiling and chuckling. *But*—toys can't smile; toys can't smile *with* the baby; toys can't tell the baby what smiles *mean*. Smiling is a communication link that holds a baby to the human family—one important reason being that neither the baby nor his parent *only* smiles. This expression is part of a whole package of feelings and actions and signals that one gives to the other, and that each responds to and acts upon.

You can talk to your baby as though he interprets your meaning, and he can give you messages that you interpret on an adult level of thinking. It doesn't matter that you're not on the same wavelength. You've been learning to "read" each other since your baby was a newborn. By now you're both pretty good communicators. Babies arrive in the world equipped by nature to make a parent a receiver as well as a giver of messages.

By contrast, the baby's involvement with toys is a one-sided affair. Toys can please him but they can't be pleased. Thus there's no feedback to nurture a warm human relationship. Only people can make the baby a social being.

Tit for Tat

You've reinforced your baby's good feelings with a multitude of smiles, nods, tendings, and loving words. Now she can not only reciprocate with happy expressions, she can start the interchange herself by smiling and vocalizing to you directly. She may even hit upon a little game that many babies play to capture a parent's attention. The "coughing game" gets its start when the baby takes notice of that strange noise coming out of you. Soon she finds she can imitate it, and she exchanges coughs with you for fun. Then one day when you least expect it, she initiates the game by making her fake little hacky cough, you rush to see if she's all right, and she beams you a big smile. She's sprouting a sense of humor!

One way that works with many babies to encourage happy behavior is to discourage fussy, irritable behavior. But it doesn't help to use a frown or an unpleasant voice. If you

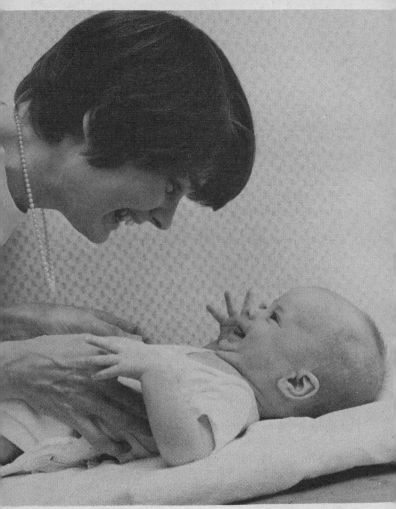

keep your face expressionless, your baby will probably feel uncomfortable with a familar face that's suddenly become strangely immobile that she'll try to change it; she'll begin to smile and murmur to make it change expression. And, of course, you let her succeed by bringing your face to life again with smiles and talk.

Parental Behavior Patterns

By the time the baby is a few months old, many couples have settled into loosely defined roles of who does what with the baby and how they do it. Each parent's interaction with the baby has its particular style; and this can be different with one baby in the family than with another, because each child's characteristics have a lot to do with shaping the parent's responses. In turn, the baby learns to adjust and appreciate differences in the persons close to him.

But it's important to keep a balance in the parent-baby relationships. If you get stuck in one role you can't know your baby in all *his* roles. He's changing fast, and you need the insight that tells you how to keep abreast of his sensitivities, how to give praises, subtle pushes, and the kind of comfort that fits his developing personality. There are times when you can't be alert to the baby's feelings or cues. And when he can't "reach" one parent, he ought to be able to depend on the other. If both of you are equally capable of taking over the baby's practical and emotional needs, the interaction between the three of you thrives.

Routines and Care

Feeding

The big project coming up for your baby is learning to eat from a spoon. This start on "solid" food is looked upon as a prideful event by many parents, a step out of pure infantile feeding on the way to "real" eating—even to feeding himself, after a fashion, before he's a year old. The start of spoon feeding *is* an important event, but there's plenty of time for the feeding progression to take place. Parental pride is misguided if it consists of boasting about how young the baby is and what a quantity of baby food he's consuming.

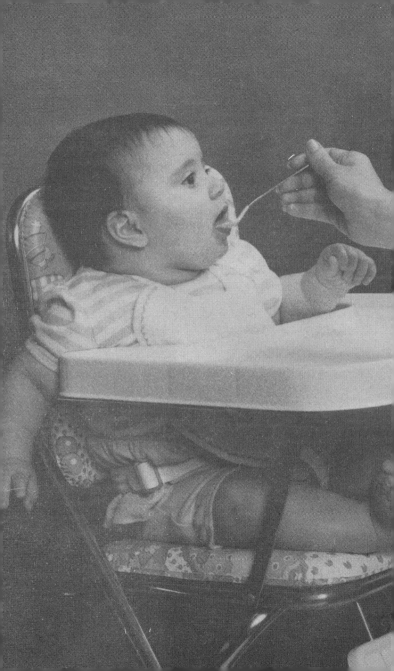

Nature's Guidelines

For one thing, starting solids too early serves no purpose. Breast milk or prepared formula is the only food a baby needs for a number of months after birth. And at an early age, his body can't properly utilize other food; most of it passes right through without doing him any good—and it may do harm. For example, if a child is prone to food allergies, the risk of allergic reactions is greater in early infancy. This is because the digestive and intestinal defense system for warding off these reactions is still immature. The older a baby is when new foods are introduced, the less chance there is of allergic reactions.

Between four and six months is the current medical consensus for introducing solid food. Before four months it isn't needed; after six months it will become an increasingly important part of the baby's diet.

There are also important developmental reasons for waiting until the baby is between four and six months of age. The sucking-swallowing reflex that a baby is born with serves only for getting liquid food from a nipple. Another newborn reflex serves as a protection against choking. This is the "extrusion reflex"; any nonliquid substance that touches the front part of his tongue is instinctively pushed out of his mouth. By about four to five months of age this early reflex disappears, and the baby can learn to swallow as we do, by using the tongue to move the food back in the mouth for swallowing.

Another development the baby should reach before you're freely feeding him solids is the ability to indicate how much food he wants. When he opens his mouth and leans forward, he's obviously asking for more; when he leans back and turns away, he's telling you he's had enough. But until about five or so months of age, a baby can't express these feelings by body language, and may let you stuff him with many more calories than he wants or needs.

Weight Watching

Doctors point out that continuing to feed a baby who's

already satisfied, perhaps satiated, is really a form of forced feeding, and a major cause of overweight in infancy. Too many babies are now doubling their birth weight long before the normal age of five or six months. With this accelerated weight gain they may get too fat to exercise enough for good development of physical skills. Doctors warn against overweight in infancy as well as in adulthood.

You can simply quote medical opinion to rebuff any raised-eyebrow remarks (You haven't started *yet*?) from those who boast about all the baby food they're spooning into their young infant. Very young babies do get pureed food down, with some initial choking, a lot being oozed out, scraped off the baby's chin, and reinserted. But when fed too much food too soon, a baby may lose his pleasure in eating. And if he's urged, shown impatience or annoyance, or is tricked by having spoonfuls popped into his mouth when he's not looking, there's likely to be rebellion, leading to long-lasting feeding problems. When snacking on sweet, starchy fillers gets started (He's got to eat *something*!) good appetite is lost and so is good nutrition. The way to establish good eating habits is to avoid sowing any seeds of a problem.

The Pleasure Principle

All these months, feeding has been a primary pleasure for the baby. Now, with a slow and easy start on this new method of eating she can be launched on a lifetime enjoyment of good food. But a baby needs to feel her way in any new venture. The whole experience of taking food from a spoon is new—the texture of it, the taste, and the mouth action. Even when the baby is developmentally ready to learn the new maneuver of swallowing, it requires practice before it becomes easy and natural.

Anything strange is easier for the baby to accept if she has the secure feeling of being snuggled close to you. For first practice sessions, let her sit on your lap, leaning against you, as she does for a breast or bottle feeding. Try to be as relaxed as you want your baby to be, not holding her tensely or restraining her hands. Hand to mouth is the most natural gesture a baby makes; she'll smear the food on her lips and suck it off her fingers or fist. This lets her get a little of the food by her familiar method of sucking; and the new taste of her hand will most likely keep her interested in trying a few more bites. With a slow start and a lot of consideration for your baby's feelings, she'll probably soon be opening her mouth like a little bird for bite after bite. She'll then be happy to sit in her baby seat, making the whole procedure easier for you.

These first bites should be dabs, served on the tip of a small spoon. A small-bowled baby spoon or a demitasse spoon fits nicely between the corners of baby lips. Give her time to mouth each tiny portion before adding another. When she gives you a negative cue—closing her mouth or turning her face away—that should be it for this time.

Pleasant eating experience is far more important than the bit of extra nutrition in first spoon feedings. Milk is the mainstay of the baby's diet. In fact, when a baby has mastered the mechanics of eating solid food, and is an eager eater, doctors often suggest giving the bottle or breast first to make sure the baby isn't short-changed on milk.

This isn't likely to be an early concern; your baby will go on loving the bottle or breast for a long time. When she's just learning to eat from a spoon, you'll wonder which way to start a feeding—with spoon or nipple. Is she acting very hungry? It might seem a good time to get a little spoon food into her. Perhaps so; you can try. But this tactic frustrates most babies; when they're hungry they want to grab hold of a nipple and suck, not cope with an awkward new way of getting food. So let your baby decide. If she wants her familiar nipple, let her nurse for a few minutes or take about half of her bottle. When the edge is off her hunger she'll be more relaxed and perhaps ready to enjoy a variation in her milk menu.

For Starters

These first little meals take only a few minutes of feeding

time, once or twice a day. You'll be starting with only a teaspoonful of pureed food, probably precooked baby cereal mixed with milk or formula. Doctors usually advise starting with cereal, since the taste is bland and not too great a surprise for the baby. Also, the precooked dry infant cereals are fortified with iron, which the baby is beginning to need now, as the prenatal store of iron he was born with is being depleted. (If you're bottle feeding, your doctor will probably recommend that your baby be switched to iron-fortified formula sometime between four and six months—that is, if he hasn't been on iron-fortified formula since birth.) The cereal should be one grain, not a mixture. Rice is often suggested as a starter, but any grain that appeals to your baby is fine—with the exception of wheat, which is usually saved till later as it's more likely to cause allergic reactions.

It's usually advised to add enough milk or formula to make a thin consistency. But some babies find it easier to maneuver a soft pea-sized lump, instead of a runny bite, back in the mouth for swallowing. So experiment. What's important is (1) to keep the bites small and wait till one is swallowed before giving another, and (2) to respect your baby's "that's enough" cue. He may reluctantly take a little more, but you shouldn't let yourself be tempted to coax more into him. Keep reminding yourself that not until the second half of your baby's first year will he really be needing the extra nutrition of solid foods. If each minuscule meal is ended with a smiling "That's fine!" your baby will be pleased with himself and willing to please you with a repeat performance.

Strained fruit is a taste treat for most babies, and the doctor may suggest it as a starter if the baby is reluctant to try cereal. Among the fruits and vegetables, the order of additions isn't important. But only one food should be tried at a time, with intervals of several days to a week between each new food. Single-ingredient foods—no mixtures— help you to pinpoint any offending food.

Fruits and vegetables can be used for two to three days after opening the jar if it's well refrigerated—and if you don't feed the baby directly out of the jar; saliva in the food can spoil it rapidly. On the lid of baby food jars you'll see an indented circle. This is a special safety button. When the button is down the jar is properly sealed and when you open the jar the button should pop up with an audible sound. You should never use a jar of baby food if the lid button is up before you open it.

The introduction of strained meats is discussed in the next chapter. Traditionally these have been started after the baby has gotten accustomed to fruits and vegetables. A growing number of doctors, however, feel that these first spoon foods needn't be introduced in any special order.

Budding Tastes

As you try out different foods, your baby will show you her preferences. Keep those going and she'll come to welcome the sight of bowl and spoon. In between, perhaps every week or so, retry a food she said no to at first; babies do change their tastes from time to time. But don't try to "improve" the taste of some food by adding salt or sugar to make it more appetizing for *you*.

Your attitude can affect your baby's tastes more than you might think. You have to be careful not to unconsciously let your face show your feelings about certain foods; one that you dislike may be a favorite with your baby if you don't influence her otherwise. Overall, a matter-of-fact attitude is better than either overenthusiasm or a timid please-try-a-taste approach. If, for instance, you enthuse over fruit and act more serious about vegetables, you're expressing your own taste or food-value opinion, instead of leaving choices entirely up to the baby. There are babies who spit out banana and gobble up spinach.

There's no need to concern yourself with the vitamin-mineral-protein content of foods just yet. This period of solid food feeding is for developing enjoyment of eating. Once that has a good start, a balanced diet for your baby is not hard to achieve. A variety of foods supply essentially the same nutrients, and one can be substituted for another according to your baby's preferences. Keep in mind the urgent appetite your baby was born with, when she could hardly wait to be fed. Good appetite is the thing to preserve; and it will develop into a desire for variety if you leave the selection up to your baby—within reason.

Food Reactions

Some vegetables may cause loose bowel movements or mucus in the stool. If so, omit that vegetable for several weeks, then try a very small amount of it again. Beets may color the stool or the urine slightly red, which is no cause for worry. You might have to discontinue spinach for a while if it causes chapping on the baby's lips or around the anus. Sensitivities to particular foods may show up as a face and neck rash, hives on the body, gas pains, or diarrhea. Be sure to consult the doctor about any reactions; some could be due to causes other than food sensitivity.

Your doctor will no doubt advise you to hold off on eggs till your baby is at least six months old—and even much older if you have a family history of allergy. Egg is more likely to cause an allergic reaction than other foods, and must be started cautiously (as explained on page 200).

Milk: The Staff of Infancy

The baby is getting an *almost* complete food in either breast milk or formula, but you should continue giving any supplementary vitamins the doctor has advised. Until the baby is eating a considerable amount and variety of solid foods, his diet may be short on some important nutrients. Most babies are now satisfied with breast or bottle feedings about four hours apart during the day and one in the late evening, before the long night sleep.

Breast milk and commercial formula are the two reliables in milk drinks for a baby. Milk is such a basic food in infant nutrition that no change should be made in the type your baby is taking without first consulting the doctor. Many nutrition experts advise that either breast milk or formula or a combination of the two should be continued for the whole of a baby's first year. Some, however, believe that it's acceptable to introduce whole cow's milk after six months *if* the baby is eating enough solid foods to supply sufficient vitamins and minerals. Skim milk is definitely *not* appropriate during the first year. Its low-fat content deprives the baby of sufficient nutrients for proper growth and development. Also, the protein and sodium content of milk is increased when the fat level is reduced, and this may put a strain on a baby's kidneys.

Up to now, breast milk or formula supplied the water the baby needs, except perhaps during very hot weather or an illness. As he takes more solid food, the extra bulk might make him thirsty occasionally. But don't flavor water with sugar; if he needs water he'll take it unadulterated. Let your baby take it from a nursing bottle. It's not a good idea to try water in a cup at this stage; such an uninteresting liquid could prejudice him against his first tries at cup drinking a little later on, when he'll be sampling juice or milk from a cup.

Homemade Baby Foods

If you wish to make your own baby foods, you'll want to invest in a "helper," if you don't already own one. Blenders are moderately priced, food processors are higher priced, but food mills—especially the made-for-baby-food models—will pay for themselves in a few weeks. Of course, this equipment, to a greater or lesser extent, will also be used in preparing family meals. Another helper, until you begin to use your own culinary creative talents, will be a baby food cookbook.

Canned fruits and vegetables are not suitable for making homemade baby foods, as they usually contain large amounts of sugar and salt. And, of course, no salt or sugar should be added to fresh or frozen foods that are being pureed for baby.

Sleep

Around three months of age, *some* babies begin to sleep an

unbroken eight to ten hours at night. Parents who have already started their baby on solid food often credit this extra nutrition with doing the trick. But studies have shown that diet additions have no effect on night sleep; milk "holds" a baby as long as cereal or any other food.

Changing Cycles

Longer stretches of night sleep parallel longer stretches of daytime awakeness. The baby's fuzzy, half-awake states have all but disappeared; now she's able to keep herself going in alert active play, with two or three naps to tide her over for a long sleep at night. Her sleep patterns are becoming much more predictable. By about three months, a baby begins to sleep in four-hour cycles during the night, cycles that include both deep states and light states. But she still may not be making easy transitions into deep sleep, and it pays to consider some of the factors that promote good sleeping.

A Contented Stomach

Although sleeping and feeding are no longer closely linked, as in earlier months, you have to make sure the baby is getting enough nourishment during the day to satisfy her for a twenty-four-hour period. A feeding schedule is important so that odd-hour hunger won't disrupt her sleep. If she doesn't wake up for the late evening or "10 P.M." feeding (which is whatever hour fits your own usual bedtime) you may be inclined to let her sleep on, in the hope that she's ready to give up that feeding. But chances are she'll need it later on and wake you in the middle of the night. It's best to keep waking the baby for a bottle or nursing until she's shown no inclination to wake herself for several weeks. Then give it a try. If it doesn't work out, start the waking routine again.

Meanwhile, make sure the baby is getting all the milk she needs during the day. If she's acting unsatisfied after a nursing, you may have to give more frequent feedings for a while to increase your breast milk. If she's bottle feeding, and draining every bottle, give her a little more formula at each feeding.

Easing Baby's Sleep

"Easy" sleep is also tied in with how the baby's caregivers feel about how much and when he sleeps. In the natural life-styles of some cultures it's all very simple. The baby is constantly with people, carried by his mother or tended by older children. At day's end he is within the circle of family and friends. He plays, eats, watches others, drowses. When he falls asleep, he's carried to bed. Bed is considered a place for a baby to sleep, not a place separated from the family for going to sleep. Since the baby's own rhythms and inclinations are followed, sleep problems are practically nonexistent.

By contrast, most American urban and suburban life-styles are quite structured, in some cases even regimented. Many households must accommodate adults' precise work and transportation schedules, and often after-work activities or obligations. If the baby's sleep-wake patterns are out of key with the family schedules that he's asked to comply with, hassles may be in the offing. Some babies, of course, are as amenable to scheduled sleeping as they are to scheduled feeding. But a live-wire baby can so resent being put to bed before he's had his fill of play and companionship that, in time, he fights against sleep even when he can hardly hold his eyes open.

Although unstructured living may be impossible, prevention and/or remedies for sleep problems may be simpler than you think. After a long afternoon nap, for instance, a baby can hardly be expected to feel sleepy at six or seven o'clock. Even though you can make good use of the time while your baby naps during the day, you may need to forfeit part of that freedom to ensure an earlier bedtime. A lot of daytime stimulation helps to stabilize the baby's sleep patterns. If his waking time has been dull, without enough attention or the kinds of playthings he can make good use of, being moved to the further boredom of his quiet crib may seem like real abandonment. All the hours of a baby's day have a bearing on how he accepts or reacts to bedtime.

The bedtime feeding should be calm and quiet, without distractions of bright light, voices, or surrounding activity. Most babies, even when they're tired, can't switch from the pleasures of social play directly to the quiet aloneness of a crib. They need a calming interval for gradual relaxing.

There's a reason why rocking and lullabies are timeless inducements to baby sleep: The rhythms of sleep are related to the rhythms of falling asleep. Influences that work on the senses in a repetitive way—movement, sound, visual effects such as "counting sheep"—are similar to the synchronized waves of sleep. The baby's rhythmic sucking in itself has a mesmerizing effect that pulls her into the lulling drift toward sleep. When a baby is helped to welcome sleep by a relaxing, soothing start, she's more likely to "contain" herself in sleep during the night.

But sleep is affected by many factors, including a baby's personality. Take the increase in energy that the baby is now putting into her play. Depending on her temperament, does she work toward new skills by patient practice, or get all stirred up by frustration; will an active day be pleasantly tiring and invite a good sleep, or key her up so much that it works against sleep?

Adults differ in these same ways in regard to sleep. Some persons are disturbed by new challenges or worries; they wake in the night, find themselves working over problems and unable to get back to sleep. Others can put daytime concerns aside when they go to bed and use sleep as a restorer of energy for tackling the next day's demands.

When a baby's night waking does occur, it helps to remember that there's always a reason. It may be a surfeit of sleep due to overlong naps during the day, or a prolonged habit of night feeding when she's outgrown the need, or too much stimulating attention in the night when she might shortly comfort herself back to sleep—all causes that are fairly easy to remedy. Occasional night wakefulness may be due to some household upheaval, a carryover from excess excitement, a discomfort such as teething, the strange "blankness" of a room when she comes fully awake in the dark. Who could possibly unravel all the reasons in the often puzzling but very real world of a baby's feelings?

Sleep "problems" are so labeled by adults. For the baby, they're disturbances that keep her from sleeping. The distinction is important. A baby is not aware of affecting her parents' relaxation and rest. When she can't sleep, she simply and naturally wants relief from her tensions. If she's given calm, commonsense support when she needs it, she'll develop more efficient sleep habits in time.

True, "in time" can seem hopelessly indefinite when your stamina and patience wears thin—even though you know that your own anxious, hurried attitude will get through to the baby and prolong her sleeplessness. There's a fine line between understanding and tolerance. This is where mother-father teamwork operates best. A change of caregiver will often clear the air and turn the trick. In any case, every parent needs respites from on-duty time with the baby.

Bathing and Dressing

One thing that doesn't interest the baby about his bath is getting clean. He's discovering that water can be a fine plaything. Splashing startles him, delights him, keeps him going with new surprises. You have to really hang onto your water baby now or he'll slip and slither himself into a head dunking. To make water an even better refresher, try a preliminary gym period.

Have a Baby Health Spa

All it takes to make a gym is a mat for the floor in the room where you bathe your baby. There he can give his muscles a good workout, without clothes or enclosures to hamper his freedom. And there he can enjoy some simple calisthenics as you help his body make movements that he can't do on his own. Lead him through each exercise slowly, a few times—but only if he likes it. Any that he doesn't take to at first you can try when he's a little older.

Arms: As he holds onto your fingers, slowly extend his

arms out to the sides, then slowly back, folding them across his chest. Unfold them, raise them slowly above his head, then slowly down to his hips. Now help him "box" in slow motion: holding his wrists, alternately push and pull his arms in front of his chest.

Legs: Holding his ankles, push and pull his legs in slow bicycling motion. Now press the palms of your hands against the soles of his feet; give alternate gentle pushes, and as he thrusts out each leg, give it slight resistance with your hands making him "pump" to keep his bicycle going.

Sit-ups: Holding his hands, pull him slowly to a sitting position. As his neck and back muscles gain strength, try continuing the slow pull upward to a standing position.

Knee-bends: Hold him in a standing position, his feet planted firmly on the mat. Lower him a bit and steady him as he pushes up to stand straight. Soon he'll turn this into rhythmic bouncing.

Jumps: After a few knee-bends or bounces, make his upward push a jump: Just as he comes up erect, lift him a few inches off the mat.

Stretches: On his back, slowly bring up his right leg and touch his foot to his left shoulder; then the left foot to the right shoulder. Gently roll him onto his tummy. Place his hands under his shoulders; he'll probably go naturally into the *Yoga cobra* posture, pushing up with his arms to raise his head and chest high off the mat. When he lowers himself, stretch his arms out to the sides; now he'll most likely assume the *Yoga open bow* posture, arms and legs out straight and lifted off the mat, back arched, rocking on his tummy with his outstretched arms for balance.

As you watch your baby exercising freely on his own, look for the movements he's striving to make, such as rolling from back to stomach or stomach to back. With a little gentle positioning you can help him learn new maneuvers, and discover the thrills of new achievements.

Dressing a Wiggleworm

After a workout in his gym and a cooloff in his bath, a

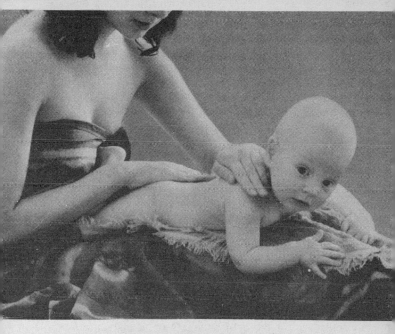

gentle body massage with baby powder or lotion may be a calming influence on your little athlete. But some babies never want to relax. If yours is an endless-energy type, and he's in training for rolling over, he can be more than two handfuls to manage. Once out on the flat firm surface of his dressing table, he's likely to start right in again on his practice routine—twisting, pushing his feet against you, flinging out an arm for a turning try. Sometimes it's hard enough just to get him into a diaper. But better not turn this into a wrestling match or you'll make each other mad.

Diversion is your best strategy. A baby's power of concentration is much weaker than his muscles or his love of fun. Try silly faces and noises to divert him, or give him a special plaything that you reserve just for dressing time. One thing that will probably work like magic is a wall mirror alongside the dressing table. Your baby stares at the baby who's staring at him, smiles when he smiles, is interested in every move his little copycat makes. A mirror captivates a baby for months, and no wonder—what could be a better toy than one that never stops interacting with him!

Outings and Travel

Even if you get your baby out of the house almost every day, and she sees people on the street and in stores, her main orientation is home. That's where she knows everyone's ways, their kinds of approaches, their voices and faces. Unfortunately, many persons in the outside world expect every baby to respond to their friendly overtures. When your baby doesn't, you just might be a little disappointed in her. After all, you'd like everyone to see her at her charming best. But try to keep your feelings where they're needed—in tune with your baby's feelings. If she cringes away, or simply gives an outsider a dumb glum stare, it's your right as protector to briskly move away, with a comforting hand on your baby. It's her reactions you need to consider, not those of strangers or acquaintances who may foolishly be offended by a baby's rebuff.

Parent Confidence

Sometimes parents need to shore up their own sensibilities—not let themselves be affected by strangers who appear critical or disapproving, either openly or in subtle ways. There are impulsive advice-givers who seem to assume that parents of a young baby know next to nothing about her.

Your strength is in the baby-parent unit, which outsiders can't know. It's a private place you can take with you wherever you go, with a special, important meaning that no one can touch. And it gives you a good feeling to let unwanted advice or opinions slide off you, and continue on your way. This is a big factor in the maturity a woman and a man gain from having children, whether they're under twenty or over thirty when they have their first baby. Being close to and responsible for a young life builds self-confidence that extends outward, and reflects back to foster your child's healthy outlook.

Visiting

Most friends, with a little prompting from you, will cooperate and give the baby time to feel at ease in their home. In strange surroundings, most babies spend a while quietly looking before opening up. If you keep the baby near you, she'll gradually overcome her shyness and "act like herself."

A baby is sociable, however, only when the spirit moves her; she wears no false smiles and puts on no airs of gaiety. If she doesn't feel like mixing, she's quite content to stare sober-faced at the goings-on around her. Unfamiliar people are interesting at a distance, but can spoil a baby's pleasure if they're overanxious to gain the response of a smile or a chuckle. When visiting, you need to follow your baby's leads and tactfully suggest to others how to do the same. Some people start right in with a boy baby, expecting him to like lively play. But personality knows no sex. Many boys are quiet and sensitive, many girls are outgoing and energetic. And few babies can tolerate a spirited approach away from home; they save their real fun for the privacy of the family circle.

But visits to other homes help to foster your baby's sociability and make it easier for her to cope with unfamiliar people and places. Try to take advantage of these months while you still have a stay-put baby. It won't be long before you have a crawler on your hands who can keep you jumping in an un-baby-proofed house.

These are the months, too, when mother and dad can more easily make nighttime visits to friends without arranging for a baby-sitter. While the baby is still little enough to fit into her cozy travel bed or bassinet, she can go to sleep before you leave, be transported (in her auto restraint if you go by car) and perhaps sleep straight through the visit, unaware that she's been away from home.

Car Trips

In suburban living particularly, shopping can seldom be done on foot, and the family car is in regular use, usually with the baby in tow. If his auto restraint is left installed, always on the ready, there's no temptation to take him along without it for a quick trip. Otherwise, the extra time it takes to properly install his restraint is your investment in your baby's safety.

The baby will no longer be sleeping peacefully through many miles of travel, and on a trip she'll need a few toys to fiddle with and chew on. As with all baby toys, no sharp edges, no small detachable pieces. Tie one or two toys on short strings (so short they can't wrap around the baby's neck) to his auto restraint—but no inflatables on strings that could obstruct the driver's road view. Take care, too, what you put on the rear window shelf—no breakable, sharp, or heavy objects that might fly off in a sudden stop.

It's not a good idea to change or add to your baby's diet on a trip. If he has started solid food, take along only the kind he's been having at home. And don't urge him to take one more mouthful than he wants. He may refuse even a taste; in strange surroundings, babies often feel "at home" at mealtimes only with a breast or bottle feeding. Keep in mind that at this age, milk or formula is all a baby really needs for good nutrition. If he's somewhat "off" milk also, give him more frequent, small feedings—but not in the car when it's in motion. Feeding a baby in an auto restraint, by spoon or by bottle, can be precarious in case of a sudden swerve or braking, not to mention an accident.

Changes in drinking water may upset the baby, so it's best to take along boiled water from home. On an extended trip, you can buy bottled water along the way. Even if your baby seldom drinks water at home, he may get thirsty in a warm car on high-temperature days. When you make rest stops, which should be frequent for everyone's comfort, try a drink of water, or milk if it's been quite a while since he's had a feeding.

Don't be surprised if your baby is out of kilter for a few

days after a trip. No matter how well he seemed to adjust to strange places and new friends, all that extra stimulation may catch up with him once he's back home. He may eat and sleep poorly, act clingy and whiney, cry more than usual. Just the fact that he was with you almost constantly enabled him to "bear up" under a lot of new experiences and to enjoy new audiences that doted on his charms. At home again, mother and dad get back into their own work routines, have less time for him, and he may have trouble coping with the change.

Adults, too, are often at loose ends after a vacation— tired, and finding it difficult to "get back into harness"— aptly put by some as needing a vacation to recuperate from their vacation. A baby needs time to adjust to the sudden loss of excitement, and the change to household quiet and normal schedules.

Any out-of-the-ordinary change or situation may have the same kind of effect. An interruption in the familiar patterns of living that a baby is accustomed to can result in a temporary setback. Regressions in behavior are natural, and trying to push a baby out of such states usually prolongs them. He needs emotional support to regain his self-confidence. Think of him as he was in his younger months, when he still asked for a good deal of tending and reassurance from you. Now he needs that same kind of "babying." If you give him that, while patiently helping him to rediscover his own interests and ways of amusing himself, he'll soon regain the independence and pleasure of relying more on himself again.

Other Caregivers

Unless you've found a tried and true baby-sitter who almost never lets you down when you need her (or him—a lot of boys are competing for equal rights on these part-time jobs), you're missing the outings you used to have as a couple. So you get in a rut, settle for TV, miss the movies or parties or whatever that used to broaden your amusements or your horizons. Most of all, you miss the freedom to be a couple together, like all the unencumbered couples you envision out there, strolling together or smiling at each other over restaurant tables.

Baby-Sitting Co-op

But how many *encumbered* couples do you know? Whether you live in a city, the suburbs, or a small town, it's a good bet that you have neighbors and friends who'd like the same chance to go out, including many who can't often afford the high cost of sitters. And simply because no one has done anything about it, all of you are sitting at home in your respective same boats. It may not be at all difficult to get an exchange system going and give one another evenings out. Talking to one parent leads to another. Why not invite a few over (bring the baby and kids!) and broach the subject of a parents co-op?

The plan's purpose is twofold: to have free-of-charge baby-sitting; and to have someone you know personally to "sit" with your baby. A parents' sitter-exchange can work something like this:

A half-dozen couples are supplied with cards marked off in four (or eight) parts, each division representing one hour (or half-hour) of time. These cards are the wampum for paying the sitter who comes to your home. Everyone is given a list of members' names, addresses, and phone numbers (including their children's names and ages). When you select a night to go out, in advance, you call from the list to find a mother or a father who's free and willing to come over. After you've paid out all your hours, you can't have the service until you earn back some hours by baby-sitting for someone else on the list.

Your co-op can grow, perhaps faster than you'd like, as other parents get wind of it. Experienced co-opers usually advise limiting the group to no more than ten or so couples. If your group is functioning well as it is, everyone may prefer to keep it to the original small size, adding other interested parents only as some of the founding group move away or drop out.

Small pools are usually informally organized, with an even-steven exchange of payment hours. But there may be instances where it's fairer to pay a higher rate; at one home it may be mostly "sitting," at another it may be playing with, reading to, or putting preschoolers to bed, or helping an older child with homework. But most parents don't narrow it down to specifics; the arrangement evens itself out through the different families you sit for and the circumstances on different occasions. Your own baby might need considerable attention from his sitter one time, and sleep straight through your absence on another night.

Depending on how familiar the various children are with the various parents, you might want to arrange some preliminary visiting. But these small co-ops sometimes grow naturally into family get-togethers, even though the original, and continuing, idea is to give parents free time away from their children.

There are benefits on both sides, for the children as well as the adults. Actually, it's a shortened form of the extended-family idea. In this parent-exchange version, the children periodically have affectionate care from surrogate mothers or fathers, become accustomed to their different ways, and share close friendships with them. The parents have an extended family of various-aged children to form warm attachments with, and they learn a lot from those other children. Taking care of a baby a little older than yours, or watching a baby and a brother or sister together, can give you some advance preparation for what may be ahead in your own family unit. It's a great feeling to have someone else's baby greet you with big smiles, or to hear your name happily shouted when you arrive to be a substitute parent for a few hours.

Men often participate as sitters. Being with other children is a change from "the same old routine" at home. And a man, being a change from the customary female sitter, is often a favorite with the kids. He may even fill a special need. Some co-op groups make an effort to include friends or neighbors who are stuck in a one-parent situation. The one parent is more often a mother; her baby or older child is missing out on close association with a father. Being a father substitute from time to time gives a man the satisfaction of knowing he's doing considerably more than sitter-service when he's with that child.

Everyone will agree that the basic considerations given any sitter should be followed: where to find all the baby's things; where you've put refreshments prepared for the sitter; where emergency phone numbers are listed, and the phone number where you can be reached. If the latter is not possible (you might not have a set destination and just want to stroll around for a while), then agree on a time to phone home. Mutual consideration and trust is what gives the parent co-op its special character. When you walk out your door, you're leaving your baby with a friend as well as an experienced parent.

Think more than twice before you join any large pool you may hear about. Some number more than seventy-five families and operate through a secretary who keeps the records and supplies members with names and addresses of the group. You're dealing with unknowns—a risky business. Also, there can be fly-by-nights in these groups who never repay obligations. A responsible teenager or senior citizen is a much safer person to depend on than a name from a large impersonal pool.

For Working Mothers—The Transition

Your maternity leave may be drawing to a close during this period, and you may be about to enter the world of working mothers. If you've found a good child-care arrangement, one you feel comfortable and satisfied with, you're starting off on the right foot. To help ease the transition, it's best to make a few trial runs. If, for example, you have an in-home caregiver, have her come a few hours each day during the week before you return to work. If you're using family day care, take your baby to the caregiver's home for a couple of hours each day.

This transition period can be emotionally bumpy. You may have feelings of ambivalence, pangs of guilt, even twinges of jealousy. All of these responses are normal, and you should be ready for them. It's important, however, to try not to transmit these feelings to your baby. If you act overly apologetic, your baby is going to sense your ambivalence. A confident yet loving leave-taking and homecoming are best for him and for you.

It's also important to have a firm routine with work schedules. A baby needs consistency in his care, and this extends to having his parents leave and return at the same times each day. It also means having a regular after-work family time. Studies of children in day care indicate that they sort of throttle down during the day, then go into high gear when they're home with their parents. It's as if they're reserving some of their energy to interact with their parents in a very intense way. There's no question that babies know their parents are special.

Pediatric Note

During this period your baby will complete the series of DTP and TOPV inoculations which were started at age two months (see page 127). These will be given at approximately four months and six months. The baby must have the full series of these inoculations to be protected against these particular diseases.

Chapter IV

Six Months to Eight Months

What to Expect

Coming up: sitting; more teeth; the cup; games; *action*. Now the baby gets all-over busy. His energy output has surged— and stays at high peak. He has much to accomplish in these months, physically and mentally.

How each baby works at his learning can make one seem quite different from another by this age. If yours is a studious type he'll still be spending a lot of time in quiet observation and tackling problems in a systematic way. If he's gung-ho on muscular work, his energy knows no bounds; he may learn to sit up or crawl or stand a month or so earlier than most babies. By now you know your own baby's personal style pretty well. But whatever his main bent seems to be, he's actually working in many directions. He has to, or he couldn't achieve the great progress that all babies make during this period.

Baby-Proofing

Expect your baby to need more freedom of action now,

whether he demands it or not. It's time to encourage free enterprise, and it's time to put your house in "baby order." How many more things there are to think about now! He can reach out for a tablecloth or a cord and pull a heavy object down on himself. He can snatch up someone's glasses or cup of hot coffee, grab a cat's tail, reach for the scissors. And who knows what he'll find, get into, put in his mouth, once he can scoot around on the floor. Survey the scene now and do all the babyproofing you can think of. It won't be enough when he finally gets into high gear, but you can be basically prepared, then add to your ideas for outwitting your baby's healthy curiosity.

Advance preparation is also an aid to habit forming— the habit of thinking where you lay things down or store them, remembering to close or lock certain doors and cupboards. On pages 287 to 289 you'll find a list of rules and reminders for baby safety indoors and out. You can't expect no-nos to protect your baby; and if you overuse them they'll have less and less meaning for him.

Equipment

The baby carrier-seat that you've probably been using for feedings becomes precarious now, easy for a sit-up baby to topple. He's safer in a sturdy high chair—*if* he's safely strapped in. Whether you buy or borrow a high chair, check these safety features: wide-stance legs for stability; a tray that locks securely and can't pinch the baby's fingers; no sharp or rough edges or sharp points; a combination waist and crotch strap that attaches securely to the chair itself, *not* to the tray. A waist and crotch strap keeps the baby sitting down and keeps him from sliding out, under the tray. The strap must always be used.

Any piece of baby equipment must be used correctly to be safe. The crib's mattress support must now be kept in its lowest position —another habit to form *before* the baby can stand. (The adjustable crib side should *always* be in the highest position, except, of course, when you're tending the baby.) Once the baby is learning to pull himself up to standing, crib bumpers should be removed as well as any large toys that could be used for climbing.

The play yard may now offer less than ideal space for the baby. There's not much roll-over room, and not far to go when the baby learns to propel himself forward or backward. And what about his visual life? He's oriented to an expanded world now, mentally as well as physically. The mesh of a play yard enclosure hazes his view of people and surroundings; that, too, frustrates some babies, making them feel imprisoned. Some psychologists frown on the idea of a play yard at any age. So do some parents. There's apparently no consensus among babies, since some will be wildly rebellious at this age, and others still tolerant.

These differences partly depend on parents' use of confinement. Timing—when and how long—has a lot to do with how many months a play yard can be put to good use. In the baby's younger months, it was a nice change of place from his crib. He wasn't yet into all-over exercise, and his short-range vision kept him interested in nearby toys. Then, too, he wasn't awake for such long periods as he is now. As with other kinds of confining equipment, overuse is usually what turns a baby against the play yard.

But you can discover those times when he likes it. For instance, an early-awake baby isn't always ready for starting the day in high spirits, but he'll usually resent staying in his crib. With just a diaper change, leaving on his pajamas, and a quiet nursing or bottle feeding, he'll often be satisfied to play calmly awhile in his play yard, and may fall asleep right there for a catnap with his toys. A tired baby in the evening may like to wind down in his play yard, in the same room with his family, till he becomes drowsy. During the day, even after a baby has learned to crawl, he'll usually accept around a half hour in his play yard when you're outdoors with him.

But even babies who are unusually placid about staying put—in any kind of baby equipment—should be encouraged to want to get out and moving. They need to learn how to use and enjoy their bodies, and feel the emotional lift that comes with exercise.

More Teeth?

By the end of this period your baby may have anywhere from no teeth to six. Although the first to erupt—the lower central incisors—come in around six months of age on the average, a *few* babies get them as early as three months or as late as twelve months. A few months after these first two teeth appear, come the teeth that give a bright new look to the baby's smile—the four upper incisors.

Teething bothers some babies very little, others a lot.

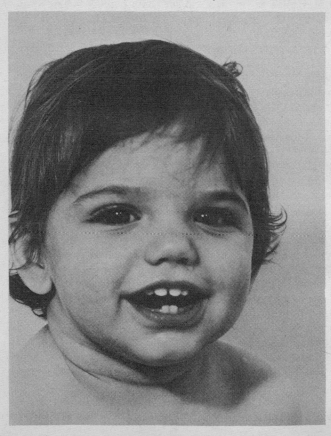

But there are all kinds of reasons for a baby being out-of-sorts occasionally, and one cause could be the beginning of an illness. That's the important distinction to make, so if you have any doubts, get in touch with the doctor. (For more on teething and tooth care, see pages 284 to 286.) As for chomping on things, most babies have enjoyed that pleasure for months back. The baby will be a little more vigorous about it now, so take care what he gets hold of and make sure his teething toys are in good condition. If he has annoying tingles in his gums, something to chew on at least acts as a soothing diversion.

Understanding Your Baby

Behavior

The wiggleworm is becoming a versatile performer. She can imitate an inchworm, hunching up in the middle and flopping down, to cover a little ground. She can belly-drag herself along, using her forearms as pushers and pullers. Sometimes she performs perfect push-ups, her body stretched straight and stiff as she balances on hands and toes. She'll rock back and forth on hands and knees, and pluckily recover from an overpush that pitches her onto her face. On her back she'll push with her feet, arch her body, and stretch her head back for a look at the world upside down.

With all these acrobatics, it seems that crawling should come easy for the baby. But crawling requires more than muscle prowess; it needs brain direction. Crawling is a difficult mechanism to work, actually more so than walking, since four separate parts are involved. The baby has to direct each arm and leg in proper sequence to propel herself in efficient, if jerky, chugging motion. Since bodily controls develop downward, the baby can't learn to direct her legs as soon as her arms and hands. Hence she first makes use of her upper body to move herself, with legs dragging uselessly behind for a while.

Sitting Up and Taking Notice

Having this temporary handicap, the baby gets busy on another maneuver—sitting without support. All the practice she's had in using her arms and hands has given her some balance mechanism. Now when you help her into a sitting position, she puts her hands on the floor between her legs to steady herself. But she shouldn't be left in this slumped position long; it's hard on the lower back muscles. As the baby gains strength and confidence, she stretches her arms

out sideways to hold a wobbly balance—while beaming you big look-at-me grins. There'll be spills; reaching for a toy, over she topples (and she'll appreciate a few strategically placed cushions). But she soon learns how to take the tumbles, curling her body ball-like and tucking in her head to save it from a bump.

When the baby can pivot her body freely to reach for toys, she may also bounce up and down on her bottom to move herself around. By this time she can get up there with ease; from her stomach she turns to one side, pushes with her arms, and pops up to sit solidly with straight strong back. Once the feat of sitting is mastered, the baby is quite nonchalant about it, no longer looking for praise—in fact, turning her attention to other important matters.

The baby's hands are still in the forefront of her activities. Give her any new object and she'll turn it and study it from every angle. She can transfer a toy from one hand to the other, and soon she'll be able to hold an object in each hand and whack them together. The more racket she can make, the better. A couple of pie tins can work her up to a feverish joy as she blinks and startles herself with every crash.

But the baby's interests range from excitement to quiet contemplation. One new interest is littleness. It's as though up to this time, the baby's eyes skipped right over any small things in her path of vision. She has been capable of seeing well since she was about four months old. But now she seems fascinated by tiny things. You'll find her staring at a particle of food, a tiny clump of lint, a bit of string, an unwary ant—and trying to poke or push these things around on the floor or her tray. There's no telling what she may find to investigate, so scan her surroundings well! This new eye work may well be a preparation or a catalyst for a new development in hand dexterity; very soon the baby will be able to use her thumb and forefinger to pick up tiny objects.

Mixed Feelings

The baby's perceptions have sharpened in many ways. The eighth month is generally considered to be the time when

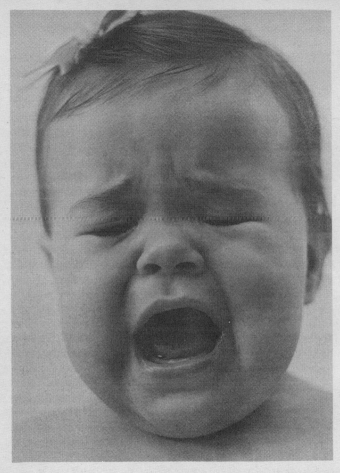

babies develop a real fear of strange persons. Yet, as with
all baby behavior, reactions are surprisingly individual. One
eight-month-old may shriek when a grandmotherly woman
comes close enough for the baby to discern that it's not *his*
grandmother. Another baby may sit in the lap of a depart-
ment store Santa, smiling, fondling his beard, and even cry
when he's taken away. A baby's fear of people may seem

quite capricious, giving you no chance to know what to expect. All you can do is abide by your baby's reactions and rescue her quickly whenever necessary.

You, too, may sometimes wonder where you stand with your baby. He'll alternately hang onto you and turn away from you. He is trying so hard to do things for himself that he may *seem* to reject you while you hold him for his bottle. He may be able to hold it well by himself, and even push your hand away. But what he is actually saying is that he wants "to eat his cake and keep it too." Even a baby who is strong on independence still wants the close body comfort that has always come with feedings. And he needs that even more than a less aggressive baby; being held for this always meaningful event reinforces the security he needs to do things on his own. Don't let your baby fool you; do let him feed himself this way if he wishes, but try to find time to hold him while he holds his bottle. Every baby can make good use of the love-rests that come with bottle or breast feedings.

Those poor toys, however, are really in for some ambivalent treatment—cuddled and caressed one minute, swung, banged, and flung the next. Even a favorite toy isn't spared a variety of experiences. What makes it a favorite is that the baby selects it—something very familiar to him—as a companion when he's upset, anxious, or sleepy. It may be a rubber frog or an old glove. It "ought to be" a soft cuddly animal or blanket. The "security blanket," in fact, has Webster dictionary status, as well as being a prop in a famous comic strip. But the baby who wants a "lovey" selects his own. He may become so dependent on it that he drags it around continually, or he may want it only as a going-to-sleep aid.

What a security object is, of course, is a substitute for the close parenting of the early months, a kind of comfort-insurance to ease the baby's transition from full dependence to the beginnings of independence. Many babies never become attached to any such comforter. Those who do may switch their affections from time to time, or keep the same one they started with for months—making it a bit difficult for parents to keep the thing looking reasonably clean and decent. Some parents think such object-attachment should be discouraged. But why? Are they revealing a touch of jealousy? A lovey doesn't mean the baby needs his parents any less; they're not "losing" the baby, just gaining a helper.

Mislabeling Baby's Behavior

A baby's behavior is often misinterpreted because it's put in an adult concept that the baby is incapable of experiencing. Sometimes an amusing label given to the baby's actions is covering very sensitive feelings that should be respected—for example, she's just "jealous."

Do babies this age experience jealousy? Not in the usual sense of the word. They have no sense of "mine," and they have only a fragmentary beginning in realizing themselves as separate persons. But by six months of age, babies have developed a strong attachment to parents, and they are now very vulnerable to separation from a parent. This accounts for the pitiful expression and crying that may overcome your baby if she sees you holding another baby. That other baby creates a definite separation, a barrier to reaching you—as well as changing the "normal" you that she has always known to a very strange you; it's almost as though you've suddenly acquired a frightening appendage! This kind of reaction is not a quirk to laugh about; it's an emotional shock that the baby should be quickly spared.

Twin babies, or close-together babies in a family, seldom show such reactions, although one of them may have become generally submissive to the other. A less demanding twin often acquires the habit of giving in to the other in matters of parent attention or toys—a situation that most big-family parents also have trouble trying to equalize. It's the "only" baby, conditioned to an only-child home, who may experience a real hurt when another baby takes her place in her parent's arms. She shouldn't be compared to the baby of a multichild family, and no one should make light of such feelings by mislabeling them "mere jealousy."

Learning

Advances in physical skills are easy to follow. You can see the effort and dogged determination when the baby is learning to roll, sit up, and move about. But what's going on inside the baby's head, what is he doing in those long, contented silences when he's asking for no attention from you?

Hand Business

Watch what he's doing with his hands, how he actually studies their actions. He picks up a toy with one hand, carefully watches that hand transfer it to the other, then back again—back and forth, demonstrating to himself that not only is the toy separate from himself, but that his two hands can act separately.

He picks up a small block, looks from it to another in front of him, picks up the second with his free hand. Now each hand is doing the same thing; he looks from one to the other. Can the two of them do something at the same time? Try it. He bumps the blocks together; they make a nice sound. He hits harder, makes louder clacks. The sounds excite him, he speeds up, misses, drops one, uses the other to keep banging away on the floor. Finally tired of that, he calms himself down by using the block for a chew-toy.

Gazing around, he spots a new item among his playthings, a wide-mouthed plastic carton. He drops the block, picks up the carton, turns it round and round, upside down, pats its closed bottom, turns it over, sets it down, sticks his hand inside its open top. Very interesting. If his hand can go in, can something else? Try it. One by one, the two blocks go in. Turn the carton over, out come the blocks. Pick up a block, bang it on the thing's bottom. It won't go in. Turn the thing right side up, in go the blocks again. Now, in and out, proving to himself the permanency of this discovery.

Clear the decks and give your baby a few wood blocks in two sizes. Does he look from one size to the other, pick up a small one, put it down, then pick up a large one and put it down, look from one to the other? It's clear that he's comparing size differences; and if he looks from one to the other while holding a block in each hand—a small one and a large one—he's also comparing weight differences.

All this elemental knowledge that we never give a thought to was *learned*—not taught to us. We learned bit by bit, added one snip of learning to another, expanded it through the years, until what each of us knows, without even thinking, would stretch—how many times around the earth? And here is your baby, just starting to fit his tiny mental pieces together. Could anything command more respect, admiration, parent-patience, than this nucleus of learning?

Sticks and stones and the simple accouterments of daily living are all that millions of babies have to feed their learning processes. Many come through the infancy period with remarkable faculties for getting along in their world; a few can advance into broader areas of life. But if you've ever seen the expression on a so-called deprived baby's face when he's given a colorful modern toy, you know what joy means in learning. While there's certainly no reason to go overboard on buying toys for your baby (an excess, in fact, is more confusing than helpful), a few well-chosen toys and safe household playthings increase his incentive to learn. Play = fun = learning is the only formula you need to satisfy your baby's thirst for knowledge.

Linkage Learning

The baby is not only putting two and two together now, she's adding many facets of information to make a whole. Because she is becoming more selective in her listening, she attaches meaning to certain sounds. She turns to look at the telephone when it rings, and obviously finds the sounds of adult talk interesting, for her babbling is taking on some adult intonations. She may alert to her own name and perhaps to a few other words. In very gradually learning that speech has meaning, the baby combines what she hears with what she sees and feels. It's the whole "setting" surrounding a word that gives it meaning for the baby.

The linkage of various abilities, trials and errors, and observations, combine to make many opportunities for advancing the baby's learning. She can solve simple problems. She can simplify problems. Sitting on the floor, she eyes a toy she wants. Reaching out her hand, it's still out of range. Then she notices, near her, the toy's attached cord. She pulls on the cord and voilà! she has the toy. Far more often than anyone notices, the baby is integrating mental and physical abilities to achieve a goal.

Some of the "wholes" a baby makes out of her experience seem really mysterious. How does she know these things? She hears the car on the gravel driveway, or footsteps on the apartment stairs. She stops what she's doing, waits, looks at the door expectantly, begins to smile or squeal or move toward it *before* it's opened—knowing this means the return of a parent. She does this only at a certain time of day! At other hours, she shows only mild interest in these same sounds. And if she's fooled, if some unexpected person appears, she looks puzzled, downcast, even a little embarrassed. This is a big mental advance; not only can the baby remember past actions of her own, she can recall a past *event* if it's one that's been regular and important to her.

The remarkable sense of timing that a baby develops during her eighth month is a facet of memory evolved from all the perceptions and happenings she's been linking together in her mind for a long time. Now it takes only a few cause-and-effect happenings for the baby to know what to expect of *some* things in her environment. Her sense of timing narrows down to such precision that she can anticipate the result of many of her actions. Pushing her feeding dish over the edge of her high chair tray, she blinks her eyes *before* the dish hits the floor, sensing the time interval between the push and the crash.

The thrill of creating loud noises and exciting disturbances impels the baby to try all kinds of ways to affect her environment—including the people who rush to the scene! Yes, a baby's learning involves a lot more than quiet study. So if you don't want to "cure" her learning, you'd better use prevention for some of it. Any moment she can barge into dangers or produce disasters.

Gestalt

There's another facet of memory that a baby acquires around eight months. Termed "gestalt," it's a mental perception of the whole of a situation or a place—an impression of the complete pattern rather than its separate parts. This kind of remembering does not involve analysis; it is simply experienced. Months ago the baby had a limited sense of this, when he differentiated a strange person's handling from your own. But now when he looks into a room, his memory of the whole as he last saw it makes him aware of any change that may have taken place. Perhaps a small table was moved to the opposite end of the couch, or a new chair was placed in a corner, and he looks around, puzzled. Or he may be aware of something that's missing—a potted plant that was on a windowsill—and he stares at the empty spot.

A baby's gestalt memory of a situation or a person may not only puzzle him but sometimes may make him uneasy. Entering grandmother's house has always meant a lot of happy activity. This time she's not bustling around; she's lying down, resting a turned ankle. She smiles, laughs, talks to the baby the same as ever. But the whole atmosphere is not "right"; his gestalt of grandmother and her house makes him sober up as though he's in a strange place with a strange person. The development of gestalt gives the baby a different and important kind of hold on the past—a memory for impressions that are apart from his own involvement.

As the baby's learning expands, you can't always tell what causes certain reactions or frustrations, or what he's accomplishing with each bit of activity or period of quietude. But if you try to keep pace with the rapid development of his mind, you can provide him with a great deal of "food for thought." You'll recognize what types of toys encourage different stages of learning, what kinds of people-play over- or understimulate him, and why he looks to you for both help and freedom to pursue all his new interests and abilities.

Parent-Child Interaction

All along, parents and baby have been affecting each other's behavior. Just for example: If you're an outgoing, enthusiastic person, your lively interest in your baby will have brought out similar responses in her. Even if she was a very quiet younger baby—at times a bit startled by your actions—by now she knows what to expect of you and reflects your delight in her; you've helped her discover qualities in herself that might otherwise have remained subdued. If she had a high-keyed personality to match yours when she was tiny, she's now a joie-de-vivre type that even you have a hard time keeping up with. She lives and learns by action,

loves an audience, and can even be her own—squealing her delight in her own antics.

Again, for example: If your personality is on the quiet, serene side, you've helped this high-spirited baby to tone down enough to spend part of her time in relaxed play and sensitive relationships with people. And with a baby who's placid by nature, like yourself, you've been in beautiful harmony, each of you profiting from all you've learned about each other.

Most people, of course, are a blend of traits that come and go, and both baby and parents learn to adapt to what manifests itself at different times. But even when there are decided contrasts in personality, a meshing takes place that generally satisfies both parents and baby in daily living together. Yet it's up to the parents to foster that; a baby only knows how to "act herself" until she's helped to find all the shades of personality that are in her.

"Acting oneself" is important in an adult sense also. Some new parents, feeling insecure, have a tendency to try to be "a mother" or "a father." They feel it's a role they should step into, and perform, in a special manner, however unnatural it feels. But parenting isn't a role to assume— it's an experience that has to be grown into. It becomes natural by living it. You've no doubt discovered that, however you started out. Being yourself—letting your natural personality guide you—gives the baby a genuine person whom she can respond to much better than to any "model" role a parent might try to acquire.

In any old-young relationship there's bound to be boredom or annoyance on either side at times. Fortunately, there's often enough contrast in the two parents to satisfy the different aspects of a baby's personality—or there are uncles, aunts, brothers, sisters, friends to give plenty of variety to the baby's relationships.

But the main thing that helps a baby to blossom in her own individual way is the on-going response she gets from her environment. If she has always had that, she has learned to trust people, and learned to be flexible. Knowing she can count on you, she can now pare down her demands on your attention. Be glad when you see that happening. A baby has to become more and more interested in herself to concentrate on all the intense developmental tasks that confront her. If it sometimes makes you a little sad when she seems to need you less, look at if from the baby's point of view. She's not growing away from you, she's growing because of you. You've given her the chance to grow by providing her with what she needed—including yourself—at every stage. And the more ventures she takes on her own, the more she needs you for backup.

Fun and Games

Completely together time is just as important as it ever was.

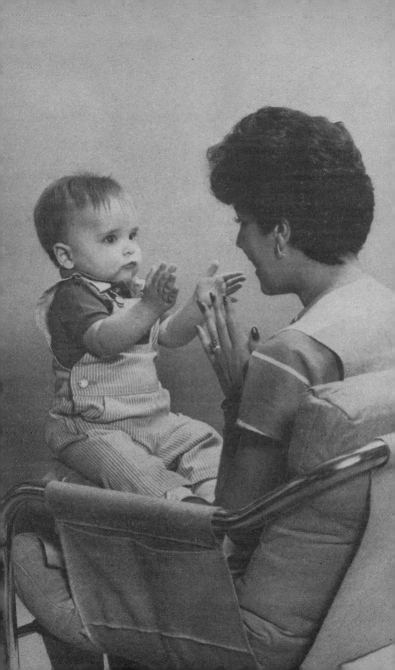

Some of it is tranquil, some of it is lively, and some fits in nicely with the kinds of things your baby is trying to learn.

Age-old nursery games are essentially the same all over the world, and key words in the songs that go with the action help the baby to learn that words have meaning.

Pat-a-cake starts by doing it for your baby, gently moving her hands in and out in rhythm to the traditional song. (Don't know it? It's high time to have someone teach you the nursery songs that delighted your infant ancestors for generations back.) With practice, the baby will be able to guide her own hands—with occasional missed contacts—and finally to know what to do when you simply say pat-a-cake.

Rock-a-bye-baby can progress from the rocking chair to open space, wide swinging and circling, along with the song. And you can taper off your flying trapeze to a gentle swaying "in the tree top"—a good way to make a transition from lively play to the calm that should come before bedtime.

Ride-a-cock-horse is an all-time favorite nursery game and verse. But have you ever wondered what a "cock" horse is? It's a rocking hobbyhorse, or a stick type that tots ride; but for now your knees will have to substitute. Make this an easy ride till your baby is a good equestrian. Then put a high finale on each ride with a pause on the last up-bounce, singing out the word that goes with it. Your baby will learn when that word is coming, open her eyes wide in anticipation, and shake with laughter when you come to a halt—then immediately start bouncing herself to ask for more.

Bye-bye is fun as a game, so long as it's not you who really means it. Your baby learns best when you're holding her and waving her hand to someone who's leaving. Soon she'll wave when you say the word. But don't be surprised if she waits till the person is out of sight; babies often have a delayed reaction and wave to a closed door.

Peek-a-boo has all kinds of progressive variations. First is your hands over your face, with the quick peek-a-boo when you, or the baby, pull them off. She likes this because she can see you're still there. And when she learns to hide her own face, she can peek through her fingers to see you. Then try a towel loosely draped over a mirror; slowly lift it up and let the baby find herself there. She'll probably poke or pat, maybe "kiss" herself in the mirror. After discovering herself a few times with your help, she'll learn to pull the towel off by herself. Another variation is a towel over the baby's face. Wait just a moment, pull it off, and give her the peek-a-boo greeting. Don't wait long, just enough to see if she'll pull the towel off herself. After a few games she may sit very still, waiting; you say, "Where's baby?" and get a chuckle or a squeal. She's fooling you now. But wait a little longer, without saying a word, and she comes out of hiding fast, looking surprised, but smiling her relief at finding you again. In the next version, you become the hider under the towel. Again, don't stay hidden long or you'll find a puckered up face instead of a smile waiting for you. You're too important a loss to be taken lightly— until the baby gets the idea that she can find you by jerking on the towel. In time she'll invent her own hiding games, sticking her head under a blanket or holding a scrap of paper over her face. And she may be swept into the height of excitement, playing the game with older kids who leap out of hiding with wild shrieks and roars—a version best kept under control.

Another kind of play with the baby that too often gets out of hand is tickling "games." Tickling can produce a lot of laughing, but it's not the best kind of fun; it's an involuntary reaction of the nervous system that doesn't need a mental connection to set it off. It's better to let your baby develop her own sense of humor, and laugh at what tickles her fancy. Lightly "walking" your fingers on her arm or leg is good for chuckles and giggles—instead of a wild laughing jag.

Back to Nature

While the baby is rapidly learning more about his environment, he's also learning more about himself. He's fascinated with what his hands can do; he's pleased with the new control over his body that lets him flip over and sit up; he pats his stomach, sucks his toes, rubs his face with a soft blanket, snuggles into your hair. Feeling and handling are basic pleasures; you like to see your baby enjoying himself in these natural baby ways. Do you have any feeling that some ways are not natural?

Now that the baby can sit up, he can see a part of the body that scarcely came into view before—the genital area. The baby may have touched it occasionally, but most of the time it was—and still is—snugly enclosed in a diaper, inaccessible to handling. Now when the baby is unclothed, here is this "new" part of the body to look at and investigate.

Touching and handling the genitals apparently gives the baby a new and special kind of sensation, at least a more pleasurable sensation than touching other parts of the body. It's a sensitive area that probably reacts to touch in a similar, though much milder way than an adult's stimulation of the genitals. Boy babies have erections since the first days of life, perhaps not noticed by parents because they often occur when hidden by a diaper—stimulated by a full bladder or urination; girl babies may have similar sensations, when being handled or dressed. So all that's new is that the baby can now make the pleasant sensation occur.

Unless it's a very deprived baby who lacks toys, attention, and freedom of action—as some babies in institutions do—the baby will not develop any dependence on genital play. It will simply be an occasional and brief interest. Only if it's interfered with will it become more important to the baby. It's amusing to see a baby discover the "belly button" hole and poke a finger in it. Suppose he was thwarted every time that happened. The forbidden spot would become so enticing the baby would go after it at every chance.

All present-day medical doctors and psychologists assure parents that genital play is natural and harmless in babies. Yet it may come as a rather significant surprise when you first see your own baby discovering this part of the body. Some parents are pleased, taking this as evidence of normal sexuality. Some parents have reactions ranging from embarrassment to serious worry. If you have any difficulty with your own feelings, search around in your past for old wives' tales you might have heard, or childhood experiences, and talk over these feelings with your spouse or doctor. This is an important area in parent-baby relationships; and this is the time to give "sex education" a wholesome start.

Give and Take

With your baby growing out of "little" babyhood, some of

her new behavior upsets the harmony you've established in young baby routines. Week by week she gets less placid about what you want her to do, more resolute in what she wants. Now you wonder what to do about controlling her.

The A-1, perfect, nonpareil, pure gold answer to that is: Nothing, except in life-threatening situations. This, of course, would require A-1, perfect, etc. parents, living in an out-of-this-world setup. Just in case you can't measure up to the requirements, the better question is: How can you control your baby's behavior without hampering her learning or spoiling her good disposition?

Here is this young, inexperienced person trying desperately to gather experience. And along with all her learning problems, she's got to contend with people, each of whom, from children to adults, wants her to conform to their particular view of things. Just when she's engrossed in figuring out how to tear pages out of brother's book, he comes along and snatches it away. When she's busy learning how to pound the loudest possible noise into the floor (right over a neighbor's ceiling) mother whisks her up and puts her in the high chair.

Certainly she'll sometimes get frustrated, stubborn, angry, for perfectly natural reasons of her own. And your reactions, also natural, dart back at her. You can't possibly understand or tolerate all of each other's behavior. But as the parent, you have a decided advantage; you're much smarter than she is. And she has a saving grace; she doesn't have *enough* mind of her own to know when her actions are being thwarted—*if* she's given consideration. A baby is so easily diverted that she's usually satisfied to settle for "this" instead of "that." But she's rightfully strong-minded enough not to give up "this" for nothing. An old magazine is as nice for crumpling as the latest issue. Hanging onto a couple of toys she's having great fun with makes a transition instead of a break when she's carted off for a bath.

It's not all so easy. If she's choking the cat, you rescue the cat. You don't stop to consider that your innocent little baby doesn't know what she's doing; your feelings are with the animal. And if your sudden brusqueness with the baby makes her cry, *maybe* she'll learn something from watching you gently pet kitty. If you're nursing and those pretty new teeth give you a sharp bite, you give a yelp and push her away. You know she didn't know she was hurting you, but your natural reaction tells her something, even if she cries. Then if you soothe her, but continue to push her away whenever it happens, she'll get the idea and learn to control her nursing to pure sucking action.

About Time

There's a lot going on in every parent's life, apart from baby concerns. But a baby thrives on short chunks of attention, the kind that is fully focused on him. He soaks in the feeling of belonging, of companionship, of your interest in his world. These pieces of time, when your baby knows you are truly with him, are worth far more than a long stretch of halfhearted attention. Even a diaper change is a chance for a little chat; you can talk to your baby about what you've got to do, what's on your mind, instead of having a faraway look in your eyes. Then he can let you go, and go back to his own affairs, because you've really been together.

For all a baby's action-packed hours, his time scale is uniquely his own. A minute can be a special drop of time full of intriguing possibilities. Now and then take a close look and maybe you'll see what he sees in it. Watch him as he considers a crumb on his feeding tray. His whole being alerts to this Moment of the Crumb. Is it hard, soft, movable, mashable? Can he maneuver his fingers to close in upon this thing? Can he somehow get it up to his mouth? When it's hurriedly brushed away, so is just a bit of your baby's learning.

Stop to think about it, and there's a lot of hurry that doesn't have to be. And when you too often snip off a bit of your baby's time, to save yourself a minute, sooner or later your snitching adds up—perhaps to a quick-tempered balky little baby who loses you more time than you've ever gained. So you get together about time as best you can, each giving up some to the other. There *is* an inequity, though. While you're learning respect for your baby's precious time, he has no conception or respect for yours!

Routines and Care

Feeding

Variety is the spice that perks up your baby's meals. She's adding foods that give her an almost grown-up menu. On first try, she may not find each one a taste treat, but if you don't push, she'll develop a liking for a wide range of foods. Follow the same procedure as when you started spoon foods—a few days' wait after introducing each one to see if it agrees with the baby.

The Valuable Additions

If you haven't already introduced strained meat, this will be the biggest change in taste, yet some babies take to it right off. If your baby doesn't, mix just a bit with a favorite pureed vegetable for a starter, then gradually decrease the vegetable while increasing the meat portion till she's used to the taste and will take meat plain. Select single-ingredient foods, then mix them, if need be, to your baby's liking. But try to accustom her to taking each food separately so that she'll acquire a taste for all foods.

Liver has excellent food value, but the strongest flavor among meats. If you don't fancy liver yourself, your baby may surprise you and not object to it at all. There's no accounting for tastes. Grandparents recall the days when babies took their daily vitamin D in straight cod-liver oil, and licked their lips over its flavor—a flavor so intense it makes most adults gag. It all depends on what a baby gets used to early in life. Older children and adults who like almost everything no doubt had a good start with a varied menu in infancy—as well as parents who didn't exhibit their own food dislikes!

When egg is started, only the yolk should be given, and this in tiny portions to test its effect on the baby. Especially in an allergic family, doctors hold off on egg until the baby is eight or ten or even twelve months of age, then if there is any reaction, discontinue it and try again several months later. Eczema is the most common form of allergic reaction in babies, usually breaking out on the face first in red, rough patches. Since the white of egg is the part most likely to cause an allergy, all babies are started only on the yolk, and this is prepared by mashing the yolk of an egg that's been hard boiled. A bit of milk can be added to soften it. Try no more than a quarter teaspoonful to start, and wait several days before continuing with very gradual increases. If you mix egg yolk with some other food for the baby, be sure that food is one you've tested out before.

Egg yolk is rich in iron, so it's well worth the trouble of preparing these tiny amounts until you know your baby tolerates it well. Finely sieved egg yolk is available in prepared baby foods too, but there'll be a lot of waste for a time unless you use part of it in some family dish. (It's a good addition to dressing for potato salad, for instance.)

Your doctor will probably okay introducing wheat cereal during this period. It was omitted before because of possible allergic reactions in younger babies. Wheat and oatmeal are the most valuable cereals.

You can also add some raw fruits: ripe pear or avocado, mashed soft; apple pulp, scraped from the halved apple with a teasoon; very ripe banana, mashed (the only fruit that can be given raw at the start of spoon feeding).

You can vary the baby's between-meal drinks. A number of juices prepared for babies are fortified with vitamin C, which citrus juices have naturally. If you squeeze and strain oranges for the baby, peel them first; peel oil is hard to digest. And since orange juice doesn't agree with all babies, it's best to start by diluting it with water, half and half, and decreasing the water gradually if your baby tolerates it well. Some babies like tomato juice for a change, but it has only half as much vitamin C as citrus fruits. If your baby is getting this vitamin in drops prescribed by the doctor, she doesn't really need the juices; but they're a good between-meal treat. C is one of the vitamins that's not stored in the body, so the baby needs it every day. And it mustn't be warmed; heat destroys this vitamin.

Three Meals a Day

Few adults adhere strictly to a three-meal schedule, and few babies can wait as long as five hours between feedings. When your baby is eating enough solids to plan them as meals, formula or breast milk will be "served" *with* meals. And it's generally advised not to give milk between meals; it stays in the stomach too long and may take away the appetite for solid foods. What to do? Trust your own judgment, of course—keep your baby's stomach satisfied.

Three meals a day is actually a loose term, meaning that the baby's solid foods are distributed in that way. It doesn't mean that the baby gets nothing else. Most babies need something between meals, and a light, wholesome snack is certainly legitimate—juice and a cracker being the customary suggestion. But "light and wholesome" can just as well be a pureed fruit or vegetable left over from a previous meal. If your baby can't hold much at one time, don't worry about whether he's getting a rounded out, "balanced" meal every time. Take it easy about reaching that three-meals milestone. Some babies do better on a four-meal schedule of solids for a while. Just avoid clumping everything together into one big stuffy meal, and carrying on through the rest of the day with only breast or bottle feedings. They don't count as "meals" anymore.

As in the earlier months, the baby's customary hunger hours are best left to self-regulation. You may find he has a big appetite for lunch only three or four hours after a good breakfast, and wants only a light supper five hours later. Or he may want his biggest meal in the evening. What time he wakes up in the morning or goes to bed in the evening, when he takes his longest nap, how he occupies the rest of his time, all affect his hunger rhythms. If the baby's life is running on a consistent schedule, he'll soon settle into regulated mealtimes. That's good for his system and for your convenience.

Milk consumption will probably go down somewhat when the baby is well into an expanded diet. If he's averaging less than 24 ounces a day (including the bedtime nursing or bottle, if he hasn't dropped that) give him most of his bottle before a meal. If he's breastfeeding, you can pretty well judge how much milk he's getting by the length of time he nurses; by this age, babies are sucking for food, rarely for pleasure alone. If he doesn't seem to be getting enough, talk to your doctor about supplementary formula. Babies shouldn't be short-changed on milk; it's a valuable food they continue to need, no matter how many other foods they're taking.

Cup Tactics

By six months it's time to start the baby on cup sipping. She won't really be drinking yet, because it takes quite a while before a baby can manage consecutive swallows. The purpose of using a cup is to promote the idea that nipple and spoon aren't the only way of getting something good. But that something had better be juice at first. Most babies don't like to fool around with their precious breast milk or formula. It has always come by nipple; it "belongs" to a nipple; they don't want to be tricked out of that natural fact of life. So you start with a little juice in a cup. At first you'll have to guide it, but let the baby hold on to your hand or the cup if she tries. It may not be long before she's taking juice quite nicely this way.

Now your baby *may* go right on to milk in a cup. "Most" babies aren't your particular baby, and it's certainly best to expect any innovation to be smooth sailing. But just in case she's opposed to this one: Give your baby her empty cup to play with during the day, when you can be nearby with a cup, too, drinking or pretending to drink from it. Call any available children in for this; babies love to watch everything other children do, and the kids are delighted when a baby imitates them.

After a while, set the baby's cup—with a quarter-inch of formula or milk in it—on her feeding tray at mealtime. Have a cup of something yourself, and now and then take a sip from it. If she reaches for hers you'll want to shower her with praise. But don't. That could startle her out of the concentrated effort she's making. What follows will probably be an upside-down cup, well examined and tasted on its handles and rim, its contents now a nice little puddle for the baby to smear around with her hands. Fine. She's interested.

Sooner or later she'll get the cup right side up to her mouth, splatter its contents on her face, maybe choke on the first gulp that goes down. She won't mind that at all—if you take it casually, with just enough praise and smiles to let her know you're proud of her. After this first success, resist the temptation to hand her the cup during a meal. Simply set it on the tray from time to time so she can practice when the cup spirit moves her. (Leaving it there is courting continual messes.)

Once the baby has decided that milk from a cup is pretty good, she may or may not want you to help her drink it that way. Follow her inclination on that. And depending on how much she takes from a cup, you'll know when you can eliminate a bottle or a nursing at mealtimes.

Learning to drink from a cup doesn't necessarily mean that your baby is being weaned. Many nursing babies change to part-time bottles. And there's no real virtue in early weaning. Whether breast- or formula-fed from the start, giving up the bottle completely is usually a difficult and slow process, often ranging well into the second year.

But meanwhile, cup drinking serves a very important purpose. It encourages the baby to do things for herself, gain a sense of separateness that builds her self-image and her ability to strive toward independence. That, too, is a very slow process. Most babies want a bottle or nursing at comforting times long after they're efficient at cup drinking. A baby shouldn't be hurried out of nipple attachment. It's the link to her earliest security and pleasure in life.

The baby has an easier way, too, of finding self-satisfaction with food. She can hang onto a piece of dry toast or a teething biscuit and gum it till it's reduced to a soggy mess. She can't yet use her finger and thumb in the "pincer grip" to pick up crumbs, but she can palm a bit that falls off and maybe get it into her mouth. These things should be given to the baby only when she's sitting up; lying down she could choke on small chunks.

Sleep

Sleep needs are so individual in all persons, babies and adults, that no one can say how much any particular baby *should* sleep. Too many babies don't fit the "average." One goes to bed at 6:00, sleeps through the night, and welcomes long naps; another goes to sleep at 10:00, wakes up early, and takes only short naps during the day. But *when* your baby sleeps is pretty well set by now. These sleep patterns are partly self-made, partly family-made.

Changing Sleep Patterns

If you're away during the day, you may have accustomed your baby to a late bedtime hour in order to spend time with him in the evenings. You may not have "an" hour, just be following your baby's inclinations, and transferring him to his crib when he falls asleep or when you want to go to bed. But if something comes up that makes it more convenient to put him to bed earlier, he can't be expected to accommodate you by docilely changing his habitual time for sleep. It might help, if you have a daytime at-home caregiver, to ask her to cut down on nap sleeping time when you need to change your own schedule on occasion. But that can't be expected of day-care center attendants or even a family day-care mother. And in any case, to suddenly interfere with a baby's accustomed sleep habits usually doesn't work. Deprived of naptime sleep, he may get overtired, nervous, cranky, and be all the more difficult to put to bed at night.

But changes in the baby's sleep patterns can usually be made smoothly if you go about it consistently and gradually. He won't notice a difference of ten minutes or so each day in the time he goes to bed for a nap or at night. If you want to shift him to an earlier bedtime, for instance, count on about two weeks to accomplish a two-hour change. And shift other routines accordingly, to fit the pattern in progress—move back morning and afternoon naps, mealtimes, and bathtime, as well as going-to-bed time.

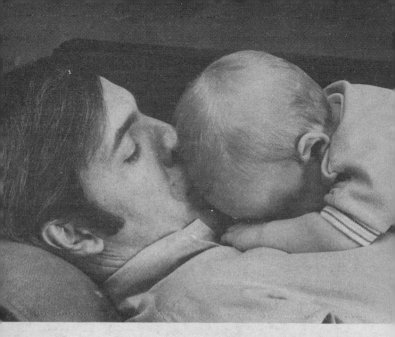

If at first it's hard to terminate family playtime in the evening, try to arrange for it to taper off. Let the baby stay with the family, but with no one entertaining him. It might be a good time to get dishes done, or a letter written, or for story reading with older children. The baby may then be willing to trade this calming down—even boring—period for the comfort of his crib. And he may be asleep before he gets there if you've dressed and diapered him for the night so that he doesn't have to be disturbed.

The Sleep Resister

But what about the baby who's a chronic bedtime resister? He may have gotten that way because of some upset that interfered with sleep, or because for months back, no fairly regular bedtime was ever set for him. Now he's staying awake till all hours, demanding attention, giving his parents no time to themselves. They're finally fed up with the situation; they want to change it. But how?

It's often advised to make a baby's bedtime *your* decision—to be pleasant but firm, consistent and decisive when you put him to bed. This may work nicely with a baby who's used to following routines, or one who's content to play awhile alone in his crib and then fall asleep. But a baby who isn't, and who resists sleep, can pester his parents for hours.

In a difficult case, it's advised to ignore any amount of protests, not even look in on the baby, however long he cries. This easy-come advice is always accompanied by the promise that after several nights of screaming for you, the baby's bedtime problem will be solved. (Meanwhile it is hoped you can handle any alarmed neighbors.) The same method is often advised to break the habit of waking and crying for attention during the night.

Perhaps some parents can do this, and perhaps it will work. But many parents can't bear the thought of this method. They've spent months building up their baby's confidence in them, making themselves his security in this world. How can he understand this sudden break in the sympathetic attention he's used to?

He can't understand it, he can't reason out the why of any sudden change. His reactions at this age still tend to be "raw" feelings—in this case, intense frustration and anger. What he succumbs to—if the treatment works—is exhaustion that ends in sleep, and "conditioning" that may lead to subsequent conformity to his parents' wishes—in this particular matter. But will it teach him anything about conforming in other situations?

The cry-it-out method is an ordeal for any caring parent. And what is it for the baby, what is he going through during this several nights' "lesson"? Will it have any lasting, hidden emotional effect? No one knows. Your opinion on that is as valid as any expert's who offers the advice.

Perhaps the most important considerations are whether you want to pit your will against your baby's whenever you're at loggerheads with him; whether strong-arm methods are really necessary, except in instances of real danger; and whether you can get yourself out of the bind you're in through nondrastic, gradual methods.

Babies do adjust fairly easily to changes in handling. An experienced baby-sitter may have no trouble putting a "difficult" baby to bed; or a father who's not in the least harsh about it may get more cooperation from the baby than his mother does—in both cases simply because their handling breaks a cycle of timid, "expecting-trouble" handling. Indecisive and inconsistent care of a baby can prolong a troublesome habit and slow up his progress in adjusting himself to family life. It's far better for a baby to learn, little by little, what's expected of him than to have to cope with haphazard impatience and irritation when a parent's "fed-up" feelings suddenly erupt.

Parents' Rights

But parents' feelings have to be considered too—all kinds of feelings. Don't think you're a weak parent if you prefer to let your baby take her time in outgrowing her dependence on you. Those going-to-sleep cuddlings and night-waking soothings can be as important to you as to your baby—part of the largess of parenthood. You needn't be deprived of babying your baby, no matter who says it's time to stop. Maybe, even subconsciously, you know about night feelings from childhood experiences of your own. So long as you give your baby the freedom and the encouragement to explore all her other avenues of "growing up," she won't be held back by loving attention.

By the same token, try not to feel that you "owe" your baby for the privilege of being away from her, during daytime hours on a job, for instance. That attitude can interfere with your commonsense judgment and change the way you would otherwise be handling her routine care. You'll, of course, be making some compensation. Babies naturally cling to their parents more after an absence, especially during a transition period of adjustment to new caregivers. And you shouldn't let one of those intimidate you with remarks or insinuations that "She never acts like that with *me*." Your justifiable answer is "I *mean* more to her." That says it all—why a baby clings to the persons who've been closest to her from the beginning, and why those persons can tolerate a considerable amount of clinging with little resentment. Neither parents nor child would willingly let their bond be weakened.

But what about this thing of resentment if it does crop up? That's another feeling some mothers (or fathers) have to deal with. You may never have felt it to any extent. You may keep it under cover, or be able to keep it under control. But suppose a time comes when it really hits you.

You're tired, you've been going hard all day, on your job or doing the housework and tending the baby. You've still got things to do before you go to bed, and you'd like nothing better than some peace and quiet for yourself. The baby seems to want just the opposite for you. She won't go to sleep, no matter what you try. Your energy is at low ebb, your nerves are wearing thin. Still—resent a dear little baby? But, of course, you do! Only a bona fide saint wouldn't.

At such times you may wonder why you ever let yourself get into this parent role; who dreamed up this idea of all-enduring motherhood; why doesn't somebody give you a break. Certainly somebody should. Husband, grandparent, sister—someone ought to be there when you need a stand-in. It's all very well to be advised (as it often is on a printed page) that mothers should "get away from it all" now and then. But what ought to be often isn't.

So what do you do about resentment? First of all, admit it, with all the vehemence you can muster—out of sight and earshot of the baby! That actually gets some of it out of you. Call up a friend, preferably one who has a baby, tell her you want to sound off, does she have time to listen. If she does, and if she's normal, it's an invitation dear to her heart; she knows what you're talking about and she probably has plenty to talk about herself, along the same line. She may even have some useful advice. But the funny thing is, these conversations usually veer off to far-removed other topics. By the time you cradle the phone, you're smiling over some tidbit of gossip, or the prospect of something to look forward to in the way of a break.

And miraculously, there's your baby, curled up asleep in her play yard where you left her fighting off sleep with that endless perseverence that drove you to truly resent her presence in your life. And you melt at the very thought that you have her.

And that's just it. That's what resentment of a baby amounts to—temporary indignation toward her because she's monopolizing you when you need a respite from any kind of interference with yourself. That's why resentment must always be hidden from a baby or child. Not to be wanted, even temporarily, is hard enough for an adult, but a devastating feeling for a child, who can't possibly understand what may be behind it. Analyzing it, for instance, you may find that you're transferring feelings you have about another person, or a situation, to the baby. Watch out for that; it's a treacherous field that no baby should be dragged into.

Reassuring Your Child

Another thing to question is whether your baby is defying sleep, or whether at times he *can't* sleep. During the second half of a baby's first year, it seems that by all rights he ought to be sleeping well. Colic is long gone, feedings are spaced out, and he's capable of long stretches of sleep. Unfortunately, that culprit teething may sneak in and spoil the scene.

Between six and eight months, *some* babies are cutting as many as six teeth. There are wide differences in how babies are affected by teething. But even when a baby shows little discomfort during the day, he may have trouble going to sleep at night. Rocking him, you can almost put yourself to sleep before his head is heavy on your shoulder, you're sure he's "ready," and you gently put him in his crib. A few minutes later he's wide awake and crying.

Yet if you let him stay up in a lighted room, he's content to play quietly, not asking for any attention. His eyes droop from time to time, he jerks awake, and goes on drowsily handling toys. Not until he finally slumps down and completely "out" will he stay asleep when you carry him to bed. Why wouldn't he go to sleep in his crib?

If you've ever had a toothache, even a mild one (or a burned finger or the like) you know how it nags at you when you're trying to go to sleep in a dark, quiet room— though it hadn't seemed so bad earlier, when you were with other persons, or busy, or interested in TV. It's being alone in the dark with a persistent throbbing or little intermittent shooting pains that makes even a small hurt loom large and impossible to ignore.

Granted that there are many other reasons for a baby's going-to-bed difficulties. One is wanting to be with you. If that seems simplistic, compare it to feelings you've had when someone dear to you is leaving for a time, even though you know he or she will be back. A baby can't look ahead. Sometimes, especially if he's been through some absences from you, every leaving is hard for him. Even going to bed is a detachment.

Certainly, ordinary separations from you are not traumatic. But the second half of the first year is a vulnerable stage for many babies, when emotional attachment to parents is especially strong—for the very reason that the baby is reaching away from them to develop independent abilities.

At some point you want your baby to be able to handle routine happenings without any fuss. Yet you want to be sure—does he really need you, or has he developed an unnecessary habit of hanging onto you? You can give him the benefit of your doubts by making concessions. And those concessions can help him to overcome bedtime reluctance.

Darkness makes some babies uneasy, alerting them to what they're missing instead of soothing them into sleep. Try a nursery lamp. A soft glow of light dispels the cheerless feel of a room; and if the baby is willing to play awhile with crib toys, he needs some light to see what he's doing.

Try soft music—a cassette of tunes or songs that keeps to a steady volume. Radio music hasn't the same mesmerizing effect; it's interrupted by talking and sudden changes in volume.

A really anxious baby needs to be sure you're still there. Try going quietly in and out of his room, not speaking to him, just going about some natural chores of folding a few clothes, putting things away in drawers. If whimpers begin after you've left, don't let them crescendo into crying. Repeat your little act, busying yourself very quietly, still not talking or looking in his direction. If necessary, sit just outside his door, where he can see you, reading or writing a letter perhaps. Through all this he'll be watching you, somewhat puzzled that you're paying him no attention, but assured that he hasn't "lost" you.

This kind of silent treatment has a much more calming effect on a nervous baby than sporadic attention. Close attention, even a few words or pats, raises his hopes of being picked up. Left to himself, but not "deserted," lets him relax—which is usually all that's needed for sleep to take over. And usually only a few nights are needed for this kind of subtle reassurance to get a baby over a nightly resistance to sleeptime.

Bathing and Dressing

It's not likely that your baby is spending her bathtimes placidly anymore, daintily dabbling in the water. And you must be tired of mopping up after her bath. So as soon as she can sit steadily, it's time for the family tub.

Safe and Sure Fun

But this is a big body of water, frightening to some babies when they first survey it. You might want to use your baby bath inside the family tub for a while; then she'll feel "at home," and all the splashed water will go down the drain. A baby bathseat is a big help; it suction-fastens to the tub bottom and has a safety strap to hold the baby in. If she takes to the family tub right off, be sure to seat her on a rubber mat. Whatever arrangement you make, don't leave her alone for a second. If she topples over and can't quickly

right herself, she can easily inhale water that's only an inch in depth.

Until the baby is used to being surrounded on all sides by water, it should be very shallow. An inch or two is plenty for getting her clean, and for play. Water itself is the main plaything, but a few bathtoys help to keep her occupied while you wash her. On that score, a baby this age doesn't differ from a newborn. A soapy backrub feels good; a face washing is still an intolerable nuisance. The wet washcloth, however, has high status among playthings; it's great for batting the water, flinging and recovering, and most of all for sucking.

As the baby gets braver she'll want out of any confining

seat. And as you add a little more depth to the water she'll discover its buoyancy and the slippery, slithery fun she can have. She'll want to try some of her dry-land stunts, flipping onto her stomach, trying to scriggle around, reaching for toys that go shooting away. Watch that she doesn't get near a faucet. (When filling the tub, always run cold water in last so that the spout isn't hot to the touch.)

Courage grows fast for most babies, and they have no experience to warn them of danger. In the midst of fun, even a slip that gives a head dunking rarely daunts a baby. But the sides of a tub can give bumps, and it may take only one hard one to frighten the baby off from the family tub for quite a while. Be right there on guard every moment.

There's one fear that many babies have—the sound of water going down the drain, and the feel of it, too, swishing past their body as the tub empties. If your baby seems frightened at the end of a bath, that's probably the reason. Take her out first, and come back later to empty the tub. Even if you're holding her, wrapped in a big towel, she may be afraid of that sound and resist getting into the tub the next time.

When a baby does remain timid of bathing in the big tub, there's a quick-fix remedy. Take a bath with her. Holding onto you, or just propped against your body, saves her the anxiety of being alone in all that expanse of water. Soon she'll welcome an older child as a bathmate. Just be sure it's one old enough to know how to play gently—no water tricks like face splashing. You'll probably be surprised, though, to see how fast the baby gains courage and plunges into some high jinks of her own.

Family tub baths for the baby aren't going to be as easy for you as the stand-up kind at tabletop height. You've got to be right down there next to the tub, doing safety duty while the baby has her fun. A foam cushion to spare your knees is a good investment.

Clothes for Action

Knee and leg protection is a clothing need for your baby

now. Long pants ease her workouts on the floor as she's practicing rollovers, rocking on hands and knees, maybe hitching forward or backward.

Stretch fabrics are for freedom of movement, but clothes are not meant to stretch beyond the *baby's* stretches. Pajamas and jumpsuits with feet, in particular, can be uncomfortable and hamper free movement if they're only a bit too short. Shoulder to crotch length should also be checked regularly so that the addition of a diaper doesn't make the garment tight-fitting. It's always better to buy clothes with room for growth. Something that fits just right when you buy it will have a short use-life—the reason so many mothers have hand-me-downs to offer that look like new.

By this age, babies usually decide that sunhats, winter hats, all hats are for jerking off. It's a fun game you don't always want to play. So get the kind that snap or tie under the chin; even those may not be foolproof. But you have to make sure a hat isn't really uncomfortable. Check that the chin strap is loose enough, and that there's no pressure, particularly on the ears or forehead, and check inside for any scratchy places.

Feel the inside of shoes, too, for any irregularities; and the toe when the shoe is on, for ample length. Only all-over soft shoes ("crib shoes") should be worn by a baby under walking age, and these must have room for foot movement and growth in both length and width. Check socks, too, to be sure they're nonbinding and at least a quarter-inch longer than the longest toe. A baby around this age may outgrow shoes in a month—all the more reason to forgo them for the healthful practice of barefootness. Bare is best for baby feet except when shoes are needed for warmth or dress-up. Otherwise, unrestricted exercise and air circulation keep the baby's feet healthy and happy. And she shouldn't be deprived of those ready toe-toys for grabbing and sucking.

Outings and Travel

Front carriers are out; back carriers are in. The baby no

longer needs head support; now he needs back support for the piggyback rides he takes with mother or dad. While a stroller is limited to fairly smooth terrain, a back carrier can go anywhere a parent chooses. Vacations with a baby may include sandy beaches, mountain slopes, cobblestone streets. Any-day trips may cover window shopping, crowded store shopping, bookstore browsing. Parents with babies on their backs are common sights in foreign countries as well as among the residents of your own neighborhood. Many parents like to backpack the baby because he likes this kind of riding and because it's an easy piece of equipment to take along anywhere.

Carrier Safety

When selecting a back carrier, check for these safety and comfort features: sturdy materials with strong stitching, especially at stress points; leg openings that are not constrictive; a well-padded covering over the metal frame near the baby's face; no sharp edges and points or rough surfaces; wide well-padded shoulder straps with secure rings and latches; a safety waist belt so the baby cannot fall or climb out.

There are also some precautions for using a back carrier. Always fasten the baby in with the safety belt. In addition, to minimize any chance of his falling out, make a practice of bending from the knees when you lean or stoop. Take care where you walk or "park" yourself. Your baby is now an active reacher and grabber. Outdoors there are thorny branches and poisonous leaves and berries. In stores, the stacked up displays of merchandise are particularly hazardous. With your baby in a back carrier, always remember that he's behind you, where you can't be sure what he's up to—"shoplifting" maybe!

In the Car

When your baby can sit well without support, he can ride facing forward instead of rearward. If you have a "convertible" auto restraint, adjust it to the forward-facing upright position. Most restraints are of this type—designed for use by both infants as well as older babies and young children. A rearward-facing infant auto restraint is not safe for babies weighing over 17 to 20 pounds. If you have this type, keep check on your baby's weight and, when it's time, change to an auto restraint that will carry him through toddlerhood. Information on selection, installation and safe usage of child auto restraints is given on pages 73 and 74, and travel tips on pages 116 to 121 and pages 168 to 169.

Other Caregivers

By the end of this period, the baby may protest being left with a sitter—the same one she's known and been happy

with for months. The minute she sees you put on your coat, she may begin to whimper and you may have to leave hearing her crying after you're out the door. It won't last; she'll shortly be busy and satisfied with her own affairs, as you will be with yours.

Day-Care Evaluation

If you're working parents and your child-care arrangement is working out well, you may be giving it less attention than you did in the beginning. But continual evaluation is necessary. The success of any day-care arrangement needs your thoughtful participation. The more involved you are, the better the care will be.

On-going communication between parents and caregiver is essential. Try to make time each day to talk with the person who is caring for your child. This may be easiest if you have an in-home caregiver or if your child is in a family day-care home. At a group center, it's important that you speak as frequently as possible with the person who has primary responsibility for your child. A good day-care center encourages parental involvement and regular meetings between staff and parents. And whatever type of child-care arrangement you have, do drop in occasionally to see how baby and caregiver are getting along.

Pediatric Note

During the second half of this first year, most pediatricians see their well-baby patients every two months instead of at one-month intervals as before. If your baby has had all his required immunizations so far (the third set was at six months) the doctor won't be annoying him with more shots until he's fifteen months old, although a tuberculosis test will be done at one year.

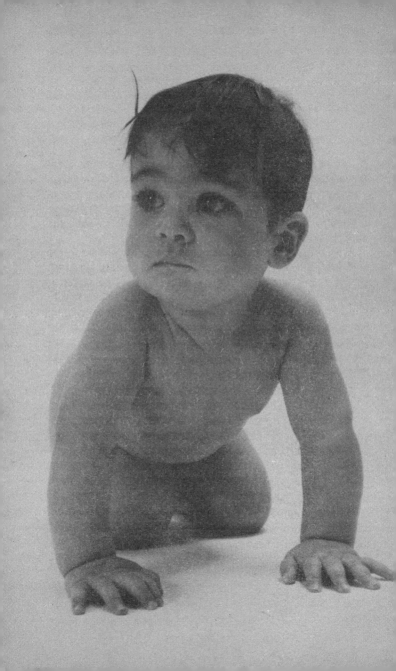

Chapter V

Eight Months to Twelve Months

What to Expect

Better get ready, get in trim, jump out of bed and into warm-up exercises every morning. Your baby is on the go! Whether baby care has seemed easy or hard so far, from now on it will at least be different. Keeping track of a mobile baby is a whole new scene. And the scene is irresistible to the baby. The box your little Pandora opens is chock-full of curiosity, whose offshoots are without end. If you think you've done everything possible to babyproof your living quarters, your baby will quickly show you what you've missed. She can ferret out fascinating things in the farthest corners. Your eyes and ears have to be open whenever she's on the loose. She'll often bypass toys for more novel items of interest. But if you've stocked certain cupboards and closets with can-have things, eliminating the important or dangerous, you can keep a good deal of her investigation within safe bounds.

Hares and Tortoises

During these months there are wide differences in how babies get about. These differences can make one baby *seem* much older than another. But the one who is concentrating on bodily skills may not be so interested in other kinds of endeavor, such as solving mental problems or gaining an understanding of speech. Hidden accomplishments don't get the attention and admiration that action does, but a baby who is "slow on her feet" may be very busy in her head.

You'll be naturally proud when your baby learns to crawl or stand or walk. But if you know a baby who's been walking for a month, and your baby has yet to take a step alone, don't succumb to envy or worry; your baby may be beating that baby when they're both racing into kindergarten together, and yours may be winning in other ways as well. Let her know she's a winner, whatever she can do and whenever she reaches any milestone.

Many factors combine to make one baby faster or slower in motor skills: how much freedom she has for practice—and has had for months back; what kinds of activites are encouraged or curbed; her natural tendencies and style in learning; whether she's outgoing or self-contained in personality; whether she's overweight or lean and lithe. Even the living quarters may make a difference in how a baby chooses to direct her energies. After she learns to pull herself up to stand, a small apartment may encourage cruising—stepping along from one support to the next. With close together furniture, the baby can cruise a whole room never lacking support. Large rooms, with more open space, require more daring for taking a few steps alone.

It's in the last few months of the first year when each baby becomes more distinctly herself. While personality differences were apparent before, now accomplishment differences vary widely and much more noticeably. But overall, you can expect a decided firming-up in your baby's spirit of independence; she'll be more determined in wanting to do things for herself, less tolerant of interference or restraint. To forge ahead she has to demand her rights. And her rights have changed since the months when she demanded only food and comfort and gentle play. Now her new directions require new attitudes from her caregivers.

This into-everything baby is eager to get her hand into her own food, the dog's dish, brother's or sister's toy shelf, everyone's belongings. She'll alternately harass and delight her family. Her sense of humor is growing, and you can make good use of your own sense of humor in handling her. Now you need to be more inventive in your methods of care to keep on good terms with your fast-changing baby.

But expect your big baby to remain a little baby in many respects. In fact, she's often more dependent on you than ever. A great deal of courage is going into the learning of physical skills, and she needs not only encouragement, but understanding parenting for her bumps and mistakes and frustrations. The time-outs she takes to snuggle close to you are her way of renewing confidence in herself.

Don't expect your baby to know what her limited world is all about, what you're all about, what herself is all about. She is gathering information and understanding little by little, but most of it remains quite a jumble. Only experience—a great deal more experience—can help a baby sort out the pieces, fit more of them together, and make sense out of her adventures in living.

On the big occasion of the one-candle cake, your baby

arrives on foot or all fours to take the seat of honor. Here is this charming one-year-old, the center of attention, looking somewhat bewildered by all the goings-on. Everyone sings the happy song, everyone is smiling and laughing as the pretty paper and ribbons are ripped off, crumpled, strewn about, and played with more than the toys inside. Everyone sees the "finished product" of twelve months of growth and development. You see a blur of 365 days and nights. How did you ever get through them all? How did this marvel of a little person come about? Only you, the parents, can give a vague answer to that; and only your congratulations to each other really mean what it's all been about. When your baby tries to grab hold of the pretty flame atop that first birthday cake, you also know what a long way you still have to go together.

Understanding Your Baby

Behavior

One way or another, the baby is constantly trying to get somewhere. He's no longer rooted to one spot, but he still has to figure out how to manage his freedom. Some primitive locomotive systems are rather odd, and your baby may try them all before settling on the most efficient. One way is to bump along on his bottom, using hands and arms for the power pushes. Or he may take off from a whole-body push-up and propel himself on hands and feet, little bottom humped up in the air. He may do a lopsided hitch, using one foot and one knee with his two hands. When he learns the mechanics of hands-and-knees crawling, he may have to go around in reverse for a while until he learns how to shift into a forward gear. Before he can walk he'll be climbing—over obstacles, up stairs, if not down, and pulling himself up to stand. And if by year's end he doesn't achieve that ultimate means of locomotion, getting there on two feet in an upright posture, he'll have a fast sprinting crawl to take him where he wants to go.

The energy a baby puts into physical activity is truly amazing. A famous Olympic star, Jim Thorpe, who in his time was called the world's greatest all-around athlete, once performed an experiment to test his own stamina against a baby's. In the normal course of a day, he followed a baby's activities, imitating every move the baby made. Jim Thorpe quit, exhausted, after four hours; the baby was still going strong!

Crosscurrents

But the baby's new freedom isn't always smooth sailing. With all her derring-do, she encounters problems, indecisions, fears. The very independence she's pursuing is making her more aware and more wary.

Sometimes she seems to be a bundle of contradictions. She scrambles down off your lap, heads for the next room, and suddenly scurries back to you, whimpering. You try to give her a snuggly hug, she pulls away and is off again. She's tempted by that shiny key chain a visitor dangles in front of her, reaches for it, then pulls her hand back and buries her face on your shoulder. What's gotten into her? Why doesn't she know what she wants?

She does, and that's the problem. When a baby wants independence, she also wants the security that she has always had. She's been pretty well protected by being "stationary." Now, what she can do physically is often frightening as well as thrilling. Having found out that she can't always trust herself to handle what she encounters "out there," she's hesitant to trust an outsider's friendly advance. Some days her insecurities follow her around till she's following you like a forlorn little puppy, content to play only where you're practically stumbling over her. And even there, right next to you, a sound that she paid no attention to before—perhaps a flushing toilet or the vacuum cleaner—may frighten her like a pursuing monster. A game that used to delight

her, being whisked up in the air and swung around, may now make her shiver or even cry with fear.

Learning to stand, in particular, makes the baby aware of and fearful of heights. She pulls herself up, looks around proudly, considers sitting down again—but how? Looking down, the floor is an alarming distance away. Afraid to let go of her support, finally tired and trembling, she cries for help. You help her down, but very shortly she's up again. Yet she'll persevere, trapping herself in this same predicament over and over until she masters the maneuver of easing herself down.

Because the baby's ambitions get ahead of her abilities, and her abilities get ahead of her reasoning power, she creates many problems for herself. She'll repeatedly try to pull herself up to stand under the same table, giving her head a bump every time. Crawling, she gets stuck in dead ends where she can't figure out how to turn around or back up. Being unable to distinguish the possible from the impossible, she often flares up over a problem; she's learned the fun of manipulating take-apart toys, but suddenly gets furious when some immovable part won't yield to her tugging. She's fascinated by stairs. She'll climb three steps on hands and knees, look back, not know how to go down, and not dare to go ahead. You rescue her, head her in another direction, she twirls around and hurries back to re-create the same problem. Some days you seem to do nothing but extricate the baby from her predicaments.

But kids often have great tolerance for an active baby's vagaries. They don't wear out as fast as an adult, and they make up whimsical games to keep the action interesting for themselves. For her part, the baby is not only tolerant, but so enchanted with older children's attentions that the risks are well worth the rewards; without a whimper, she puts up with all the dragging around she gets. And she learns to comply just to keep an older child with her; she'll welcome the child's help with a meal when she won't sit still for a parent. And usually when a child settles down to show her a book, the baby obligingly turns on a studious mood. In time, she'll point to pictures, and in time learn to make the appropriate moos and meows.

Older siblings will usually work out their own ways of keeping some control over the baby. They learn how to lure her away from their things with one interesting toy as they quickly rescue and put out of reach the things they don't want her to touch. They know the value of "mine" and so respect the baby's grabbing of her own toys as she begins to exercise her own property rights. "Who had it first" hasn't much validity in settling any children's disputes, and overall it's best to let siblings and the baby find their own ways of getting along together—so long as it doesn't come to blows. But a baby can usually take anger from a brother or sister without having her feelings hurt to any extent; she's used to their flighty ways and doesn't take their quick-change emotions as seriously as a parent's mood changes.

But in another house, or the park, your baby may shun the friendliest of children. She'll stare at them, watch every move they make, but take little interest in any toys she's

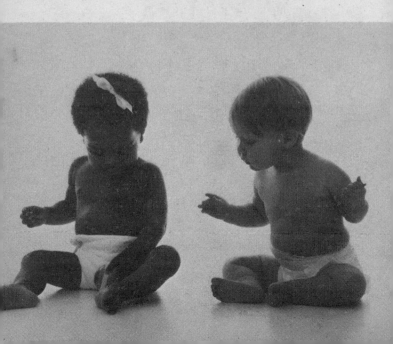

offered. In strange places a baby may do nothing but stare for an hour or more, only taking care to keep you nearby.

With a visiting baby who's near her own age, yours will probably do little or nothing to make her welcome; in fact, she may start a tug of war if that baby so much as touches one of her toys. You never know, however, how babies are going to "fit" together. If your baby is a placid type, and the visitor is aggressive, yours may take to a corner and leave the field to her unfriendly caller. But more often the two babies will play separately, only occasionally glancing at each other.

The Super Chair

Pounding, clattering, jangling, any kind of noise-making is still a favorite pastime. It's a way to feel important, and to get instant feedback from play. Now, imagine the baby's thrill in combining locomotion with noise, even before he can walk. You'll be treated to this if he discovers a chair that when pushed around on the kitchen or patio floor makes a wild screeching that babies consider the height of pleasure in sound effects. If it gives you auditory shivers you can reduce the volume somewhat by turning the chair on its back and letting the baby hold the legs like a wheelbarrow— that is, if you don't mind the wear and tear on the chair. Or you can put casters on the chair's feet. Cutting down on the noise won't please the baby, but it won't spoil his pleasure too much. After he can stand, and before he can walk steadily, chair pushing gives him a nice way to get around in a kind of pretend walking. He has constant support and gets good practice in making one foot follow the other.

Clever Fingers

The baby's hands are beginning to act almost grown-up, with all the new tricks of manipulation they're performing. That visual interest the baby was recently showing in tiny things has developed into an ability to handle them. His thumb and index finger now work nicely together; he can pick up a pea, a bit of string (or a nail or dead fly he finds

on the floor!). At first he uses the side of his hand for balance as he closes in on the object; but soon he can aim straight down with precision, using thumb and finger like a bird's beak. Keep close scrutiny, for whatever his fingers find, his mouth gets; and there are many edibles, such as nuts, popcorn, raisins that he can choke on, as well as the dangerous things he could swallow.

And what's all this interest he's beginning to have in holes and cracks? It's the baby's busy forefinger at work. He has just discovered that it can now work independently, not only for pointing but for probing. He'll poke it into a knothole on the floor, a hole in a blanket, your ear, his belly button, the crevice of an open door, an electric outlet. Be sure that all outlets are sealed off with safety covers; and check for little fingers before you slam the refrigerator or car door! This one-finger control is such a novelty, the baby is compelled to keep practicing it, testing its accuracy.

His hand grasp is also showing new understanding. Spoons and cups are usually picked up by their handles. But the best thing—from the baby's viewpoint—is that he can now release his hand grip at will. He did let go of things before, of course—at first accidentally, then on purpose. But even this later letting go wasn't easy; it lacked full control and timing. Now his release becomes deliberate and precise, and he practices this new skill happily and endlessly. One by one he'll drop an array of toys over the side of his crib or high chair, watching each one land on the floor. He's interested in their different sound effects; one lands with a soft thud, another with a bang. And, being an avid seeker of knowledge on the nature of all things, he also studies how some things change shape when dropped. A spoon remains the same; milk from his cup spreads out in interesting rivulets; when a china saucer hits the floor it changes from one piece to many. Naturally, his experimentation has to be kept under control. And at some point his supply of safe dropable things will give out—when you've had your fill of picking them up and returning them.

These growing-up months are full of surprises. Every day your baby diverts you with some new trick; every week you see him turning another corner. A baby's road to independence is paved with excitement, fun, stumbling blocks, and dangers. He can't yet read the road signs, so he stays his course with a mixture of physical, mental, and emotional energy. He's reckless and cautious by turn. No wonder he often regresses to enjoy safety and comforting with you.

Learning

Space exploration is an undertaking your baby may or may not choose to pursue in later years, but she's already studying some of the fundamentals. Having learned a few months ago that she could get a toy by reaching her hand out into space, she now learns that she can get a toy by taking herself out into space. She has entered the space age of babyhood and she's ready to begin her research.

Space Observations

In her explorations the baby discovers that things "change" size—get bigger—when she's closer to them. Some things "transform" themselves; a tree seen from her stroller becomes a totally different thing when she crawls up, feels its trunk, and looks up into it. She becomes more aware of the distances between herself and objects. When she first began to reach for objects, she often missed her aim; when she begins to crawl and walk, she misjudges distance and bumps into things.

Space perception doesn't come easy. Watch a toddler learning to sit down in her little chair. For some time she can't trust her distance judgment. She may first back up to the chair, take hold of the seat and pull the chair to her; then she may turn herself and the chair around in a circle before sitting down. She seems to be testing out the maneuver she'll use later when she faces the chair, holds onto it, and turns herself around to sit down.

Actually, the beginning of spacial concepts is when the baby senses that an object is not an extension of herself, but exists apart from her and from other objects. Reaching and grasping gave her some conception of this; but now, moving herself around through space gives her a much stronger sense of herself as a separate entity in the world. She senses this, too, from getting herself trapped in places when she's making her rounds of the house; you rescue her from a tight spot between the couch and the table and she sees that she has been separated from those objects. She can send a ball out into space, and with her marvelous new ability to propel herself, she can now pursue and retrieve. By detaching that ball from herself and then attaching it to her again, she not only gains a perception of space, but of herself as distinct from an object.

Upside-down space observation continues to intrigue the baby. She'll pause in her crawling, turn onto her back, arch up, and take a look around at this changed perspective. Even before she's toddling, she may be able to balance herself, leaning over with her hands on the floor, and look backward through her legs. And when you're holding her you've got to hang on—she'll suddenly swing herself back and hang head down for this fascinating study of an upside-down world.

The Dawning of Reason

Making things happen. Think of the significance of that from a baby's viewpoint—a baby who has lived through many months with things happening to him and around him. He *did* learn from all that, constantly; he even made things happen when he was totally unaware of doing so. For instance, he cried and you came; he smiled and you smiled; he waved a rattle and made it make noise. But he had no goal in mind when he did these things.

Even when the baby gained a limited concept of cause and effect—that a toy tinkled when he batted it, for example—it was a closed-in bit of learning. He was not able to keep a series of ideas in mind, or to imitate something he had seen others do, or even to retain many of his own separate performances long enough to repeat them.

But now—what a difference. The baby can foresee the results of many of his actions, decide on a goal, and deliberately make many things happen. This is no sudden burst of enlightenment. For months the baby has been hard at work, checking his repertoire of actions against one another, discovering what happens after he does this or that, learning to make the same things happen again. This required memory development and endless experimentation, and it's still riddled with many misjudgments. But the hold the baby now has on making his world go round adds great scope to his learning.

You've been seeing many effects of your baby's learning without being aware of all the complex factors that led up to each accomplishment. Indeed, the most renowned experts are not in full agreement on how a baby's learning develops. What's important, and most fascinating, is that somehow the baby emerges from that early stage, where learning was largely sensory experience, to this present stage, where reasoning enters into learning.

With two blocks the baby can invent a machine—and make it go, using one block to push the other. He can build a tower of two—and collapse this engineering feat with one swipe, to study its two separate parts again. With push and pull toys he can make action reverse itself. With nesting cups, plastic "donuts" that fit on a pole, shape sorters, many simple take-apart and put-together toys, he'll carry out his experiments in size, shape, and space relationships.

But there is no "right" way to play with any toy. A baby makes of his toys what pleases and interests him at any moment. A stuffed toy will be snuggled, swung about by its ear, sat upon. A fit-together toy will be used in its separate parts for chewing on, pounding with, scattering; then used "correctly" for size and shape learning; and later become anything the baby wishes it to represent as imitation and imagination broaden his play. Nor can a baby be expected to know what is and is not a plaything. In these free-wheeling, curiosity-driven months, you've got to keep your eyes and ears on the alert. Be especially aware when you *don't* hear any activity from your little mouse; he might be sitting in a corner quietly chewing on an electric cord.

Yet in the midst of the baby's wide-ranging activities you'll be able to discern which learning skills he's working on and what kinds of playthings he needs. He should have the chance to reinforce each piece of learning with plenty of practice, even though one—pounding—may play on your nerves.

Pounding is a basic human skill. One of the first evidences of developing intelligence in the human race was the use of a pounding tool; and one of the first musical instruments was a drum. All babies discover and thrill to the action and the sound of their own pounding. As you put up with it as best you can, be assured that the interest will eventually slack off; it's while an ability is new that the baby is most intent on practicing it.

Monkey Business

Doing what others do, however awkwardly, is becoming a new interest for the baby; and imitation is beginning to play a large part in learning and in shaping the baby's attitudes. Much as he hates to have anyone wash his face, you'll find him swiping at his face with a wet washcloth. If you blow on your hot coffee before you take a sip, he'll blow on his cold cup of juice. You scold the dog for good reason, he "scolds" at him for no reason. Perhaps you have a habit of humming over some restful work; sometimes you'll hear your baby humming during quiet play, imitating your moods of calm concentration.

The baby learns a great deal from watching other children play. You may be surprised by his skill with a toy you thought was beyond him. He watches a visiting child intently as she puts rings on a pole, takes them off and puts them on again; later, you find your baby performing the same skill with ease, although he had never tried it before.

At the park he sits silently on the sidelines, staring at children in the sandbox, refusing to get near it. The next day at home you find him in the midst of a sugar mess, dipping and pouring in creditable imitation of the park kids. (And you find a new location for your sugar canister.) During these months you'll have surprises—amusing, annoying, praiseworthy, and the "Oh, no! where did she learn *that*!" kind—as your baby tries to shape himself in the image of others.

Memory Building

Without memory development, the baby's learning would be coming to a slow halt about now. She would have impressions to go on, and certain actions that would be more habit, or conditioning, than actual remembering. She would not be able to build new abilities by adding the memory of one action to the memory of another to learn something new. And she would continue to live within the confined circle of present time. Future time is still beyond the baby's mental grasp, but she now has a hold on the past. This gives her the valuable concept of what is called "object permanence."

When the baby was younger, anything she didn't experience through her senses did not exist for her. In her play she was bound in particular to touch and sight experience. Now, a toy that isn't here at the moment hasn't vanished into nonexistence; the baby can see and feel that toy in her mind. Persons, of course, are included in "object" permanence. Because the baby can now retain a mental image of you, she no longer thinks you're gone for good when she can't see you. She'll play alone for a while, then confidently go back to the room where she last saw you; only if you're not there does she become anxious and begin to whimper.

But don't be disappointed if your baby forgets things that she seemed to know well. New learning keeps overlapping the previous, and she may lose interest in some accomplishments, or forget them for lack of regular repetition. Many babies refuse to perform any of their new skills away from home, and even with the family, may become shy or stubborn with too much urging. This is actually a kind of strength, a refusal to be "manipulated" in their actions.

Hide-and-find is a new game to play with your baby. If she sees you hide a toy under a pillow or a scarf, she'll usually retrieve it immediately—unless she's diverted by something else of interest. A short time ago, the baby couldn't do this; out of sight was out of mind. The baby will also invent her own hide-and-find games—tuck a book or a toy under a rug, leave it a short while, then go back and pull it out. When this game develops, you can suspect your baby when some item of yours mysteriously disappears in the house. But don't expect much help in recovering it. Some babies so enjoy hiding things that they soon forget about most of them; days later you come across your glove stuffed into a crevice of the couch.

A thing must be fairly easy to find for the baby to really try to find it. In fact she'll use a kind of quirky logic on a search problem. If her ball keeps rolling under a table and she keeps crawling there and retrieving it, then she sees it roll under the sofa, she'll correctly go to the spot where it

went out of sight. Realizing that she can't go after it there, she'll ponder a moment, then crawl back under the table to search where the ball "ought" to be. Such convenient bits of reasoning are really remarkable; no matter that the solution doesn't work, the baby has put her mind to work on a problem.

As the baby's memory span increases she'll think of a plaything she wants, one that was gathered up in a recent clean-up of the floor. Going to her toy shelf, she'll fling aside half a dozen other interesting items till she finds what she's looking for. Keeping a thing in mind and refusing to be distracted is a big step in learning to concentrate.

The baby's memory is not only holding pictures of things, but of situations and events. This enables her to learn by imitation and also to recreate a game she played with someone else. Suppose dad comes home and playfully puts his cap on the baby's head. She yanks it off and puts it on his head; he puts it back on hers. She'd keep the performance going indefinitely, but dad has other things to do. The next morning the baby finds the cap, crawls to dad in the kitchen and tries to start the game again. Six months ago the baby had a memory span of about six seconds; now she recalls something she was doing the day before!

The baby's memory continues to stretch, but slowly. Not until late in her second year will she be able to remember something that happened as far back as two weeks. But by the end of this first year, memory will be leading the baby into the most complex of human skills—the learning of language. Hearing the same word or phrase many, many times, in association with the same object or action or circumstance, she'll recognize this bit of speech as a symbol of specific meaning, and finally will attempt to imitate it. In time she'll retain a memory of many sound symbols and begin to string them together. Gradually she'll be able to extend herself into a world where many meanings can be shared. With the aid of memory, the baby's learning can expand to any horizon.

Parent-Child Interaction

When your baby is able and eager to take off into a wider world, you know he has to go where his development leads him. To gain self-reliance, you know he's got to steer his own course. You know he must be given freedom to explore, examine, test, and try out his abilities in his quest for independence. All well and good—the admirable aims of good parenting! But idealistic concepts are as abstract as the hum of a motor when your freedom baby is heading for disaster. You throw the honored guide words to the winds, too, when he's trying to bathe his teddy bear in the toilet.

To both kinds of situations you react—fast. But if your voice and handling is the same for impending danger as for imitative behavior or innocent investigation, your baby won't be learning much about his wide open spaces. You're likely to hurl that handy little word *no* at your baby more times than you realize in the course of a day. And he'll pick it up and use it, one way or another. Before he can say the word, he can wag his head no in a fun kind of mimicry.

And before he does that, he has plenty of ways to act out his no in defiance of yours if frustration grabs at him too often. Only you—not the baby—have control of the nos in his life. Before you even start to use the word, it's well to take a long-range look at the months ahead. Looking through your baby's eyes, you can do a first-rate job in your role as copilot in this adventurous new phase of his life.

Curiosity on the Loose

The baby wouldn't be getting anywhere without the power of curiosity; it's been the driving force of all great achievements back through the ages. And since the earliest days of your baby's life, curiosity has compelled him to learn. Why else did he peer out and fasten his eyes on a patch of window light; gaze at your face intently; listen to your

whispers; watch the movements of a mobile; study his own hands; examine textures, colors, shapes? None of this was necessary for his survival; nor had it anything to do with his comfort. It was a pure inner drive for infant knowledge.

For many months, the baby's seeking of information about the world was limited to what others provided for him. Now, imagine the compelling power of curiosity as the baby sets out to explore all that was unreachable before. And you, now, are faced with the problem of freedom versus containment. Your baby must be protected from hazards, and things precious to you must be protected from him.

Not all babies are house-wreckers. Babies have their own styles of handling new experience, and this follows through in their new-found mobility. But a baby who's been penned up too long, clamoring to exercise his independence, may go a bit loco for a time. Given the chance, he may ransack the house, strewing rooms with crumpled magazines, streamers of toilet paper, contents of waste baskets, drawers, and cupboards. His darting curiosity makes his first freedom a sea of confusion. By contrast, a baby who's quietly me-thodical in learning-style may settle into long periods of interest in one thing at a time. As he makes his rounds he may spend an hour tugging all the cushions off the sofa and struggling to get them back on again, or keep returning to a cupboard door to concentrate on moving it on its hinges.

When the baby gets involved in some unacceptable busi-ness, such as turning the knobs of the TV or stereo, he'll be more accepting of a substitute for play if it's in his line of interest—perhaps one of the multiactivity toys that has things to dial, slide, turn and spin.

Even after a baby is used to having the run of the house, he'll often show feelings of insecurity about exercising his rights. Just the fact that he can take himself away from you makes him more aware of the meaning of separation. In a typical scenario, he plays awhile with pans and lids on the kitchen floor, crawls over to investigate a crumpled scrap of paper near the doorway. He looks back at you, hesitates, then on he goes, into the next room, under a table and out again. He finds a crumb, eats it, examines the rung of a chair, tries to climb onto it, fails, looks around for other interesting possibilities. But suddenly—seeming to sense the large loneliness of where he is—he scurries back to the kitchen to sit at your feet.

A baby is often a little pathetic as he struggles with the counter pulls of independence and dependence. He may want to stay in a particular room where he's having fun, but he keeps interrupting his play to check on your where-abouts. Voice contact is a good means of reassuring him. When you leave to go from room to room, keep a little "conversation" going with him. Your voice takes the place of your presence, gives him companionship, and dispels his nervousness in being alone.

Even the most daring baby needs to know you're nearby to protect him. He learns very soon that curiosity is fraught with hurts and with unpleasant accidents and messes that he had no intention of causing. He's confused by much that happens, but fascinated by many discoveries. Freedom lures him on, and his driving force is the curiosity he was born with. This is what you need to preserve while you protect him from the dangers lurking in his environment, and protect your own rights of possession in the home you share with your baby.

What About Discipline?

It's easy to enjoy a baby's budding self-confidence and independence of spirit when she's struggling to pull off a sock or scramble up on a sofa. She's wonderful to watch and easy to live with when she goes happily on her way, seldom cross-cutting your wishes or convenience. But what do you do about her troublesome and willful behavior? How do you discipline her healthy curiosity?

One dictionary definition of discipline is "strict control to enforce obedience." How handy it would be to have a little crawler with such an abnormally high IQ and angelic nature that you could enforce obedience with every barked-out order! Assuming that you have a normal baby, you'll want a better definition, and the dictionary gives you one

that has wise application to a baby: "training that develops self-control and character." With this commonsense approach, you won't be running roughshod over your baby's trust and confidence in you. To destroy that would be to undermine the foundation you've built through all the past months—the sense of security and self-confidence your baby has for developing her love of learning.

Naturally, a baby needs controls. She hasn't the reasoning ability or experience to understand hazards or the rights of others. But neither can she understand why someone is mad at her, why her hand is slapped for touching one thing and not another, why people scold or yell at her.

There's no cut-off age for keeping a baby happy. And keeping her happy is not avoiding discipline; it's a way of gaining her compliance with your guidance. Certainly you can't always give in to her. But a baby doesn't always have to win in order not to lose. Whenever you steer around a clash of wills, you avoid making her a loser. With a little ingenuity you can find easy ways to handle many situations.

You've given the baby a long playtime in the bathtub, and still she starts to struggle and yell when you try to take her out. But start a game of peek-a-boo with the bath towel, then drape it over her head, lift her out, and tub fun is forgotten with her fun in the game. Diversion has worked for a long time to avoid conflicts with the baby. Now that she's older, and her attention span is longer, the simplest form of diversion—handing him one thing as you take away another—won't always work. A more advanced ruse is to provide a substitute that fits in with what the baby is *doing*. If she's rolling a ripe peach on the floor, she'll be willing to trade it for a ball but not for a block. If she's dragging around a clean pair of pants, she won't be interested in a clackety toy you shake at her, but an unwashed pair will do just as well for her mission of the moment. When you have to pounce and whisk her away from her objective, make it a rough and tumble game that gives her no chance to feel frustrated.

Why all this "indulgence"? Well, think for a moment how many natural, unavoidable frustrations there are in a baby's life—not only those imposed on her, but all those she encounters in her play. She works through her own problems, seldom crying for help, because of her intense interest in trying to learn how to do things for herself. But being thwarted in her aims and interests is quite a different thing—a different kind of frustration that goes against the grain of her endeavors. A baby's play is continual learning; the fact that it's fun doesn't change its importance.

This new mobile life has brought the baby a lot of perplexities to cope with and try to sort out—do and don't, yes and no, good and bad. Sometimes the green and red lights are flashing so fast she can make no sense at all of what's expected of her. And even when she has learned a small measure of control over her impulses, her reaction to a sharp no is little more than a startle that stops her in her tracks—momentarily. The minute you turn away she goes right back to the thing she was after. Her inner urge to act is much, much stronger than your verbal control over her.

But the baby *will* learn the meaning of *no* and *don't touch* if you use them sparingly. Sometimes you'll shout to stop her fast—and the alarm in your voice will tell the baby how urgently you mean it. But in general she'll learn best if you keep your cautions calm, and reinforce their meaning with an "explanation" whenever possible. Before she can understand words, your expressions and gestures can tell the baby that something is hot, will hurt, belongs to daddy or mommy, is not a plaything. Sometimes—perhaps as early as the tenth month—you'll see her looking at something and shaking her head no. It doesn't mean that she has any more than a vague sense of this whole *no* business. Nor does it mean that her own no will "stick," any more than yours will, for some time to come. But it reflects your patience in helping her learn to think about what she does.

The real test of discipline is whether it changes behavior for the better. Barked-out orders, threats, or punishment will only deter a baby for the moment. If she's squelched too hard, her will to learn levels off; she never knows what actions will be approved or disapproved. She either becomes timid and uncertain of herself, or she becomes a fighter, intolerant of so much as a restraining hand, and finally succumbing to tantrums.

A youngster in a tantrum is a miserable, pitiful little creature. All her controls are shattered. She can't be reached until her kicking and screaming have worked off most of her intense frustration. But when she comes out of it she needs you. She needs soothing, comforting, and quiet words that let her know you don't blame her, you understand her feelings and how hard it all is for her at times. Babies seldom have real tantrums before their second year, but milder and briefer attacks of anger and frustration are warnings. They tell you it's time to question your handling of the baby. Does she have too many controls, or inconsistent controls? Are you showing more disapproval than encouragement and praise?

One important thing the baby has learned throughout her life up to now is that she can please you. She knows this, it gives her great pleasure, and it's her strongest incentive to comply with your wishes. When there's harmony between you and your baby, she can learn from your guidance; when there's friction and anger, she resists. It's a matter of understanding that all your baby's behavior, whether pleasant or unpleasant for you, is legitimate for her. Keeping that in mind, you'll find ways to keep things under control without upsetting the good feelings you have about each other.

The Copycat

Watch your words and actions now! Your baby is watching you. He'll pick up not only delightful little expressions and gestures, but attitudes best not included in his learning. If you point to an airplane in the sky, he'll point and smile when he hears that roar; and he'll have the same reaction to a rumble of thunder if you don't transmit a fear signal. If you do, he'll retain that fear, and perhaps also be afraid when he hears the rolling of drums in an approaching parade. Consider a beetle; it's an interesting creature for a baby to watch. If it gives you the creeps and you sweep it away, all tiny creatures are to be feared, including an innocent ant lugging a bit of leaf, or a lovely butterfly on a flower.

You'll sometimes see more than you like revealed of yourself as your baby mimics you. A sudden swear word or sharp gesture of anger gets instant attention because it's charged with emotion, and the baby reflects that in not-too-cute agitation and jabbering. If you have a habit of slamming doors, you'll have a hard time teaching your baby that doors can be hazardous to hands.

All along, of course, imitation is working in many good ways. It helps the baby in learning to eat with a spoon, drink from a cup, undress himself (taking off being much easier than putting on at this age). The baby's sense of humor is in such ready use now that he's not only amused by things *you* do, but he's amused when you imitate *him*. Bump your head right after he bumps his, imitate his startled expression, and you'll most likely intercept his crying with laughing. Boom! for a fall turns a minor hurt into a funny hurt and dispels a lot of anxiety in learning to toddle. In fact, there's a fine line between sympathizing with a baby's small hurts and fears and reinforcing them. Prolonging "poor baby" can hold him back, when actually he's ready and willing to try again.

Play-acting is a useful and fun form of imitation. Because the baby is now capable of simple symbolic thinking, he can even learn something by imitating a stuffed toy. Suppose he's learned to climb onto the couch, but he's had some falls trying to get down; now he's afraid to try. Get his attention, then nudge his teddy bear off the couch. Pick it up, comfort it, then make it climb back on the couch. Now "show" the bear how to turn on its stomach and safely slide down. After several repeat acts, which the baby will surely demand, he'll try the maneuver himself—and be thrilled with his bravery.

Keep that play-acting bear, or a big doll, on hand. It may help your baby over various problems or anxieties. It can show him how to pat a friendly dog, slide down the little tots' sliding board in the park while you hold his hand.

It may even help the baby get over his fear of the vacuum cleaner if that appliance becomes an ogre to him. Turn the motor on and off, making the bear give a little jump each time it comes on; in between, have the bear pat the machine; then have him help push it, first with the motor off, then on. The baby *may* soon join in, laughing at the bear's jumps and finally doing his part in pushing. Play-acting works fine with some babies, and it's always worth a try.

To get a baby over his fear of letting go when he pulls himself up to stand, a doll may not be much help. Your best bet is to put the baby through the action yourself. The crib is a good place to practice so that he has a soft surface to plop down on. Let him hold your arm instead of the crib rail, bend him slightly at the hips and give his shoulders a little push forward and down. After he's gone down with a bump a few times, he'll catch on to the natural knee and waist bend that will let him down easy.

Imitation has its limits in learning and teaching, but it's well to keep it in mind—especially for the things you *don't* want your baby to learn.

Gibberish and Jargon

Now your baby is beginning to imitate some of the actual forms of the words he hears. But language learning is far more than imitation. The baby is still playing with the sounds he makes, stringing them together in longer and more varied patterns. Jargon is a stream of gibberish in which you detect an occasional "real" word. But that word may have no more meaning for the baby than all his cooing and babbling had. Speaking is not just making sounds, and mimicking words is not always understanding them. Language is interwoven with situations, emotions, attitudes and responses of others, and all the milieu of circumstances that accompany a word or phrase.

So keep on talking to your baby. Gradually he'll connect a few words with their meanings, and he will understand many words and phrases before he can speak them. You won't really know for sure when your baby does speak that "first" word and actually understand it. But when you hear ma-ma or da-da or pa-pa, you can be pretty sure he knows what it means. Those words are the same in many languages all over the world, and they are often the first to be spoken because they are filled with meaning for the baby. Starting with the earliest universal speech sounds, the baby gradually acquires the distinctive phonetics and "music" of his parents' native language.

In a bilingual family, the baby has no trouble learning two languages simultaneously. One will not take precedence over the other unless he has much more exposure to one than the other. Even if both parents are bilingual, it's generally best for each parent to speak only one language—always the same one—to the baby. Then he falls naturally into understanding and using that language without confusion. But if the baby sometimes mixes the two languages he shouldn't be corrected; that could confuse him. A young bilingual child can't translate; he hasn't the slightest idea what you mean if you say, Yes, this is an apple, but what is it in Spanish (or French or Korean—whatever)? Yet, speaking the other language, the correct word comes out naturally. The baby doesn't think back and forth as he's learning two languages; it's the pattern that he learns; and one pattern can't be superimposed on another in the beginning of any kind of learning.

You can help your baby with the highly complex skill of language learning by speaking clearly, in short phrases, with emphasis on the most meaningful word. Long before he can speak, he'll learn the names of many familiar things, and point to their pictures in a book or magazine when you say the word. He'll also learn to follow simple directions if you phrase them simply and briefly. The one language to avoid in talking to your baby is "baby talk." It could say what you meant way back in little baby days; now "I love you" says it much better.

Routines and Care

Feeding

All those months of round-the-clock feedings are far behind you. Three meals a day is established. And now comes the baby's personal project—self-feeding.

Well, at least it starts out without too much mess. It's when the baby starts to wield her own spoon that the whole business gets really sloppy. But letting her try any way she likes to get food into her mouth assures that you won't still be spooning it into her at the end of another year. By that time, babies who have enjoyed the privilege of self-feeding aren't exactly eating with polite society manners, but they're usually eating with relish.

A baby who's held back in feeding herself loses her interest in learning. That's because any developmental skill

is more easily learned when the baby is eager to try it. Denied that, a chain reaction usually sets in: The baby has less interest in meals, is urged to eat, resists being fed, and begins to subsist mainly on between-meal snacks. But when a baby is allowed to feed herself as soon as she shows an interest—whether she has a naturally big appetite or a small one—she finds her meals appetizing because she can choose what and how much she wants to eat.

The baby has had some practice in self-feeding with the teething biscuits and toasted breads she's been holding in her fist and chewing on. But small bits of food have eluded her. Now, new finger dexterity comes to her aid. She learns to use her thumb and forefinger to pick up small pieces of food and carry them to her mouth.

Lumps? That Depends

Almost all babies start out with an aversion to lumps—when the lumps come by spoon. That's understandable; all these months a spoon has contained soft, smooth food. So when the baby's tongue encounters a mouthful of coarse food, there's something wrong—like finding bits of egg-shell in your fluffy omelet. The baby spits out the first spoonful and refuses the next. You can try easing her into the change by mixing just a bit of coarse food with a tasty, favorite pureed food. Add a spoonful of vegetable or fruit, mashed with a fork, or mix a little "junior" baby food with the strained. Some babies will gradually accept this, others continue to object.

But the best way to get a baby used to lumps is to let her feed them to herself with her fingers; this way, they take on a whole new character. Accustomed to feeling lumps in her mouth, she'll then accept some by spoon, and many of her meals can be prepared from what's cooked for the family.

While she's waiting for some good solid food, she has a scattering of dry cereal flakes to push around, select from, and pop into her mouth. When they've done practically nothing to appease her hunger, she wipes the remainder off her tray in a couple of decisive swoops. She's ready for the next course.

Lined up in front of her are three little cubes of cooked carrot, three cooked green beans, three little clumps of crumbled hamburger. She looks from one to the other, decides on the basis of color, then on the basis of taste, finally on what's left. Eating this bird's ration takes time. She's still hungry, but a bit tired from the concentrated effort of getting food into herself unaided. With a little more finger food to fiddle with, she allows you to feed her occasional bites from a spoon. This rounds out a meal with the foods that won't adapt to fingers. To be sure, the whole procedure will drag out the mealtimes. But every minute lost now is a minute gained in the time it will take for your baby to become a full-time self-feeder.

Think of everything you can to make foods manageable by fingers. If you settle only for the quickest—dry cereals— your baby will be stuck with having to take everything else by spoon, and you'll probably be stuck with a number of foods you think she ought to have. When babies begin to be choosy, they often resist being fed everything except their favorites; but they'll usually finger-feed themselves almost anything offered, if it's served first, when they're hungriest.

Try: scrambled egg; crumbled hamburger; chicken, lamb, pork, well cooked and minced; broiled, nonoily fish, picked through with your fingers to remove any bones; cottage cheese; tiny cubes of soft yellow cheese; any cooked vegetable in small cubes; cooked peas with the skins broken; tiny pieces of soft fresh fruits—seeds and thick peel removed; tiny (half-inch) sandwiches spread with smooth peanut butter or prepared baby food meat. *Just remember to give the baby only things that her mouth can prepare for swallowing by tongue-mashing or gumming—without actual chewing.*

On to the Spoon

With early practice, your baby may be pretty efficient in

spoon-feeding herself before a year of age. Some polite babies start by "helping" as you feed them, holding your hand that's holding the spoon. Some, on a sudden urge, snatch the spoon away from you. Your polite answer to such rudeness is simply to get another spoon for yourself, and resume the feeding while the baby jabs his spoon around in the dish of food.

Poor little thing. He had no idea, when he got hold of that spoon, it wouldn't be a simple matter to do what you're doing—get food onto it and up to his mouth. But once this ambition gets hold of him, he's got to try. He'll try for weeks before he has any regular successes. When he can get a bit to stay on the spoon, it spills off on the way up, or he tips the spoon at the last moment and the food lands on his nose or chin or shirt. He has to remember to open his mouth just when the spoon gets there—a trick that requires perfect timing to be synchronized with the difficult balancing act he's performing with his spoon.

You can't really teach a baby how to hold a spoon in the most efficient way. You may find him looking intently at the way you hold yours—the usual adult way being thumb on top, handle between first two fingers. But that won't be the best way for the baby. He'll do better with his fist gripped around the handle, thumb underneath—which he'll finally discover by trial and error; for a while he'll keep switching his hold, even if you manage to start him off right.

Baby spoons with a looped handle used to be popular, at least with baby-gift givers. But most babies seem to prefer the short, straight-handled baby spoon, which is easier to grip properly. Mashed potato is a good stick-to-the-spoon food. It's easy to scoop up, and not likely to drop off on the jerky way to the baby's mouth, even when he gets it there upside down. A suction-bottom dish prevents slipping, and a dish with divisions gives the baby a choice in what to try next. With a combination of finger and spoon foods, he'll soon be able to get most of a meal into himself, and he'll have a great time doing it!

The Mess of It

Yes, the mess is what makes this learning pretty nerve-racking to watch. The baby's persistence is admirable, but the fun he has with food is another part of the picture. Feeling and handling, remember, has always been his way of examining everything, along with the taste test. Now here is this interesting stuff to get his hands into, smear, lick off his fingers, dig into with a spoon, drop overboard to see chunks land on the floor. Here are these interesting morsels—soft ones, slick ones, sticky ones, some nicely squishable, others crunchable—a veritable laboratory for investigative study—all with the added attraction of taste variety.

Each of these things has a different feel in the baby's hands and in his mouth. He'll munch on a mouthful, take it out of his mouth, look the pulpy thing over, and put it back in; mash and mix a few together, scoop up the mess and try to push it into his mouth with the palm of his hand. When he's eaten all he wants by spoon and by fingers, there's plenty of mushy leftovers to smear around on his feeding tray. Considering that this is the same kind of artistry preschoolers perform with finger paints, it's possible that food smearing is the beginning of creativity!

At this point in life a baby can't be expected to differentiate between which things are for play and which are to be "respected" for one reason or another. He doesn't know why he's allowed to pound on a pie tin but not on a china dish—or why turning his spoon every which way to examine it is more acceptable than doing the same with his cup of milk. In his view, the cup proves more interesting; turned upside down, it makes a nice puddle to swish his hands in. Not for a long time will a baby have any conception of food as something to be respected. Unless he's living in unfortunate circumstances where he gets little to eat, he'll want to play with food as well as eat it. What's wasted won't matter to him—only to you, after the trouble of fixing him a tasty and pretty little meal.

How much messing is "within reason" varies from one

parent to the next. If all of it makes you squeamish, it's a good idea to busy yourself with something else, nearby, while the baby works his way through a meal. If you can tolerate quite a lot of mess, but his awkwardness makes you nervous, you'll keep wanting to help him. You have to remind yourself that this is *his* project. Too much help or interference can be a handicap, making him lose interest, or lose confidence in what he's accomplishing on his own. When the baby is tackling the difficult—albeit pleasura-ble—job of self-feeding, try to think of it as a develop-mental skill like any other that he has to teach himself. After all, you can't show him how to place one foot in front of the other and keep his balance. There'll be a lot of spills on the way to steady walking, and a lot on the way to capable eating.

That Quirky Appetite

"Capable" encompasses more than the mechanics of eating. A baby knows how much food she needs, but to trust her appetite is difficult for many parents. With all that energy she's expending, it seems she should want three full meals a day. Sometimes she does; other times she eats practically nothing at one or two meals. Her appetite may wane for a few days, then pick up again. These natural variations have no significance; a fluctuating appetite is common to persons of all ages. Worrying, and urging the baby to take even a little more than she wants, is the surest way to spoil her pleasure in mealtimes. And *what* a baby chooses to eat—given a selection of good foods—is apparently what her body needs. Evidence of this was made clear in an experi-ment conducted a number of years ago, and now famous in the chronicles of baby feeding.

Dr. Clara Davis arranged for a small group of babies to be given completely free choice in selecting what they wanted to eat from a variety of wholesome natural foods at each meal. Their nurses refrained from influencing the babies in the slightest way, or restraining them from any bizarre eating patterns they indulged in. Sometimes a baby would choose

the same food for several meals in a row, passing up practically everything else. Babies went on food binges, eating
great quantities of eggs or meat or greens, for instance, in
addition to other foods. A baby would drink a quart of milk
with one meal, then want almost no milk at the next. No
matter what kind of food they ate in excess of normal portions, there were no digestive upsets. Appetite varied in
quantity and selection; a baby would concentrate on vegetables for a while, then change to starchy foods. Meals were
often quite unbalanced on a day to day basis, but over a
week or several weeks, the babies selected the foods that
gave them a balance of good nutrition. Dr. Davis carried
out her experiment later with older children and found that
their instincts were as trustworthy as the babies' in selecting
a proper diet.

Outside influences should definitely be out when the baby
eats with the family. She'll be quick to notice if someone
makes a wry face over a particular food, and quick to resist
if she's coaxed to eat something she wanted yesterday, and
may want next week, but doesn't want today. You can do
some fancy figuring on a computer to determine which other
foods will supply the same nutrients as the foods your baby
doesn't care for right now. But it's just as reliable, and a
lot easier, to abide by your baby's decisions—*if* you provide
wholesome choices and let her appetite be what it may.

The Fine Art of Chewing

Until the baby has a set of molars, she'll be chomping
crunchy food as best she can, and she mustn't have chunks
she could choke on. And before she advances from lumps
to chunks, she'd better know something about chewing.
Imitation is her best bet for learning. So demonstrate. She'll
look on, amused, but try to keep your chewing "serious"—
somewhat exaggerated, but slow and steady. When she offers you a bite of her toast, chew it thoroughly, then offer
her a bite of yours. She may pass that up and keep plying
you with bites to keep watching your funny face. It takes
quite a few sessions before a baby gets the idea of imitating;

meanwhile, you'll get pretty tired of her ragged toast and cookie offerings.

When she does decide to copycat, it may be when you least expect it. She'll be sitting in her high chair, staring at you while you're munching away at the breakfast table; then she'll take a bite of her breakfast and do a nice imitation of you. To round out the scene, pour a little milk in her cup, add a little to your cup of coffee, take a drink from your cup. If she follows suit, don't even comment; keep the whole performance casual and natural. You've got a nice little breakfast companion—until she decides it's more fun to start banging her cup and making a mess with her food. Well, all good actors start out with bit performances. You have only a few years to wait till you can proudly include your child at table in your favorite steak house or gourmet restaurant.

Sleep

For the mobile baby, sleep is simply a means of refreshing himself for more rounds of thrilling experience. He's charged with energy now, pushing himself toward many new capabilities, and often he's not able to curtail his drives long enough to want to sleep. But if he enjoys his day to the fullest he can more easily welcome sleep. Thus, the best approach to a happy bedtime is through the baby's daytime hours.

Families and household setups differ as to when it's best for the baby to be bedded down for the night. If you liked having the baby awake in the evenings during his earlier months, and more or less let him choose his own bedtime, you may want more say in the matter now. There's not much chance to relax with this older baby who's all over the place, having to be watched. If you do want him asleep at a reasonably early hour, start by trying to arrange his napping times.

Day Sleep

Even with all the urgent business the baby has to accomplish, he usually doesn't resist naps during the day. He seems to know that he'll soon be back to take up his interests where he left off. The trouble during these months is that neither you nor the baby can always tell how much daytime sleep he needs. Most babies are taking two naps a day, but the hours may be shifting, and one may be skipped for a few days, then resumed, and finally dropped altogether. If the baby's usual pattern is a long morning nap, lasting till close to lunchtime, he'll be good for hours of activity; then late in the afternoon he's likely to fall apart. He's too tired and cranky to be kept awake for an early supper and bedtime, so you give him a nap, after which he's beautifully revived and ready to keep going into the night hours.

The pattern to aim for is a long, early afternoon nap—with a short one in the morning if he wants it. Odd as it seems, many babies are willing to go back to bed for a short sleep soon after breakfast; perhaps they need time to come out of the relaxed state of sleep and work up to their full energy. Without a morning rest, the baby is likely to collapse just before lunch. You find him curled up in some corner; or you seat him in his high chair, and while you're putting a few finishing touches on his tempting little meal, he falls asleep sitting there. There's nothing to do but carry him to bed to sleep it out, which throws off his mealtimes schedule as well as an early afternoon nap. This is your cue to move lunchtime a half hour or an hour earlier, to catch him before he's too sleepy to eat. If he's not very hungry at this earlier time, make it a small meal and give him the rest when he wakes from his nap, to tide him over till suppertime.

Night Sleep

Bedtime is hard for a baby to accept, for at day's end he senses that when he gives up his waking life it will be a long time before he gets it back again. Some babies, instead of gradually tapering off their day, seem to put on full steam ahead when they near their bedtime. But this is a kind of false energy that can work up to a giddy state. If an older child (or an unwary adult) carries the baby into rambunctious play, all inclination toward sleep is chased away, however exhausted the baby gets. Bedtime is much easier for him, and for parents, if it's preceded by a relaxing hour in the household.

But there's no point in trying to stick to a precise bedtime hour. For one thing, the baby's sleep needs are changing as he gets older. If he's shifting back and forth between one nap and two, he'll be sleepy later and earlier on different nights. Watch for the clues, and remember that even this older baby appreciates the cuddle time that he always enjoyed before sleep. He often needs it more now, to relax his muscles and mind and help him let go of the day. Holding him for a last bottle or nursing, rocking and singing to him for a while, makes a comfort bridge that is well worth the half hour it takes to ready him for sleep.

The baby's night sleep may continue to be interrupted by teething. Now, when he wakes in the night he may compound his problem in getting back to sleep. When he can pull himself up to stand, but hasn't yet learned how to get down again, he'll be yelling for your help—perhaps many times over if the urge to practice gets hold of him in the night. Try the method suggested on page 247 for helping him learn how to plop down. He may still prefer to call you, but if you know he can do it in the daytime you can be pretty sure he'll make it in the night when he gets really tired from standing. After you've helped him a few times, give him a while to try before you go to him again. In any case, he'll probably master the maneuver in less than a week if you encourage daytime practice.

A soft nightlight is more soothing than darkness for many babies. And a few toys to play with during night wakings may also help to keep the baby from calling you. Don't worry about toys keeping a baby awake. They really help to calm him down from all his physical exercise. If you find him soaked—when he's awake—a diaper change will make him more comfortable. But you won't need to worry about keeping him covered for warmth if he wears a blanket-sleeper for his night capers.

Bathing and Dressing

Water is for fun! No finer toy or play material has ever been invented that can surpass water for pure fun in playing. And now your baby may discover a new way to "use" water.

About the time a baby begins to walk, she'll also begin to show the rhythmical movements of swimming, a pattern that was a part of her newborn reflexive behavior. The newborn baby makes stepping movements when supported, then loses that ability for many months; her swimming ability also goes underground; around the end of the year, the two skills return in voluntary form. If you give your baby light chest support in the bathtub, she'll begin to move her arms and kick her legs in natural swimming motions. This is fine exercise for her learning-to-walk legs. Can the baby learn to swim unsupported? Yes. But there are special methods of teaching. Refer to the discussion of baby swimming programs on pages 266 to 268.

New Tricks with Clothes

First you had a limp rag doll to dress and undress, then you had a gymnast, now you have a nice little helper whose help is often quite a handicap. The trouble is, the baby can't understand your inconsistent attitude about her self-help skills. You praise her for pulling off her shoes in the house, and fail to appreciate the same performance when she's on an outing. Some mornings you smile when she unsnaps her sleeper. But if she gets to work on it before you're there, and jerks off her diaper too, she'll wonder why you make such a fuss about the wet mess she's made of her bed. When the undressing skill gets out of hand, your best bet is to outwit the baby whenever possible—tying double knots in her shoelaces, for example.

The baby learns undressing considerably earlier than

dressing, but she's beginning to help with that too. Sometimes she'll obligingly arch her back and push up with her feet to let you place a diaper under her bottom. She'll push her arm through a sleeve and thrust out her leg to get pants on. Soon, though, comes that recurrent problem with standing. Babies who want to do everything in standing position see no reason why they should lie down, or even sit during dressing. They even insist on standing for a diaper change. Rather than struggle, you might as well change your long-standing habits to fit your baby's changing posture. Use the floor now, instead of the dressing table. Stand the baby with something to hold onto for balance, and she'll be as co-operative as she can, lifting one leg, then the other, and changing her hand holds to accommodate the shirt sleeves. You can even get the diaper on neatly with a little practice. After all, why argue with progress; your baby is making valiant efforts to grow out of that infant behavior of just lying around.

Shoeless to Shod

Now you'll be thinking in a different way about shoes for your baby—not only for warmth and as a dress-up addition, but as foot protection. Barefoot is best for learning to walk, but before you set the baby loose outdoors, you have to be sure of your ground. Uneven ground gives the feet extra exercise, but a cut or bad bruise could impede practice for a week or more.

In walking without shoes, the toes can grip the floor or ground, the foot and ankle have maximum freedom of move-ment, and through this exercise the muscles are strengthened to hold the foot and ankle straight. For this reason, most doctors recommend—for outdoor use—a soft oxford type rather than a high-top shoe that allows less exercise for the ankle (although high-tops do have the advantage of resisting the baby's efforts to pull them off).

First walking shoes should have flexible soles and soft uppers. While you take care that the length and width doesn't cramp the baby's foot, also take care not to get shoes too big. Shoes that are too long or loose cause tripping and awkward foot action. Examine the baby's feet regularly for any thickening of the skin or red spots indicating pressure or slipping. If the shoe soles are slick, rough them with sandpaper. And forgo highly waxed floors and scatter rugs for your toddler's safety; floors cluttered with toys are also hazardous. Learning to walk is difficult enough without such handicaps.

Sneakers are generally approved for babies as well as

older children. Their suppleness gives the foot better exercise than most shoes, and their soles have good grip. The doctor will keep check on your baby's feet, and if he detects any problem he'll recommend a foot specialist who will advise on any correction or type of shoe that may be needed.

Outings and Travel

Your baby's wariness of the outside world may put you in an awkward position at times. He may be fearful of persons in your own neighborhood who have always spoken to him, or act nervous and clinging in friends' homes. The baby's drives toward independence naturally weaken the security he felt as a little baby. But you can often ward off his fearful reactions to people and places by advance preparation, or even spur-of-the-moment help.

When you set out from home your baby has no idea where you're going or what's going to happen. If it's a visit to an unfamiliar place, try giving him an "explanation" just before you leave. While he can't understand your words, your warm voice, gestures, and expressions can give him an idea that something different is coming up. If he seems nervous when you arrive at a new place, hold him close and talk to him reassuringly. He may be tense with persons he's familiar with at your home when he sees them in *their* home. Explain that he needs a little time to feel at ease away from home. Most people understand that babies go through phases, and will keep their distance until the baby warms up to them of his own accord.

On the street, if you see that sweet old lady approaching who always got a smile from the baby with her chuck under his chin, give him advance support with a firm hand hold or your arm around his shoulders—and explain to the lady that you're in a great hurry today. By avoiding a pause for a chat, you'll probably avoid an incident that might hurt her feelings.

It's not always easy to balance consideration for other persons' feelings with support for your baby's. But urging

a baby to make friends, or to be brave in unfamiliar places, will make him more timid and fearful. Respecting his feelings in this phase—which to some degree appears in almost all babies—helps him to overcome it, and to gain an outgoing personality for the wider world he's entering.

Mother Nature at Work

The bustle of a shopping trip or travel to strange new places may key up a baby to a nervous state that makes it hard for him to relax when he arrives back home. By contrast, a day in the open air, away from a plethora of people, noise, and activity going on around him, has quite a different effect. Coming home, the baby may go instantly to sleep in the car, and not wake up when you put him to bed, or all through the night. Benevolent Mother Nature expects him to go to sleep with the birds and all her other little creatures, and he does.

A long outing in nature is different from the stimulation of other kinds of experience. It works on the nervous system in a tranquilizing way instead of building up nervous energy that's hard for the baby to throw off. A contributing factor, of course, is usually your own relaxed mood, induced by the same natural soothers that have been working on your baby. You can't have a long picnic every day, but whenever possible, weekends and vacations planned for a restful environment are good for the whole family.

If you're camping enthusiasts, your baby will be happy to curtail his explorations for the pleasure of being backpacked on treks to new territory. He'll probably even be agreeable to short periods of penning up, since the whole environment and atmosphere is so different from home. You might want to invest in the collapsible, fencetype corral that gives the baby four times the space of a regular play yard.

In summer or winter, heat seems to bother the baby more than cold. He'll let you know if you've bundled him up too well on a wintry day—not always by pulling on his clothing, but by fussing and crying. But most babies and toddlers don't seem to know when they're getting chilled. In late afternoon at the beach, for instance, the baby may go on playing in water and pay no attention to the chill creeping up on him; then you suddenly discover that his little hands and feet are cold. Just as in his infant days, you have to keep check on the baby's comfort, especially when he's involved in big-baby fun. And, of course, a very watchful eye.

Water Safety

Big babies usually have no fear of water. When they first experience an ocean, lake, or pool, it's the cold that frightens them. Accustomed to tepid tub water, the baby needs time to get used to the surprise of a different temperature. Dabbling is her approach and privilege in water sports. If she plays in the sand on the edge of a large body of water, she'll gradually begin to play with gently lapping waves that reach her. When she can toddle, she'll like to wade in shallow water. And when she crawls or falls in and gets wet all over, she's launched on the real excitement of water play. Watch her every moment! After the first few shocks of cold water, a baby will keep going, and toddle in right over her head—and come up spluttering but undaunted when you rescue her.

A baby has to find her own way in water play. She feels much more secure touching ground than being held and dipped in and out. A really sad spectacle is a screaming baby and a laughing parent trying to demonstrate the "fun" of water play. Water is for fun, but a baby has to make it so herself.

Baby Swimming Programs

These are popular—and controversial. Actually, no claims are made as to lasting swimming ability unless the child has continual practice; with even a couple of weeks skipped, a young child forgets all that she's learned, and the teaching method has to be started from scratch again. The system is that the instructor teaches the parent how to guide the baby's lessons, and the parent carries on with the baby.

Proponents of these programs emphasize the value of shared parent-child pleasure; opponents are concerned about the risk of developing confidence without sufficient stress on survival. Some programs require a doctor's checkup and okay before the baby can join. And some doctors have health concerns, such as possible middle ear infection or water intoxication, if a baby swallows a large amount of water. Of course, you should always consult your doctor if you're considering joining a parent-infant swim program.

Perhaps the most valuable aspect of water-baby programs is what they attempt to teach the parents—to keep the baby's pleasure in mind, to guard against being overanxious and transmitting fear of water to the child, and to be right there on guard every moment to protect the child's safety. Overconfidence in a young child's ability is one of the main objections that many authorities have to early swimming programs.

Under three years of age, a child can't even begin to learn anything about water safety. Backyard pools should always be fenced off, and young children should never be allowed to use the pool without constant adult supervision. Nor should an older child ever be entrusted with looking after the baby, even in a roped off shallow end; the lure of water fun is too great to be mixed with responsibility.

In any outdoor water setting, remember the sun! Your baby's tender skin is highly vulnerable to burn even after it has a gradually acquired tan. A collared, long-sleeved shirt and a sun-screen lotion for the face are always good precautions for the water baby. Before she dives into this greatest of play materials, review the sun safety precautions covered on pages 114 to 116.

Traveling

Trips away from home with your baby may be a bit more difficult than they were when he was content to stay put for play, and inclined to sleep for long daytime hours. But at any age, and whatever mode of travel you use, you need equipment for carrying the baby when you're on the ground— either a lightweight, collapsible stroller or a carrier (a back-pack type for this age). It's good to have both for differences in the places that you'll be covering on foot. A stroller, for instance, can be difficult to maneuver up and down stairs or through crowds. Information on buying and using back carriers is given on page 217.

Now that the baby has long waking hours, he needs exercise breaks during long trips by car, where he's confined in his auto restraint. When planning the approximate time to cover distances between destinations, allow for periods to pull off the throughway and let the baby crawl or toddle around in a grassy place. On a plane, he may be difficult to manage in the limited space between rows. There's more space in bulkhead or front-row seats, and you should request these seats when you make your reservations—several weeks in advance of your flight and much earlier during holiday seasons. However you go, a roomy diaper bag with several compartments can carry a day's supply of clothing, formula, and baby foods.

It's safer to feed the baby from jars of baby food, but be sure to discard any unused portions. You can give him chopped bits of your hot meal. But avoid cold meats, cold hard-boiled eggs, milk puddings and custards, and pastries with moist fillings; any of these could be more easily contaminated than hot foods. Fresh fruits, and some fresh vegetables, are fine for the baby—if they're washed and peeled just before eating. For those that you can't mash with a fork, or he can't easily chomp with his gums, you may want to take along a baby food mill to add fresh-food variety to his diet. And wherever you are, bottled water (boiled and brought from home in a sterilized jar, or purchased along the way) is a safeguard; changes of water from one locality to another may upset the baby's stomach.

(You'll find other travel suggestions on pages 116 to 121 and pages 168 to 169.)

Other Caregivers

You might think it would be easier for a baby to do without his parents as he grows older and learns to crawl or toddle and voluntarily take himself away from them. The independence he is gaining is exciting; but it's also sobering for him. An independent spirit doesn't grow without some glimmering of a sense of loss. The very fact that the baby *can* separate himself from you physically, and do without the complete care he had as an infant, gives him a strange, unsettling feeling. You can tell this by his ambivalent behavior, how he resists you one minute and clings to you the next. You can tell, too, by the way he tries to monopolize you after you've been away. A baby who was busy and happy all day with another caregiver often "changes character" when his parents come home. He follows them around, wants to be held, tries to keep their full attention on himself. It's as though, when he sees them again, their importance floods back to him.

It may seem strange that a baby's parents continue to be the primary meaning in his life, even if he has had care and attention and amusement from other persons right along. But the first attachments that a baby makes are his security base for branching out to other relationships.

A one-to-one relationship is important for the newborn. His transition from womb security to the outside world is a fragile period, and his adjustment is eased by consistent interaction with one person in particular. This is usually his mother, and their intimacy is actually a continuation of their nine-month union. But a baby who has close contact with his father early in life soon forms this same kind of attachment to him, and looks to either parent for comfort and help. Perhaps the baby has an instinctive sense of "belonging" to his parents, or perhaps they transmit that security to their baby by their deep affinity to him.

Now in these late months of the baby's first year, he has some sense of what this parent tie means to him. It's the support and comfort he feels when he returns to find you after venturing into another room alone, or the joy of seeing you again after a whole day without you. Sometimes that joy changes to irritable or aggressive behavior. A baby may hold himself in with other caregivers, then let out his pent-up feelings and nervous energy on his parents (just as older children and adults reserve many feelings for airing in the privacy of the family). But cranky or clinging or eager for fun, the baby is telling you how important you are in his life.

Once he's in the routine of his parents' absences, the baby gets along very nicely, because he knows that this routine also includes their return. As long as someone who cares about his all-around welfare is looking after him, the baby keeps busy and happy with his own affairs. If you're working parents, you'll know very soon whether the care-giver arrangement you have is good for your baby. Not by his eagerness to be with you again—that's natural—but by his general health and spirit. To reassure yourselves, drop in unexpectedly now and then to see how baby and sitter, or babies and caregivers in a group arrangement, are occupying their time. The general tone of the atmosphere will tell you whether this setting is what you want for your baby.

For the working parent or the stay-at-home parent, these months are a time of adjustment to a baby who is making his own adjustments to the changes taking place in himself, as well as to any alterations in his daily life. Some of his natural tendencies may be misinterpreted by others and blamed on you willy-nilly—you're not with him enough, you're with him too much. That overworked word *spoiling* may have cropped up on and off since your child's newborn days, whenever he tucked in his angelic wings for a time. The fact is that you know this little character better than anyone else, and the love bond between you is your guide to his needs. This gives you the right to expect from your baby's other caregivers the kind of care that closely approximates your own.

Pediatric Note

Your doctor will be extra kind to the baby on his ten-month checkup—no shots! But the baby probably won't warm up to his doctor. Stay close, and hold the baby for as much of the exam as possible. At twelve months, his unfriendliness may be even stronger. During this well-baby visit, the doctor will do a test for tuberculosis. (At fifteen months, the baby will be immunized against measles, rubella and mumps. See page 276 for a complete schedule of recommended immunizations and tests for babies and young children.)

What you'll be waiting to hear is: "You've done a great job with this baby's first year—keep up the good work!"

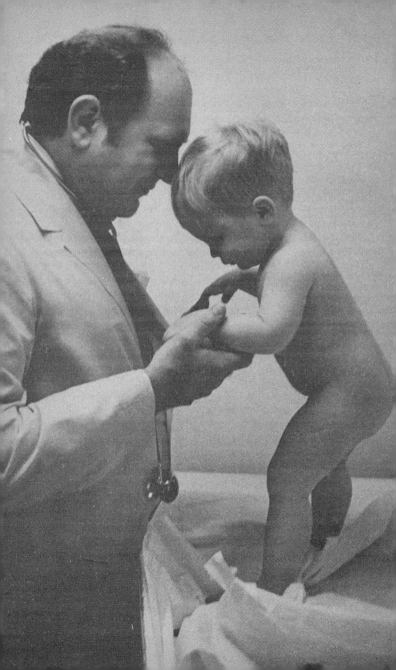

Chapter VI

Health

Keeping a Health Record

A health history is an important document. Memory is never as reliable as a written record, and accuracy is extremely important. Your pediatrician or health clinic will, of course, keep records. But the record you make for each of your children will be an invaluable reference in the months and years ahead. Ours is a mobile society; if you move to a new locality and your children change doctors and schools, their health records will save hours of time in obtaining the necessary information to fill out requested forms.

Basics of the health record include: blood type; birth weight; dates of all immunizations and tests; illnesses; medications and any reactions to them; injuries; dental information. Also noted should be developmental abilities by age, as well as behavior and personality profiles at progressive ages.

All that you know of your own families' health histories should be recorded too—those of parents, grandparents, and other blood relatives on both sides of the family. This information may be important in medical diagnoses for your child, eliminating extensive detective work in searching out possible causes in case of an illness or problem; and it can subsequently be of use for future generations in the family.

Also remember that your baby's health record begins at conception. Notes on any pregnancy difficulties or illnesses, medications taken during pregnancy and childbirth, the nature of the delivery, are all pertinent information to be included in your baby's records. You may want to include your newborn's Apgar score in the record, and you can request a copy from the obstetrician. This is a numerical rating of an infant's condition at one and five minutes after birth, based on heart rate, respiration, muscle tone, reflexes, and color.

Have a photocopy made of your baby's birth certificate for his record book. (The original should be kept in a safe place with other valuables.) Be sure to check this certificate for accuracy; a misspelling of the baby's name or the parents', or an error in the sex of the baby (for instance, a female Dale or Lee recorded as a male) could cause problems at some point in the future. Don't delay in having any error in the birth certificate corrected; this is too important a document to neglect. If you should decide to change your baby's name, do it legally; problems can follow when a person is commonly called by a different name than the one on his or her birth certificate.

Routine Check-ups

Well-baby medical checkups are usually scheduled once a month up to six months, then every two months to the end of the year. These routine checkups are as important as contacting the doctor promptly when your baby is ill. Many serious diseases are prevented with the immunizations given periodically. Even if your baby is not scheduled for a shot, and you feel confident she's in good health, don't neglect these doctor visits. There's always the possibility that the doctor will detect some condition that has escaped your notice.

Usually the nurse will record your baby's weight and height before he is seen by the doctor. She may also ask you a few questions and make notes on the baby's record card. During the examination, the doctor accomplishes much simply through observation. Experience with many babies helps the doctor judge your child's state of health and development in comparison with other children of the same age. This doesn't mean that all babies develop at the same rate; there are often wide differences in all phases of development. But it does let the doctor know if there are any unusual deviations from the norm. The baby's build and general appearance, his skin condition and nutritional state, his behavior—all combine to give a pretty clear picture of his present health and his progress since the last visit.

You may be unaware of many of the doctor's observations and impressions throughout the examination. There are differences in medical procedures and differences in doctors' personalities. One may say little as he or she checks the baby; another may chat with you and ask a number of questions. Private office setups and clinic systems also vary, depending on the size of a pediatrician's practice or a clinic's scope, and on individual preferences in how doctors handle their work. You may feel well satisfied after a leisurely medical visit, or somewhat shortchanged after a rapid but equally efficient checkup. Your own manner also influences the kind of rapport you have with your baby's doctor. If you're embarrassed to ask questions for fear some of them may seem foolish, you may leave the office with worries still on your mind. But if you don't hesitate to ask the doctor to clarify some point, you'll get the most satisfaction from your baby's checkups, along with more confidence in caring for your baby.

It's best to reserve most of your questions until the end of the examination; many may be answered by what the doctor tells you. Then ask him or her about anything that puzzles you or that's been worrying you since your previous visit. It's always a good idea to have written questions to refer to; and be sure to make notes on any instructions you're given.

Many private pediatricians, as well as clinics, give printed instruction sheets at each well-baby visit. They usually suggest what to add to the baby's diet and what to expect in her development until the next scheduled appointment. Some are quite detailed, others are brief and short on explanations. You should read over these routine instructions before you leave the office, and discuss with the nurse anything that may need to be clarified. One of her duties is to be sure that you understand not only what is to be done, but how to do it. This includes any nonroutine doctor's orders. If a medication has been prescribed, for example, let the nurse explain the best way to administer it.

If you're in doubt about some detail after arriving home, or have questions before your next scheduled visit, telephone the nurse. She is authorized to answer many routine questions, but will always consult the doctor on any matter that is unusual or technical.

Immunizations and Tests

The immunizations that are scheduled to protect your baby against preventable diseases may also protect many other children; epidemics can begin with one child's illness that rapidly spreads through a community. The following schedule is currently recommended for normal children by the American Academy of Pediatrics.

Age	Immunizations
2 months	DTP/TOPV
4 months	DTP/TOPV
6 months	DTP/TOPV*
15 months	Measles, Rubella, Mumps
1½ years	DTP/TOPV
4-6 years	DTP/TOPV
14-16 years	Td

*TOPV is optional at six months.

DTP is a combination of three vaccines for prevention of diphtheria, tetanus (lockjaw), and pertussis (whooping cough) and is given by injection. Td is a combination tetanus/diphtheria vaccine.

TOPV (trivalent oral polio vaccine) gives protection against the three types of polio, and is taken by mouth.

Measles, rubella, mumps immunizations may be given in one injection, or as measles-rubella/mumps.

A test for tuberculosis is given at twelve months, and this may be repeated at one- to two-year intervals, depending on the physician's recommendation for your area.

Recognizing Illness in an Infant

When the baby is sick you may first notice a difference in her behavior; she just doesn't seem her usual self. Perhaps she's listless, irritable, or crying intermittently for no apparent reason. Then other symptoms of illness usually follow. These include: a runny nose; continuous sneezing or coughing; hoarse breathing; refusal of more than one feeding; vomiting; sudden change in the number or consistency of bowel movements, or in their color or odor; decrease in urine; unusually flushed or pale complexion; hot or dry skin; skin rash; red, irritated, or sensitive eyes; indications of pain; convulsions; temperature of 101° F or above.

Warning signs are rarely cause for alarm. It's important to remain calm when judging your baby's condition and accurately reporting his symptoms to the doctor. How promptly to get in touch with the doctor is usually not difficult to judge. For example, very labored breathing or a rapidly rising temperature would tell you to call the doctor *now*; nighttime wakefulness due to intermittent coughing would tell you to let the doctor get his or her sleep and phone in the morning. But the baby's age is an important factor to consider; a newborn has little resistance to infections, his condition can worsen rapidly, so you should take no chances. Also, you should be aware that the absence of fever is not always a good sign; young babies in particular may have a dangerous illness with little or no fever.

Fever

Fever is an indication that the body is reacting against an illness. And the best time to take your baby's temperature for the first time is *before* it's necessary for the first time. Knowing just how to proceed will help you to be calm and efficient about it when the baby is sick. It's best to use a rectal thermometer; this has a round bulb that's more comfortable for inserting than the pointed oral type.

Bring down the mercury to at least 97° F by holding the upper end of the thermometer firmly as you shake it with snapping motions of your wrist. (Better do this over a bed when practicing, in case it slips.) Lubricate the bulb with petroleum jelly or baby cream. Put a diaper on your lap and lay the baby on her stomach with her legs hanging down. Gently insert the bulb about an inch into the rectum, letting it find its own direction; then hold it in place by spreading your hand over the baby's buttocks, with the thermometer secured between two fingers. One minute is enough to give an almost accurate reading.

To read the thermometer, first wipe it with a tissue; then hold it horizontally, with your back to the light, and roll it very slightly until you see the band of mercury—a thin silver line. The point where this stops is the temperature, indicated by the numerals and markings on the stem; each short mark is a fifth of a degree. An arrow points to 98 ⅗°, which is considered as normal temperature.

The centigrade scale, rather than the Fahrenheit, is used in some areas, including continental Europe and Latin America. On this thermometer, 37° C is marked as normal temperature. To translate centigrade temperature into Fahrenheit terms, multiply the centigrade figure by 9, divide the result by 5, then add 32.

Actually, normal human temperature varies by one or

two degrees below or above the average of 98 $\frac{3}{5}$° F, so it's a good idea for each person to know his or her own normal temperature. Body temperature also tends to be a little lower in the morning and a little higher in the evening. Young children's temperatures usually rise a bit when they're very active. Always take it after a quiet period of at least a half hour, and after nothing was eaten or drunk for the same length of time. When you report a temperature to the doctor, state the time of day it was taken, and how (rectal or axillary).

For toddlers and children still too young to properly and safely hold a thermometer in the mouth, the axillary method may be less frightening and less embarrassing than the rectal method. Place the bulb end of the thermometer (either rectal or oral) in the armpit, with no clothing underneath it, and hold the child's arm flat on the chest for about three minutes. (Four minutes will give the accurate temperature; two minutes a close enough reading.)

Before storing the thermometer, always wash it with soap and warm water—*hot water will break it.*

A temperature of 101° F or above should always be reported to the doctor. But it's well to keep in mind that fever is a symptom, not a disease. Many pediatricians today don't prescribe medication to reduce a moderate temperature that accompanies an illness. Keeping track of the fever's progress, up or down, helps the doctor to diagnose and treat the underlying cause. A fever that continues to rise, or that returns after subsiding for two or three days, may indicate that the illness is becoming more serious or that a secondary infection has developed. It's also important to know that a mild fever that continues to recur every day may indicate a more serious illness than a sudden high fever that's gone the next day. Remember, too, that fever is only one symptom; it does not occur in all illnesses; and the doctor must be contacted when a child shows any signs of illness.

Liquids are extremely important during a fever, as dehydration can develop rapidly in a baby. A young baby with a stuffy nose may resist extra water or juice by bottle. If he hasn't yet learned to drink from a cup, try spoon feeding liquids; this takes time and patience, but if done frequently you'll get quite a lot of fluids into him.

Don't dress or cover the baby warmly when he has a fever. You must, however, check on his condition frequently; if a fever "breaks," he'll perspire and need a light cover to prevent chilling.

Emergency treatment of high fever (104° F or above) is necessary if you can't contact a doctor within an hour. Undress the child and cover her with a sheet. Wetting your hands in a basin of tepid water, gently rub different parts of her body—arms, legs, chest, back—re-covering each exposed part as you go along, and rewetting your hands as necessary. The rubbing brings blood to the surface of the wet skin, cooling it by evaporation. If the temperature is still high after a half hour, hold the child in tepid bath water for fifteen or twenty minutes. Cold fluids given by cup or bottle are also helpful.

The Common Cold

The common cold is by far the most frequent illness among children as well as adults. But, in general, babies have fewer colds, and milder ones, than older children. For one thing, rest is easier to regulate with a baby than with an active older child, and rest is what the body needs to combat infections. There's no cure for the common cold; the array of antibiotics so effective in killing bacterial infections have no effect on viral illnesses. There are around two hundred distinct viruses responsible for colds, and while there's a period of immunity after being infected by one or another of them, there are plenty more at large. Treatment consists of relieving the symptoms and preventing complications. Fatigue, chilling, overheating, or drafts cannot *cause* a cold, but these conditions can make it harder for the body to ward off the invading virus, and also to resist bacterial infections. A cold lowers the body's resistance to complications such as bronchitis, pneumonia, and sinusitis; babies are particularly susceptible to ear infections. A cold may also be a symptom of a serious disease—with or without fever. Young babies seldom have fever with a common cold, but toddlers and preschoolers may have a sudden high fever at the start of a cold.

How can you tell when a cold is more than a cold? Some of the signs are: rectal temperature above 103° F; a temperature that remains high longer than twenty-four hours; the child looks or acts sicker, with or without a fever; repeated vomiting; shallow, rapid, or labored breathing; wheezing; changed or weakened voice; increasing cough or a deep "chest cough"; unusual or increasing irritability; indications of pain; cold symptoms that don't improve or that worsen after four or five days.

A sick baby should be kept evenly warm in cover-all clothing, with room temperature at about 72° F during the day, and 68° to 70° F for night sleep. Moisturizing the air with a cool-mist humidifier helps to ease coughing and keep nasal passages from clogging. Since a baby can't clear her nose by blowing, breathing may be difficult while she's nursing. A stuffy nose can be relieved with nose drops prescribed by the doctor, or with an infant nasal syringe. Be sure to clean the syringe well after each use.

Medication

Give no medications (not even baby aspirin) except those prescribed by the doctor. Timing is extremely important when giving medications, and if you trust to memory it's easy to make mistakes. A chart will help to keep everything straight. Under the name of each medicine, write the date and hour started. Under this, the time each subsequent dose is due. Four times a day, for example, might be 6:00 and 10:00 A.M., and 2:00 and 6:00 P.M. If the medication is to be given around-the-clock, the timing must, of course, be extended, and you'll need to set your alarm clock for the nighttime doses. As you give each dose, check it off on your chart. Never exceed the prescribed dosage; and don't discontinue a prescribed medication when you—and not the doctor—think it's no longer needed.

Most liquid medicines for babies come with a calibrated dropper, which makes it easy to measure the prescribed dosage. Hold the baby in a sitting position to avoid choking; slip the dropper into a corner of his mouth and slowly squeeze the bulb; keep it compressed as you remove the dropper, then gently hold the baby's lips closed until he swallows.

Liquid medicine without a dropper can best be given by nipple instead of spoon, to avoid losing some in spills or dribbles. Measure out the recommended dose, then pour it into a nipple; hold your thumb over the bottom of the nipple and let the baby suck out the medicine. This way he gets the full amount in a swallow or two; if it's mixed with juice or formula in a bottle, he might not take all the liquid.

A tablet medicine must be mashed to a fine powder and mixed with a spoonful of strained fruit or jelly (not with honey, which may be potentially harmful to babies under a year of age). If a capsule medicine is prescribed for a young child, cover it with a sticky type of food, such as mashed banana or potato, and follow it with a quick drink of juice.

The most helpful "technique" for getting medicine into a baby or young child is a matter-of-fact attitude. *Expect* her to take it, act quickly and surely but gently. Exaggerated oh-so-good preliminaries can create suspicion; and you should never give the impression that medicine is candy.

Croup

Croup can be mild or serious, and the doctor should be called immediately for any attack of croup. It's an alarming condition—hoarseness, fits of a barkinglike cough, and tight, struggling breathing. Spasmodic croup, the mildest and most common type, generally comes on suddenly in the night, usually without fever. Moist air is the emergency treatment until the doctor can be reached. If you have a cool-mist humidifier, use it in a small room for fast humidifying. If you don't have a humidifier, take the child into the bathroom and run hot water in the bath or shower to steam the room quickly. When he is breathing moist air, the croup usually subsides rapidly. But an adult should stay with the child as long as any symptoms remain, and check him frequently during the night to see that he's breathing normally. Attacks may recur for two or three nights, so the air in his sleeping room should be kept moist. And it's best to sleep in the same room with the child for at least three nights.

If an attack of croup doesn't subside after a half hour or so in moist air or steam, and if you can't get in touch with a doctor, the child should be taken to the emergency room of the nearest hospital.

Convulsions

Convulsions are frightening to see but seldom serious in themselves. The body stiffens, jerks, and twitches; breathing is heavy, the eyes may roll up; there may be slight frothing at the mouth; and possibly loss of consciousness. A convulsion runs its course in a short time, and first aid consists of preventing the child from hurting herself. Put her on a bed (not in her crib) so that she won't knock against a hard surface with her spasmodic movements; place a tightly rolled cloth between her teeth to keep her from biting her tongue; loosen any restrictive clothing, such as a belt or collar. Don't try to restrain the child in any way; if she vomits, turn her on her side to prevent choking.

A convulsion is triggered by irritation of the brain; there are numerous causes, which tend to differ at various ages. In a young child, a common cause is sudden high fever at the onset of illness, even a cold. The doctor should, of course, be consulted so that he or she can evaluate the underlying cause. If the child does have a high temperature (104° F or above) and you can't reach the doctor within a short time, use the wet rub method described on page 280 to bring down the fever—*after* the convulsion has run its course.

Recuperating from Illness

Your child's recuperation from an illness may be a harder period for you than the illness was. You've lost sleep and kept yourself going on nervous energy. Then—sometimes suddenly—the baby is his old self again, full of regained vigor, and both of you would like to get out of the house for a change. Yet the doctor's instructions may be to keep the baby indoors for several more days. Now it's especially important for you to grab a nap and a good night's rest as soon as the baby is asleep. Don't be tempted to disregard the doctor's instructions for your child's care after an illness. Following through on medical advice can mean the difference between a relapse and renewed good health. Take care, too, to protect yourself from your child's illness. Foolish as it may seem, some adults take no precautions against catching a baby's cold. There's, of course, no such thing as a harmless little "baby germ"; the infection spread by an infant's sniffles and sneezes can result in a whopping big cold for her mom or dad.

Teeth

Teething varies widely among normal healthy babies—in timing, trouble, and sometimes in order of eruption. One of the lower central incisors (biting teeth) is almost always first; and some babies have their eight incisors—four above and four below—by a year of age. The eight molars and four canine teeth are cut during the second year and first half of the third year. This gives your baby his set of twenty first teeth. At around six years of age, the permanent teeth will begin to push up through the gums, displacing the baby teeth.

All babies do a lot of biting when they're teething, and you must be especially alert to what the baby may be chewing on. Do be sure the baby has safe teething toys, as chewing on things is some help in relieving irritated gums. But don't let the baby have a spoon to chew on unless he's in his high chair; a spoon can be dangerous if he falls. Some teething babies are cranky during the day; some have a hard time going to sleep or are wakeful during the night. The so-called pain threshold varies greatly among different persons, babies included, and this partly accounts for the differences in the amount of irritability or sleeplessness that babies may have when teething. Sucking sometimes causes discomfort for a teething baby. If he pulls away from the breast or bottle when he's obviously hungry, give him as much milk as possible by cup, or mixed with cereal and other foods. Yogurt, milk puddings and soups, and yellow cheese will also help to fill out the baby's calcium needs. (One ounce of yellow cheese supplies about the same amount of calcium as eight ounces of milk; for the same value in cottage cheese, however, ten ounces are needed.) Colds, diarrhea, and fever are often blamed on teething. These illnesses are caused by germs, not by teething, although it's thought that teething may lower some babies' resistance to infections. Any illness or a fever of 101° F or higher requires the doctor's attention. You should also consult your doctor before using any teething preparation on the baby's gums.

Baby teeth can be cleaned with a small piece of gauze or with a soft baby toothbrush and a tiny bit of fluoridated toothpaste. By two years of age, a baby is trying to copy all kinds of grown-up ways, and it's a good time to let her start brushing her teeth herself. However sketchy her early attempts are, she'll be accomplishing some cleaning and taking pride in learning to do it by herself. After a while, to get a better job done by helping, you'll probably have good cooperation if you let your child have a turn brushing *your* teeth.

Baby teeth need professional dental care. The fact that they'll be lost doesn't make them unimportant. These first teeth are the space-savers for the permanent teeth, helping them to grow in straight. Decay can cause pain or infection, sometimes making extraction necessary. Dental visits should start by age three, and be made every six months. If there are no cavities, so much the better; a pleasant visit to the dentist dissipates the fear of this place with all its strange apparatus. If there are tiny cavities to fill, there'll be much less discomfort than with big ones. Select a dentist who has "a way" with children; a professional's personality has a strong effect on lifetime fear or acceptance of any necessary medical treatment. Pedodontists (specialists in the care of children's teeth) are versed in handling and calming nervous children, and generally have attractive waiting rooms with play materials for various ages.

One of the major causes of dental caries in young children is allowing them to go to bed with a bottle of milk or juice. If a child must take a bottle to bed with him, the bottle should be filled with water.

The Medicine Chest

Medicine-chest supplies for a young child should be limited to a few essentials, and it's best to keep them on one shelf, apart from family supplies. Your doctor can recommend particular brands, but he or she might advise you to have on hand: baby aspirin or aspirin-free substitute, a decongestant, medicine for diarrhea, nose drops, a painless antiseptic, gauze bandage, adhesive tape, absorbent cotton, petroleum jelly, zinc oxide paste, ointment for diaper rash, bicarbonate of soda, rectal thermometer, nose syringe, and hot-water bottle.

No medication should be given without first consulting the doctor; but having particular basics on hand saves valuable time in an emergency. Most prepared medicines (but not all prescriptions that the pharmacist fills) are marked with an expiration date for safe usage, and must be discarded after that date. Those without dates should be marked by you, with notations on the condition they were used for, and any adverse reactions. But these should never be used again when you *think* your child has the same ailment she had before; always check with your doctor before giving any treatment.

Syrup of ipecac is one other essential for the medicine chest. This is an emetic in case of accidental poisoning. In certain situations, however, vomiting should *not* be induced. If your child ingests a toxic substance, and if she is not unconscious or having convulsions, give her water or milk to dilute the poison, then telephone your physician, poison control center, or hospital emergency room for further instructions. Vomiting should *not* be induced if the child is unconscious or having convulsions; if the child has ingested a petroleum product, such as gasoline, kerosene, paint thinner, cleaning fluid; if the child has ingested an acid or alkalai, such as toilet bowl cleaner, drain cleaner, oven cleaner, lye. In these situations vomiting could cause further damage.

Safety

Safety guidelines are given throughout the age-category sections, but equipment and toys must be checked periodically, and the baby's environment constantly, for hazards. Remember that babies and young children have no conception of many dangers; also that their urge to do is much stronger than their self-control, even after they have learned the meaning of no. Calm, serious words have a much better effect in teaching safety than any kind of punishment; a child should feel your concern for him rather than your anger. Following is a capsule course in safety measures for a baby:

Keep a few steps ahead of your baby in anticipating potential dangers. A baby who cannot roll over, reach an object, climb, may do so tomorrow. And never leave baby unattended, especially on a bed, couch, dressing or bath table; in the tub; in a room with a gas heater or burning fireplace. An accident could happen in seconds. Also, never leave him in the care of young children; they haven't the judgment to take care of an emergency.

Place crib, play yard, high chair well away from wall

decorations, electric outlets, fan, window, hot radiator, burning fireplace, gas or electric heater.

Install smoke detectors in your home. Test them periodically to be sure they work. Use sturdy screens in front of all fireplaces.

Do not use a pillow under the baby's head. Keep crib sides up and locked when not tending baby.

Examine baby's clothing frequently for loose snaps, buttons, decorations; anything she can pull off goes into her mouth.

Select toys with care. They should be nontoxic and sturdy, with no sharp edges or points, detachable small parts.

Tie plastic wrappings in several knots before discarding; this material can cause suffocation.

Scan floors for small things the creeper or toddler might swallow. Check furniture for sharp edges and corners. Put safety covers on electric outlets not being used. Put adhesive strips or decals on sliding glass doors.

Know your house plants; many are poisonous. Keep all plants well out of baby's reach. Check the floor frequently for fallen leaves.

Remove breakable, sharp, heavy objects from tables and shelves. Check for unstable floor lamps, top-heavy table lamps. Be wary of hanging tablecloths; a baby could pull the cloth and be hit by falling objects. Bolt bookcases to walls.

Firmly secure cords of small appliances, lamps, telephones to prevent baby from tugging them down. Disconnect appliances not being used. Shorten the loop ends on drapery and blind cords so the loops are well out of baby's reach.

When cooking, turn pot handles toward rear of stove. Never leave the oven door open. Keep a fire extinguisher in the kitchen; be sure baby can't reach it.

Install child-proof latches on drawers and cupboards baby should not get into. Put high hooks on doors that may lead to hazards. Provide top and bottom stair gates. Be sure window screens are securely fastened to window frames or install childproof window gratings.

Store cleaning agents and all household chemicals in a high, locked cupboard. Never put nonfood substances in a dish or soda bottle. Keep all medicines in the medicine cabinet and install a lock on the cabinet. Be sure all medicine bottles have childproof lids. Leave medicines and toxic materials in original containers for identification in case of ingestion.

Keep any potentially dangerous objects or substances— cosmetics, perfume, deodorant, shampoo, conditioner, hair spray, nail polish and remover, shoe polish, ink, spot remover, lighter fluid, matches, scissors, needles, pins, knives, etc.—in childproof cabinets. Get in the habit of putting such things away immediately after using.

Use a diaper pail and kitchen trash can with childproof lids. Never leave hazardous materials in an open wastepaper basket.

Record phone numbers of doctor, hospital, poison control center, police and fire departments; keep numbers near the telephone for quick reference. Keep a first-aid book on hand.

Do not expect a baby or toddler to recognize hazards, to be safely stopped by nos, to control his urge to explore. Curiosity is a natural force in learning.

Epilogue:

Looking Ahead

Crawling or toddling, your baby has crossed the threshold into the second year. This entrance into the busy months ahead is not an exit from babyhood. What the first birthday celebrates is the amazing transformation that's taken place from Day 1 to Day 365 in your baby's life. The second year will be far less spectacular in outward change. But inwardly your baby will be shaping and firming himself into a very substantial little person.

The one-year-old is working hard at developing his self-confidence. *Being* a skillful crawler or a toddler has caused him to regress a bit in that respect. It was easier to feel sure of his caregivers when he couldn't "run away" from them; they came to him. Now he must intermittently reassure himself that they'll be there when he needs or wants them. He's not always sure when he does. But there are times when he feels just like the little baby he used to be, and giving him the full privilege of being that baby recharges his good feelings about himself.

Many babies prefer to crawl for some time after they've learned to walk. Walking is a performance that gets a lot of applause; but crawling is much more reliable for important business. The sprinting crawl that some babies acquire can far outdistance a neophyte's walk.

A skilled toddler, though, often wants to do little else

but keep himself moving, simply feeling the joy of pro-
pelling himself through space, selecting his route, turning
corners, reversing direction, coming back to home base and
setting out again. His legs may seem tireless. But suddenly
this freedom of spirit seems a lonely state. He hurries back
to you to be picked up and held close and rocked in your
arms for perhaps no more than a minute or two. He may
close his eyes in perfect quietude, soaking in this interlude
of security. Then he wriggles away and is off again.

Quick-change moods are typical of the second-year baby.
As he moves ahead in toddlerhood, he hangs onto his babyhood like a security blanket, pulling it along with him for
the comfort he may need at any moment. He rejects any
comforting not of his own choosing, using only what he
needs to bolster his courage for what he's working toward—
firm declaration of his independence.

By fifteen or eighteen months, the baby may be well into
this phase. Besides saying "no," she can act it out in all
kinds of ways. Tell her to put down your book; she scuttles
off with it. Insist that she come this way; off she goes that
way. This behavioral phase is referred to as negativism. But
is it?

Turn the coin over and look at the baby's side. There's
the "positivism" of what's going on. A toddler's "no" is a
little show of importance that she needs to realize herself
as an individual. She has to act out her aims—even when
they're no more than whims. She often has no definitive
goal in mind until she's crossed in what she's starting to
do. Then she quickly firms up, feels the pleasure and strength
of being herself, and acts it out. It's a great feeling to be
letting go of little-baby helplessness and taking a bit of
action in decision making.

Having worked on problem solving all through her babyhood, she's now working on decision making—quite an
undertaking for a little person who knows next to nothing
about the hazards of the world, and who can't comprehend
the whys behind most of your nos. One problem in admiring
her spunkiness is how to handle it when she hasn't the
reasoning power to see the reasonable side of things. That

results in some dead ends, no matter how you try to appease her.

If she drops her cookie on the sidewalk and you thwart her in picking it up, she's lost something important to her. Another cookie is not the same as *that* cookie, and she may bat away the new one you offer and carry on angrily, still wanting *her* cookie. But a toddler is still short on attention span, and distraction still works—though it's got to be a little more inventive than what worked a few months back. Try the diversion of a quick change of scene; whisk her up and hold her on a high place, or hold her where she can look in a shop window. The one thing not to do is "argue" over that cookie—unless you know how to explain the possible harm of invisible germs to a one-going-on-two-year-old.

A toddler feels important when he imitates what he sees adults doing. Play is a child's work, and every toddler loves to work hard. Watch him lug a heavy load across the room; use all his strength to extricate his riding toy from a jam; hurry from room to room gathering up things to fill his wagon, then empty it out and start all over again. The sheer pleasure of doing and trying keeps him going. Give him a large grocery store carton and watch his inventiveness. He'll struggle till he learns how to climb into it without tipping over; dump himself out and push it around the house; fill it with all his stuffed animals and climb in on top of them; turn it upside down and sit on it; use it for a drum; and when it's finally collapsing, walk away from it as a thing that meant nothing to him. Project completed.

Toddlers play in all kinds of ways during the course of a day. Some are generally more "studious" in all their play. But stick-to-itiveness is not common in young toddlerhood. Sometimes a toddler's play seems wildly flighty. She'll abandon one thing after another in rapid succession, never settling down long enough to discover the potential of any one plaything—to our way of thinking. But how can we know? All play is serving the toddler's purpose of being in control of her own interests. If she jerks on a tiny wooden man sitting in a little wooden car, and the man won't come loose, perhaps that's all she wanted to know. She tosses that toy aside and grabs another, spends an instant on that one, and goes on. She may find one to spend some time with, or she may shift to enjoying herself in action—climbing onto the sofa and down again, toddling from one room to another with no apparent goal in mind, then taking a ride in a rocking seat or on a wheeled toy.

A toddler is self-centered simply because he's very busy trying to become self-reliant. He often acts as though he can pretty well do without people except for the necessary services they provide. You serve the food; he'll manage to eat it without help, thank you. You prepare his bath; he'll wash himself—by soaping away for five minutes on one leg, then protesting any interruption of his play for further washing. You take him for a ride in his stroller; he'll want to keep going—no stops to chat with a neighbor.

But for all a toddler's self-assertive behavior, he has plenty of cooperative spirit too. He pays little attention to children his own age, but he appreciates having an older child or adult enter into his play. He'll try hard to imitate what you do with his toys; he'll share a cookie or try to spoon-feed you from his dish. You can do a lot to reverse a toddler's possessive and negative behavior by simply *expecting* good intentions—by using thank-yous and smiles and even bids for assistance. A toddler will leave some mischief he's into if you ask his "help" in lifting a box or moving a chair or putting silverware on the table. The scramble he makes of spoons and forks is well worth his glowing smile when you tell him what a big helper he is. A toddler is quite capable of showing love and sympathy too. His quick hugs and kisses tell you how much you mean to him. And he'll notice a tiny scratch on your hand and ask you—at least with the expression on his face—if it hurts.

Language learning will be steadily increasing during the second year. This doesn't mean, however, that the baby will necessarily be saying much. The gauge of language development is how much the child understands—her receptive skill with words. By midway in this second year she may have an understanding vocabulary of around forty words. These will include not only names of persons and things, but action words and a few concepts, such as "pretty" and "big" and "hot."

It's important to keep your conversation in the immediate present when you talk to your toddler. She lives "right now"—with no understanding of tomorrow. But she may pick up on some of your abstract concepts, with a general sense of their meaning. If you often say, for instance, "in a minute," she'll know that means a delay; and when you call her, she may answer "inny-minny," feeling quite justified in keeping on with her play.

You can't be with your toddler at all times. And even if you were, he'd be letting you know that he's trying to stand on his own two feet. He has no idea how immature he is— he'll still be in diapers when he graduates from this year! There's a lot he's not able to learn until he gains more maturity, physically and mentally and emotionally. Meanwhile, when he asserts his importance and shouts out his nos, take advantage of his sense of humor and love of fun, and "turn him around" with games and jokes.

When your toddler is too busy with toys to want to leave them, ask her if she wants to go into lunch like a grasshopper or a pussy-cat, and maybe, getting in her no, but a harmless one, she'll decide, "No, a wabbit"—and come hopping along.

Rituals, especially at bedtime, become important to toddlers. Things must be done the established, "right" way. All dolls must be kissed and told bye bye, toddler must be held up to click the light switch, but when it comes to actually climbing in, she'll try to think of other important things to attend to.

Looking ahead, don't let anyone "warn" you that you're heading into the age of Big Problems, that you're going to have a difficult, stubborn, willful child to handle. This is the baby you know—as charming and determined as she's always been to grow and learn. Now she's facing new problems in trying to grow out of babyhood while keeping your love and security. You'll encourage and respect her independence by going around instead of head-on when you see resistance coming, and you'll keep her as happy as possible because that's how she's best able to learn. You can count on the fact that this bigger baby wants to be happy and wants to please you. But when she can't, she's not being bad. She's just being her immature self.

Index

About the Author

Maja Bernath is a former Associate Editor of *Parents* Magazine and the former Editor of *Expecting*, *Baby Care*, and *Your New Baby* Magazines. She has written extensively on pregnancy, infancy, and early childhood.

BRINGING UP BABY

A series of practical baby care and family living guides developed with the staff of *PARENTS™ MAGAZINE.* Explains both the whys and how-to's of infant care.